BEST OF
Bayou Cuisine

D0862206

St. Stephen's Episcopal Church, Indianola, Mississippi

BEST OF
Bayou Cuisine

Edited by
St. Stephen's Cookbook Committee

QUAIL RIDGE PRESS
Brandon, Mississippi

Best of Bayou Cuisine Committee

Debbie Allen	Vickie Hester
Jack Allen	Ferne Little
Marion Barnwell	Mary Speer
Trish Berry	Joyce Van Cleve
Karen Carpenter	Michelle Van Cleve

QUAIL RIDGE PRESS
P. O. Box 123 • Brandon, MS 39043
1–800–343–1583

Library of Congress Cataloging-in-Publication Data

Best of Bayou Cuisine / edited by St. Stephen's Cookbook Committee
        p. cm.
    Based on Bayou Cuisine, 1970
    ISBN 0-937552-78-X
    1. Cookery, American–Southern style. 2. Cookery–Mississippi.
I. Clark, Dollie. II. Bayou Cuisine.
TX715.2.S68B46   1997
641.59762–dc21   97–3982
                                                          CIP

Contents

The Story
of Bayou Cuisine

Bayou Cuisine cookbook of St. Stephen's Episcopal Church in Indianola, Mississippi, has sold nearly 100,000 copies. First published in 1970, the cookbook was conceived by Mrs. Arthur B. (Dollie) Clark, Jr., as a money-raising project for a much needed parish house and Sunday School building. The Rev. S. Ross Jones was rector and the original recipe committee members were: Mrs. J. P. Fisher, Mrs. Opie Little, Jr., Mrs. Tom Barron, Mrs. Champ Terney (now Sue Eastland McRoberts), Mrs. E. S. Van Cleve, Jr., and Mrs. Maury McIntyre.

The first 3,000 copies were sold by October, creating the exciting necessity of another printing in the same year. Eight months later another 10,000 copies were printed. These remarkable sales continued through the following decade. By 1996, St. Stephen's had reached its goal: the parish house and the Early building had been built, the church had been renovated, and the parish was on sound financial footing. Ten percent of all sales were going to Outreach, the charitable arm of the church.

A little of the history of St. Stephen's church may be of interest. The first organized congregation of St. Stephen's Mission came together to worship on November 29, 1904, with Halsey Werlein Jr., as rector. The first recorded baptism was that of Frances Eugenia Early, on December 3, 1907, with Bishop William duBose Bratton officiating. The present church building was consecrated on June 3, 1909, and the first service was held there on Easter Sunday, with the Archdeacon of North Mississippi, the Ven. R.E.L. Craig of Jackson officiating. The first marriage in the present church building was the wedding of James Martin Heathman and Inamay Hogin on May 17, 1910. St. Stephen's mission became a parish in 1921 with just over sixty communicants. Today over 200 communicants celebrate services in the original building.

In the spring of 1996, at a time when St. Stephen's Church was without a priest, a new committee was appointed to evaluate the future of *Bayou Cuisine*. At the end of what we thought was a routine discussion with Barney McKee of Quail Ridge Press as to whether or not to reprint, the discussion suddenly took a new direction, the result of which was that Mr. McKee made a proposal that Quail Ridge Press publish a new, condensed form of the cookbook. By the end of the meeting, we were all smiling over the prospects of what would become *Best of Bayou Cuisine*.

The current committee has worked diligently for months, selecting and editing what we considered to be the best recipes from the original cookbook. The ones we wanted to keep were those that had stood the test of time, in taste, accessibility of ingredients, and feasibility of cooking time. Many times, when we had the inevitable disagreements over a particular recipe, we simply voted, figuring that the ten of us made up a reliable cross-section of not only St. Stephen's parishioners, but potential customers for the current market. If we were really stuck, one of us would resolve the impasse by showing up at the next meeting with the dish in question ready for us to taste. When our selections were nearly finished, we put several dishes through the same trial by fire by giving ourselves a dinner party comprised, of course, of dishes from the cookbook. So, although we worked hard, we had a wonderful time in the process.

We also solicited additional recipes from the congregation, especially new parishioners. We were overjoyed to receive nearly a hundred new recipes, many reflecting changes in taste such as the health-conscious trends of the nineties, and many reflecting changes in food products such as the now-popular pond-raised catfish. We are proud to present these recipes.

Our hope is that *Best of Bayou Cuisine* presents the best of the old and the new. In this cookbook, we have retained the classic recipes that have been part of a tradition that has lasted over twenty-five years, and we have added exciting new recipes that will quickly become popular. (See symbol that indicates new recipes) The original cookbook was uniquely divided into sections that reflected a succession of ethnic influences over time, Indian, French, Spanish, and so forth. Mrs. Clark wrote prefaces for each of these sections. The demands of today's market made that arrangement unfeasible; therefore, this cookbook is arranged by traditional categories: appetizers, beverages, salads and such.

We would like to thank Tom Barron for the lovely new cover

photographs of Indian Bayou, for which the cookbook is named. We also thank Eleanor Failing for helping us update the names and hometowns of the authors of these recipes, a daunting task considering all the changes that can take place in over twenty-five years. We thank Laura Gresham for all the daily details she has attended to in cookbook sales, often going far beyond her duties as church secretary. We owe a great debt to our typesetter, Paula Sykes, whose patience and humor saw us through some trying times.

Best of Bayou Cuisine reflects the on-going story of life and love in the parish of St. Stephen's Episcopal Church. Although this collection marks the passing of an era, it also represents the beginning of an exciting new one.

Marion Barnwell, Chair
Best of Bayou Cuisine Committee

Appetizers

Antipasto

2 (4 ounce) cans mushroom
    pieces
1 (14 ounce) can artichoke
    hearts, drained and
    chopped
1 (4 ounce jar) sliced
    pimiento
1/4 cup chopped bell
    pepper
1/2 cup chopped celery
1/2 cup chopped salad
    olives
1/2 cup black olives,
    chopped

Mix together.

Marinade:

1 teaspoon seasoned salt
1 teaspoon salt
1 teaspoon sugar
1 teaspoon garlic powder
1/3 cup wine vinegar
1/3 cup olive oil
1/4 cup instant onion
    flakes
2 1/2 teaspoons Italian
    seasoning
1/2 teaspoon lemon pepper

Bring to a boil, pour over vegetables.

Laura Gresham
INDIANOLA, MS

 Denotes New Recipe

Artichoke Dip

1 can artichokes
1 cup mayonnaise
1 pint sour cream
1 (8 ounce) can sliced water
 chestnuts
1 package ranch dressing
1 small can shrimp
Red pepper, to taste
1 tablespoon lemon juice

Drain artichokes, shrimp, and water chestnuts. (Cut artichokes into 6–8 pieces each.) Mix with all other ingredients, and refrigerate overnight. Serve with dip style corn chips.

Ellen Clayton
INDIANOLA, MS

Bean Dip

1 can Bush's Best Chili hot
 beans
1/2 pound butter
1/2 pound grated sharp
 cheese
1 to 2 jalapeno hot pep-
 pers, chopped
1 medium onion, grated
1 clove garlic, chopped
 finely

Mash beans coarsely, put all ingredients in double boiler until cheese melts. Serve with Fritos.

Lynn Eastland
INDIANOLA, MS

Black-eyed Pea Dip

1 large package black-eyed
 peas (frozen)
1/4 cup salad oil or bacon
 drippings
1 tablespoon finely grated
 onions
Salt and pepper to taste

Boil peas in salted water until tender. Drain. Sauté onion in oil and add peas to mixture. Press peas to break skins and mix with the seasonings. *Variation:* Add Ro–Tel tomatoes and green chilies to taste. Sprinkle with grated Parmesan cheese and garnish with strips of avocado dipped in lemon juice. Serve with Fritos or fried tortilla triangles.

Mrs. Aleta Saunders
GREENWOOD, MS

Hot Broccoli Dip

3 ribs celery, chopped
1 small can mushrooms,
  chopped
1/2 to 1 medium onion,
  chopped
3 tablespoons butter
1 roll garlic cheese
3 packages frozen chopped
  broccoli, cooked
1 can cream of mushroom
  soup
Tabasco
Worcestershire

Serve from chafing dish with fritos, or other party cracker.

Mrs. Henry Crowell
INDIANOLA, MS

Smoked Catfish Ball

2 smoked catfish fillets,
  flaked or 1 can smoked
  oysters, chopped
8 ounces cream cheese
4 green onions
1 can mushrooms
1 small can black olives,
  chopped
1 teaspoon prepared
  horseradish
1 tablespoon
  Worcestershire sauce
1 tablespoon lemon juice
1 teaspoon creole
  seasoning
Salt, pepper
Paprika

Soften cream cheese. Mix with other ingredients except paprika. Roll into a ball, sprinkle with paprika. Chill. Serve with crackers.

Jackie Brocato
INDIANOLA, MS

Soused Catfish

6 (3 - 5 ounce) catfish filets
2 onions, finely chopped
1 tablespoon chopped
 parsley
3 bay leaves
8 cloves garlic
1/8 teaspoon mace
Sprig of thyme or 1/4
 teaspoon dried
6 peppercorns
Salt to taste
2 cups tarragon vinegar

Cook catfish at 350° for 20 minutes, covered with all ingredients. Allow to cool. Strain liquid. Save onions. Place flaked catfish in dish with 1 inch rim. Pour strained liquid over fish. Top with onions and crushed parsley. Serve with soda crackers.

Delicious and light.

Seymour Johnson
INDIANOLA, MS

Cheese Ball

1 (8 ounce) package sharp
 cheddar cheese
1 large package cream
 cheese
1 small package bleu
 cheese
1/2 teaspoon garlic powder
1/4 teaspoon cayenne
 pepper
Pecans

Grate sharp cheese and mix with cream cheese and bleu cheese. Add other ingredients and work until thoroughly mixed. Form into ball and roll in finely grated pecans. Makes a ball approximately 4 inches in diameter. Serve with fancy crackers.

Christine L. Chandler
GREENWOOD, MS

Olive Cheese Nuggets

1/4 pound sharp cheese
1/4 cup soft butter or oleo
3/4 cup sifted flour
1/8 teaspoon salt
1/2 teaspoon paprika
24 to 30 large stuffed olives

Grate cheese; mix with butter. Sift in flour, salt, and paprika. Make dough into balls and shape around each olive. Place on ungreased cookie sheet. Bake in 400° oven 12 to 15 minutes. Serve hot or cold. Makes 2 to 2 1/2 dozen.

Mrs. Harry Griffith
YAZOO CITY, MS

Cheese Straws

1 pound sharp cheese,
  grated
1 stick butter
2 cups flour
1 teaspoon salt
1/2 teaspoon red pepper

Melt butter and pour over cheese. Work in flour and pepper; let cool. Press from cookie press on cookie sheet and bake at 375°.

Mrs. Earl Brickell
INDIANOLA, MS

Variation:

2 sticks oleo
1 cup sharp cheese, grated
1 teaspoon red pepper
1 teaspoon garlic salt
2 cups flour, sifted

Cream oleo. Add cheese, red pepper, garlic salt, and flour and roll in waxed paper. Chill thoroughly. Slice 1/4" thick. Bake 350° for 15 minutes.

Mrs. Emily McClendon Smith
INDIANOLA, MS

Cheese Wafers

2 cups sharp cheddar
  cheese, grated
2 cups Rice Krispies
2 sticks oleo
2 cups flour
1/4 teaspoon garlic powder
1/4 teaspoon salt
1/8 teaspoon red pepper

Mix well; roll in balls and press with fork. Place on ungreased pan. Cook in 350° oven 20 minutes or until light brown.

Mrs. J. H. McPherson
PARAGOULD, AR

Chicken Liver Paté

1/2 pound chicken livers
(boil in white wine, a
little chicken broth,
(enough to cover)
1 bay leaf for 15 or 20
minutes. (Keep cov-
ered.)
Chop livers in food
chopper or blender
1 teaspoon salt
1/2 cube rendered chicken
fat or butter (2 table-
spoons)
1/4 teaspoon nutmeg
2 tablespoons minced
onions
1 teaspoon dry mustard
Chopped black olives
according to taste

Simmer the livers in broth until done. Drain
and grind them with olives, or puree in blender.
Add little of broth and wine, the minced onion
and other ingredient. Pack in a crock. May be
frozen to serve later.

James Robertshaw
GREENVILLE, MS

Miniature Cream Puffs

1 cup water
1/2 cup butter
1 cup flour
4 eggs

Ham filling:
3 cans (4 1/2 ounce) deviled
ham
1 tablespoon horseradish
3/4 teaspoon pepper
3/4 teaspoon onion salt
1/3 cup sour cream

Heat water and butter to a rolling boil in sauce
pan. Stir in flour. Stir vigorously over low heat
until mixture forms a soft ball, about 1 minute.
Remove from heat. Beat eggs in one at a time,
until smooth. Drop dough by rounded spoonfuls onto ungreased baking sheet. Bake at 400°,
about 25 minutes or until puffed, golden brown
and dry. Remove from sheet and cool.

Mrs. Charles B. Fisackerly
BLAINE, MS

Curry Dip

1 pod of garlic, smashed
1 small jar salad dressing
3 tablespoons ketchup
1 tablespoon
   Worcestershire sauce
3 teaspoons curry powder
2 teaspoons crushed onion
Pinch salt
1 teaspoon Tabasco

Thoroughly mix all the above ingredients together. Good as a dip with raw vegetables.

Mrs. Seymour B. Johnson
INDIANOLA, MS

Mushrooms in Vermouth

4 (4 ounce) cans mush-
   rooms buttons, drained
1/2 cup dry Vermouth
1/2 cup red wine vinegar
1 clove garlic, crushed
2 tablespoons chopped
   onions
1 tablespoon basil leaves
1 teaspoon salt
1/2 teaspoon black pepper
1/2 teaspoon sugar
1/2 teaspoon English
   mustard (powdered)
1/2 cup olive oil

Put mushroom buttons in attractive jar with tight fitting lid. Combine all other ingredients and beat with fork until well mixed. Pour over mushrooms. Seal and store in refrigerator, up to two months. Serve as a garnish for cold meats or as an hors d'oeuvre. Makes about two 8 ounce jars.

Mrs. Rodgers Brashier
INDIANOLA, MS

Hot Mushroom Dip

4 tablespoons butter
1 clove garlic
1 pound mushrooms, sliced
2 tablespoons dried parsley
1/2 teaspoon salt
1/4 teaspoon pepper
1 cup sour cream

Melt butter in chafing dish. Add garlic which has been minced, mushrooms, parsley, salt, pepper. Cook until mushrooms are tender. Fold in sour cream. Serve on melba toast.

Miss Margaret Ann Gibson
MEMPHIS, TN

Stuffed Mushrooms Parmigiana

12 fresh mushrooms (large)
2 tablespoons butter or margarine
1 medium onion, finely chopped
2 ounces pepperoni, diced (1/2 cup)
1/4 cup finely chopped green peppers
1 small clove garlic, finely minced
1/2 cup (12 crackers) crushed rich round crackers
3 tablespoons grated parmesan cheese
1 tablespoon snipped parsley
1/2 teaspoon seasoning salt
1/4 teaspoon dried oregano, crushed
Dash pepper
1/3 cup chicken broth

Plan 2 mushrooms per person for appetizer. Plan 6 mushrooms per person for main course.

Wash mushrooms, remove stems and reserve. Drain caps on paper towel. Melt butter and margarine in skillet; add onion, pepperoni, green pepper, garlic and chopped mushrooms stems. Cook until vegetables are tender, but not brown. Add cracker crumbs, cheese, parsley, seasoned salt, oregano, pepper. Mix well. Stir in chicken broth. Spoon stuffing into mushroom caps, rounding tops. Place caps in shallow baking pans with 1/4 inch water covering bottom of pan. Bake uncovered in 325° oven about 25 minutes until heated.

Kathy Allen
INDIANOLA, MS

Pickled Okra

Small okra pods
1 quart vinegar
1 pint water
1/2 cup salt
Alum
Dill

Pack okra in clean pint jars in which a pint of alum and dill is placed. Boil together the vinegar, water, and salt. Pour hot liquid over okra. let set for 30 minutes. Seal.

Tom Miller
BLYTHEVILLE, AR

Cheese Marinated Onions

3 ounces blue cheese,
  crumbled
1/2 cup salad oil
2 tablespoons lemon juice
1 teaspoon salt
1/2 teaspoon sugar
Dash pepper, paprika
4 medium white onions

Mix all ingredients except onions. Pour mixture over thinly sliced onion rings and refrigerate for 24 hours. Makes about one quart rings.

Mrs. Ben Himelstein
MOORHEAD, MS

Mushroom Pinwheels

2 large cans crescent rolls
1 (8 ounce) soft cream
  cheese
2 stems green onions,
  chopped
1 can mushrooms,
  chopped
Season salt, to taste

Roll out crescent roll dough, being careful not to separate. Mix cream cheese, green onions, mushrooms, and season salt and spread atop dough. Roll up crescent rolls and refrigerate to harden (about 1 1/2 hours.) Slice and bake in a 350° pre-heated oven for 8–12 minutes.

Variation: Brush each slice with egg and sprinkle with poppy seed before baking.

Michelle Van Cleve
INDIANOLA, MS

Cheesy Onion Dip

1 (12 ounce) package frozen
   chopped onions
24 ounces cream cheese
2 cups Parmesan cheese
1/2 cup mayonnaise
Fritos

Thaw onions completely. Roll in paper towels to remove excess moisture. Mix onions with softened cream cheese, Parmesan and mayonnaise. Bake 425° until slightly browned, about 15 minutes. Serve hot with Fritos.

Mrs. Ernie Baker
INDIANOLA, MS

Barbecued Pecans

1 quart pecans
Salt
Worcestershire sauce

Place pecans in colander. Pour water over pecans and drain. Place pecans in shallow pan; wet generously with Worcestershire. Tumble until well covered. Sprinkle with salt. Place in 300° oven for 1 hour, or until brown.

Mrs. Morris (Freda) Lewis
INDIANOLA, MS

Variation: Lay pecan halves on foil-lined pan and moisten generously with water. Sprinkle with salt to taste over nuts. Put in 300° oven 15 minutes. Turn off heat. Leave in oven 1 1/2 to 2 hours (door closed).

Mrs. Joe Green
INDIANOLA, MS

Salmon Party Mound

2 cups canned salmon
1 (8-ounce) package cream
  cheese, softened
1 tablespoon lemon juice
2 teaspoons grated onion
1 teaspoon prepared
  horseradish
1/4 teaspoon salt
1/4 teaspoon liquid smoke
1/2 cup chopped pecans
3 tablespoons snipped
  parsley

Drain and flake salmon, removing skin and bones. Combine salmon, cream cheese, lemon juice, onion, horseradish, salt and liquid smoke; mix thoroughly. Chill several hours. Combine pecans and parsley. Shape salmon mixture into a ball; roll in nut mixture; chill well. Serve with assorted crackers.

Mrs. Cub Amos
DALLAS, TX

Hot Seafood Dip

1/2 pound butter
1 cup flour
1 small can evaporated
  milk
2 cups sweet milk
1 teaspoon paprika
1 teaspoon black pepper
1 can mushrooms, finely
  chopped
2 cans crab meat
1 pound cooked shrimp
Salt to taste
1 bunch of onions, finely
  chopped
1 1/2 cups parsley, finely
  chopped

Melt butter in top of double boiler. Slowly add flour and then slowly add milk and cream, making a white sauce.

Add the remaining ingredients and serve in a chafing dish with melba rounds.

Mrs. Seymour B. Johnson
INDIANOLA, MS

Sherried Shrimp Dip

1 cup mayonnaise
1 tablespoon tarragon
  vinegar
1 tablespoon wine vinegar
2 teaspoons anchovy paste
1 teaspoon dry mustard
2 tablespoons sherry
1/2 cup chopped parsley
1 tablespoon onion juice
4 tablespoons capers
1/4 teaspoon garlic powder

This is the best dip for shrimp ever; good on crackers when the shrimp runs out.

Combine all ingredients a day ahead of time.

Susie Calvert
WEST POINT, MS

Shrimp Dip with Mace

1/2 pound cooked, peeled
  shrimp or 2 cans me-
  dium shrimp, drained
1/2 green pepper, diced
2 pieces celery, cut fine
1 cup mayonnaise
1 (8 ounce) package cream
  cheese
1/4 teaspoon dry mustard
1/2 teaspoon mace
1 teaspoon onion juice or
  grated onion
1 teaspoon Worcestershire
  sauce
1/4 teaspoon salt or to
  taste
Dash of red pepper

Roughly chop shrimp. Soften cream cheese. Beat smooth. Add all other ingredients. Refrigerate at least 1 hour before serving. Makes about 4 cups.

Mrs. Jeptha Barbour
INDIANOLA, MS

Steak Tartar a La Seymour

2 pounds ground top
  round
2 medium onions, minced
1/2 cup capers, minced
1/4 cup minced parsley
2 teaspoons Dijon mustard
Dash of Worcestershire
Dash of Tabasco
1 1/2 teaspoon salt
1 teaspoon pepper
1/3 cup cognac (optional)
Chives

To finely ground raw meat add all ingredients except chives and mix well. Mold in serving bowl; sprinkle with chives; set in bowl of shaved ice. Serve with melba toast rounds. Serves 8-12.

Seymour Johnson
INDIANOLA, MS

Vegetable Pizza

2 cans crescent rolls
1 beaten egg
12 ounces cream cheese,
  softened
1/2 cup mayonnaise
2 teaspoons onion juice
1 teaspoon garlic salt
2 teaspoons dill weed
Cheddar cheese, shredded

Spray Pam on a 9" x 13" jellyroll pan. Roll out dough to cover bottom of pan. Pinch seams together with fingers. Brush with beaten egg. Bake at 375° for 13-15 minutes. Cool.

Beat cream cheese, mayonnaise, onion juice, garlic salt, dill weed together until smooth. (Best done the day before). Spread over pastry. Top with bits of cut-up veggies — cucumber, broccoli, cherry tomatoes, carrots, green onions, mushrooms, ripe olives, sprinkle with finely grated cheddar cheese. Cut into serving pieces.

Mary Tucker Myres
INDIANOLA, MS

Quiche Lorraine

9 inch pie crust
6 slices thick bacon cooked
  and drained
12 thin slices Swiss or
Gruyere cheese (about the
  same size as bacon)
4 eggs
1 tablespoon flour
1/4 teaspoon nutmeg
1/2 teaspoon salt
Cayenne pepper
2 cups light cream
1 1/2 tablespoons butter,
  melted

Line pie plate with pie crust. Cut bacon, slices in half, cover the crust with overlapping layers of cheese and bacon. Beat together eggs, flour, a generous grating of nutmeg, salt, and a few grains cayenne. Add light cream; stir in 1 1/2 tablespoons melted butter. Strain this custard over cheese and bacon. Bake at 375° for about 40 minutes or until custard is set and top browned. Serve warm. Serves 6 nicely. Serve as hors d'oeuvre or main course dish.

The Rev. Edward S. T. Hale
BROOKHAVEN, MS

Soups and Sauces

Beef Stock

4 pounds beef shank slices
  with meat on bones
2–3" marrow bones
3 quarts water
2 carrots cut in thirds
2 medium onions quar-
  tered
2 stalks celery with leaves
2 teaspoons salt
1 bay leaf
2 whole cloves garlic
4 whole cloves
6 peppercorns
1/2 teaspoon dried thyme
  leaves
2 sprigs parsley

Place meat and marrow bones in a large kettle with the water. Add remaining ingredients and bring to a boil over moderately high heat (about 275°). Simmer covered over low heat for 4 hours. Strain stock. Cool. Chill overnight. Skim off fat from top before using. If stock congeals on standing, warm slightly until it melts before measuring amount needed in recipe. Makes 3 quarts.

Mrs. Honey Morris
INDIANOLA, MS

Chicken Stock

1 (5 pound) stewing
  chicken - cut up
1 stalk celery with leaves
3 medium carrots - cut in
  thirds
1 onion quartered
1 bay leaf
1 sprig parsley
2 whole cloves
1/8 teaspoon dried marjo-
  ram leaves
2 teaspoons salt
3 peppercorns
2 quarts water

Combine all ingredients in a large kettle. Bring to a boil and simmer, covered, over low heat for three hours. Strain broth. Cool. Chill in refrigerator overnight. Skim off fat from top before using. If stock congeals on standing, warm slightly until it melts before measuring amounts needed. Remove chicken from bones and use in salads and sandwiches. Makes 2 quarts.

Mrs. Honey Morris
INDIANOLA, MS

All about Our "Bean Soup"

2 pounds no. 1 white
Michigan beans
Smoked ham hock
Salt and pepper

Cover with cold water and soak overnight. Drain and re-cover with water. Add a smoked ham hock and simmer slowly for about 4 hours until beans are cooked tender. Then add salt and pepper to suit taste. Just before serving. bruise beans with large spoon or ladle, enough to cloud. Serves about six persons.

Bean soup has been a featured item on the menu of the House of Representatives Restaurant since long before that day in 1904 when the then Speaker of the House, Joseph G. Cannon, of Illinois, came into the House Restaurant and ordered bean soup. Then, as now, bean soup was a hearty, zesty and filling dish; but it was typically hot and humid in Washington that day, and, therefore, bean soup had been omitted from the menu. "Thunderation". roared Speaker Cannon, "I had my mouth set for bean soup"; and, he continued, "from now on, hot or cold, rain, snow, or shine, I want it on the menu every day."

Thos. G. Abernethy
FIRST DISTRICT, MS

Black Bean Soup a La Tampa

1 pound black beans
1 cup olive oil
1 pod garlic
1 tablespoon salt
1 ounce bacon
1/4 pound ham bone
1/2 cup vinegar
3 bay leaves
2 large onions, chopped
  finely
1 bell pepper (green),
  chopped
1 1/2 quart water

Soak beans thoroughly overnight. Fry onion, bell pepper and garlic lightly in 1/2 cup olive oil. Combine all ingredients including water in which beans were soaked except vinegar and onions, and cook with slow fire until beans are tender and liquid is of thick consistency. Add vinegar a few minutes before serving. Serve in a thick bowl with one cup cooked rice over which black beans are placed and topped with 1/2 cup chopped onions.

Tom Barron
INDIANOLA, MS

Cheese Soup

1/4 cup butter
1/2 cup chopped onions
1 cup grated carrots
1/4 cup plain flour
1 1/2 tablespoons corn
  starch
1/8 teaspoon baking soda
4 cups milk
4 cups chicken broth
1 teaspoon salt
3 jars old English sharp
  cheese or
3 cups fresh grated ched-
  dar

Sauté onions in butter, add carrots, flour, cornstarch, and baking soda. Stir. Remove and place in large pot - add milk, broth, salt and cheese. Simmer until cheese melts. Do not boil.

May add 1/8 teaspoon chili pepper or 1/8 teaspoon red pepper flakes. Keep in crock pot on low - great for Super Bowl parties. May freeze.

Vickie Hester
INDIANOLA, MS

Corn Chowder

1 can corn kernels
1 can cream style corn
1/2 small onion, chopped
4 pieces bacon, cooked and
  chopped

Mix all ingredients and simmer until warm.

Mimi Alexander
INDIANOLA, MS

Summer Cucumber Soup

"This soup signals *summer* to me!"

4 to 6 cucumbers
2 medium onions, chopped
6 tablespoons butter
  (unsalted is best)
2 cups chicken broth
2 cups buttermilk
1 tablespoon minced fresh
  basil (or 1 teaspoon
  dried)
1 tablespoon minced fresh
  parsley (or 1 teaspoon
  dried)
2 tablespoons minced fresh
  mint (or 2 teaspoons
  dried)
Salt and pepper to taste
Lemon for garnish

Stem, halve, seed and roughly chop cucumbers. Note: This is best with garden cucumbers. If you have to use the waxed grocery store variety, you must *peel* them as well, which makes the soup less green.

Melt butter in large, heavy saucepan. Add onions and cucumbers. Cover tightly and "sweat" the vegetables over medium heat for about 15 minutes. They should be soft, but not in the least, brown.

Stir in chicken broth and herbs. Remove from heat. Puree in small batches in blender. (Careful hot liquids expand in the blender). Transfer pureé to a large bowl, stir in buttermilk, and salt and pepper to taste. Chill the soup for 4 hours minimum, and taste. Correct seasoning if needed. (Occasionally a pinch of sugar is needed.) Thin the soup if desired with extra broth or buttermilk. Serve in chilled bowls with a thin lemon slice floating on top. Makes 6 servings.

Kate Failing
INDIANOLA, MS

Gazpacho

2 ripe peeled tomatoes
1 peeled cucumbers
1/4 cup green pepper
1/4 cup diced onion
1 cup tomato juice
2 tablespoons olive oil
1 1/2 tablespoon vinegar
Dash of tabasco
Salt and pepper
1 small clove garlic,
   minced

Combine in blender for 3 seconds. Serve cold with crackers. Serves 4.

Mrs. W. E. Failing
HOUSTON, TX

My Gumbo

12 slices bacon
10 tablespoons flour
12 cups water
5 pounds raw shrimp,
   shelled
5 chopped onions
2 chopped bell peppers
5 packages cut frozen okra
10 bay leaves
4 (28-ounce) cans tomatoes
10 tablespoons
   Worcestershire
5 tablespoons salt
1 tablespoon black pepper
2 cans tomato paste
4 shakes Tabasco
1 tablespoon parsley flakes
1 teaspoon celery seed
2 teaspoons soy sauce
1/2 teaspoon tarragon
1/2 teaspoon thyme
1/2 teaspoon rosemary
1/2 teaspoon savory
1 or 2 pounds lump
   crabmeat

Fry bacon and drain on paper, reserving bacon grease. Mix flour with grease and brown. Add water. Set aside bacon, shrimp and crabmeat. Add all other ingredients and cook slowly for 3 hours. Add shrimp and crabmeat, cooking until shrimp is done, about 5 minutes. Crumble in crisp bacon. Yield: 1 dozen (22 ounce) freezer jars.

Mrs. Joe Berman
LEXINGTON, MS

Shrimp Gumbo

1 ham hock
3 quarts water
4 green peppers, chopped
1 stalk celery, chopped
4 onions, chopped
4 cloves garlic, minced
2 pounds cut okra
1/2 bunch parsley, cut fine
4 tablespoons bacon fat
2 (14.5-ounce) cans
   tomatoes
1 tablespoon paprika
1 tablespoon sugar
2 tablespoons
   Worcestershire
1/2 teaspoon black pepper
2 tablespoons salt
2 pounds shrimp
2 cans crabmeat
1 jar oysters

Put ham hock in water. In skillet with bacon grease combine peppers, celery, onions, garlic, okra, and parsley; cook slowly for 30 minutes. To ham hock and water add ingredients cooked in skillet. To all this add tomatoes, paprika, sugar, Worcestershire, black pepper and salt. Simmer for 3 hours. The last 5 minutes of cooking add shrimp, crabmeat and oysters. Serve over small serving of rice.
Serves 12 or more and freezes well.

Mrs. W.H. Baird
INDIANOLA, MS

Oyster Bisque

1 quart oysters
4 cups light cream
1 tablespoon flour
1 tablespoon butter
1/2 cup chopped celery
1 bell pepper
Salt, pepper, and
   Worcestershire sauce
   to taste

Put oysters through a meat grinder. Thicken the cream with flour and butter, chopped celery and bell pepper, salt and pepper. Add the oysters and keep the soup hot; do not allow it to boil. Add Worcestershire sauce when ready to serve.

Mrs. Thomas Dominick
VICKSBURG, MS

Onion Soup

3 cups onion, sliced very
  thin
1/4 pound butter
3 quarts water
2 cups strong chicken
  stock
2 cups beef stock
Salt and pepper
1 cup grated Gruyére
  cheese
Toasted hard rolls, sliced

Sauté onions in butter. Cook until onions are golden brown. Transfer to pressure cooker, add a bit of the water, and cook under pressure for 10 minutes. Put this in large earthenware bowl or ovenware. Add remaining water, beef, and chicken stock, salt and pepper. When cool, add 1 cup of grated Gruyére cheese. Stock must be cold before adding cheese or it will curdle. Bake uncovered in 250° oven until half of the liquid has evaporated. This may take anywhere from 1 1/2 to 3 hours. Serve with Gruyére or Parmesan cheese and slices of toasted hard rolls. Makes 12 servings.

Lucy Huff Bishop
JACKSON, MS

Baked Potato Soup

4 large baking potatoes
2/3 cup butter or marga-
  rine
2/3 cup all-purpose flour
6 cups milk
3/4 teaspoon salt
1/2 teaspoon pepper
1 1/2 cups shredded
  cheddar cheese, divided
12 slices bacon, cooked,
  crumbled, and divided
4 green onions, chopped
  and divided
1 (8 ounce) sour cream

Wash potatoes, prick several times with a fork. Bake at 400° for 1 hour (may also be microwaved) or until done, let cool. Cut potatoes in half lengthwise; scoop out and reserve pulp. Discard shells.

Melt butter in a Dutch oven over low heat; add flour, stirring until smooth. Cook, stirring constantly, 1 minute. Gradually add milk; cook over medium heat, stirring constantly, until thickened and bubbly.

Stir in potato, salt, pepper, 1 cup cheese, 1/2 cup bacon, and 2 tablespoons green onions; cook until heated (do not boil). Stir in sour cream; cook just until heated (do not boil). Serve with remaining cheese, bacon and green onions. Yield: 2 1/2 quarts.

Marty Vincent
INDIANOLA, MS

Potato Soup

1/4 cup butter
4 cups potatoes, diced
1 cup chopped celery
1 medium onion, chopped
1 pimiento, minced
2 tablespoons minced
  parsley
4 cups chicken broth
1/2 teaspoon paprika
1 1/2 cups sour cream

Melt butter and sauté potatoes, celery, onion and pimiento. Add parsley and broth, then simmer until vegetables are tender. Blend in sour cream and paprika.

Rebecca Barrett
INDIANOLA, MS

Old-Fashioned Split Pea Soup

1 pound split peas
1 large pepper
1 large onion
2 pods garlic
3 ribs celery
1 ham hock
3 quarts water
1/2 stick oleo
Chopped parsley

Sauté chopped onion, celery, and garlic in oleo; put in ham hock and let simmer. Put split peas in 3 quarts of cold water and let come to a boil, then put in with the ham hock and let boil until thick. Garnish each serving with chopped parsley.

Old Southern Tea Room
VICKSBURG, MS

Eastern Serbian Soup

6 cans cream of potato
  soup
1 cup grated smoked ham
1/2 onion, chopped
1/2 bunch parsley, chopped
1 small head cabbage,
  grated
4 cups sour cream
2 cups water
1/2 cup chicken stock
10 dashes white pepper
Juice of 1 lemon

Simmer onion and cabbage 10 minutes in water. Add all other ingredients, except sour cream, and simmer 5 minutes. Add sour cream last. Makes 16 cups.

Frank Tindall, Jr.
INDIANOLA, MS

Tortilla Soup

1 onion, chopped
2 cloves garlic, chopped
2 tablespoons oil
2 chicken breasts, cut up in bite-size pieces
28 ounce can tomatoes, chopped
10 1/2 ounce beef broth
10 1/2 ounce chicken broth
10 1/2 ounce tomato soup
1/2 cup picante sauce (I use hot)
1 teaspoon Worcestershire
1 teaspoon cumin
1 teaspoon chili powder
4 corn tortillas

Brown onion and garlic in oil. Simmer all ingredients, except tortillas for 1 hour. Cut tortillas into strips and add to ingredients during the last 10 minutes. Serve with grated Monterrey Jack cheese and chopped onion.

Variation: omit tortillas and serve with tostato chips.

Julia Lewis Miller
HOUSTON, TX

Vegetable Soup

1 soup bone (with meat) or 3/4 pound lean meat
1/4 stick butter
3 1/2 cups tomatoes
2 1/2 cups tomato sauce
1 stalk celery, chopped
1/2 bell pepper, chopped
1 large onion, chopped
1 package frozen mixed vegetables
1 teaspoon parsley flakes
1 teaspoon oregano
2 teaspoons salt
1 teaspoon pepper
2 1/2 quarts water

Brown soup bone and meat in 1/4 stick butter; remove and reserve soup bone and chop meat. Add celery, pepper, onion and cook until tender. Add tomatoes, tomato sauce, vegetables, soup bone, chopped meat and seasonings and 2 1/2 quarts water and simmer at least 4 hours. Return meat to soup. Serves 8.

Serve with corn meal muffins and salad for a winter lunch.

Sue Eastland McRoberts
JACKSON, MS

Tangy Barbecue Sauce

2 tablespoons oil
1 onion, chopped
2 stalks celery, chopped
1 bell pepper, chopped
3 small cans tomato sauce
1 small can crushed
   pineapple
1/4 cup molasses
1 teaspoon ginger
1/2 teaspoon cinnamon
1 teaspoon Worcestershire
   sauce
Salt and pepper to taste

Cook over low fire—15 minutes. Makes enough to cook 3 pounds of meat. Chicken and ribs are best. Let the meat get room temperature. Brush on the sauce. Barbecue over a charcoal fire or broil in the oven.

Mrs. T. H. Campbell, III
YAZOO CITY, MS

Lemon Barbecue Sauce

4 cups oil
1 1/2 cups vinegar
1/2 cup black pepper
1/3 cup salt
4 lemons
1/2 cup brown sugar

Slice lemons. Combine with other ingredients. Cook on low heat until lemons are falling apart. Store in the refrigerator. This is delicious on chicken. Marinate the chicken in a small amount several hours before cooking over charcoal. Yield 1 1/2 quarts sauce.

Jimmy Failing
INDIANOLA, MS

Beet Sauce

1 pint beets, cooked and
  chopped
1/3 cup onion, chopped
1 cup celery, chopped
1 cup mayonnaise
1/2 cup Heinz chili sauce
1 tablespoon
  Worcestershire sauce
Pinch of salt
1 clove garlic, mashed

Serve sauce over green string beans that have been cooked in salt water (no meat). The sauce will keep in the refrigerator for several days. Mix together beets, onion and celery.

In bowl of food processor, combine mayonnaise, chili sauce, Worcestershire, salt and garlic. Pulse briefly. To mixture in bowl, add beets, onion and celery. Pulse again briefly.

Serve sauce over green beans. The sauce will keep in the fridge for several days. Delicious.

Mrs. Guy Robinson
INDIANOLA, MS

Carne Adovada

Excellent sauce for pork tenderloin.

1/2 small onion, chopped
1/2 tablespoon olive oil
1 teaspoon minced garlic
4 dried, whole chile
  peppers
1/2 teaspoon cumin
1 teaspoon coriander
1/2 cup fresh lemon or
  lime juice
1 tablespoon
  Worcestershire sauce
1 cup chicken broth
1/4 cup roasted bell pepper
  or pimiento
1/2 teaspoon sugar, salt,
  and pepper

Cut chile peppers open and discard seed. Rinse and soak in water. Bake on cookie sheet 5 minutes at 300°. (Do not burn.) Remove while damp. Puree with a little chicken broth in blender. Sauté peppers, onion and garlic in olive oil. Add bell pepper and spices. Continue to cook and add the puréed chile peppers and liquids. Bring to a boil. Simmer for 20 minutes. Serve with grilled pork.

Claiborne Barnwell
JACKSON, MS

Chili Sauce

12 over-ripe tomatoes, peeled
6 medium onions
6 large green peppers, cored
1 cup vinegar
3/4 cup sugar
1 tablespoon salt
2 teaspoons cinnamon
2 teaspoons cloves
2 teaspoons all-spice
1 teaspoon red pepper
2 teaspoons black pepper

Finely chop tomatoes, peppers, and onions. Add other ingredients and, if necessary add a can of tomatoes to make it juicier. (The equivalent of canned tomatoes can be substituted for the over ripe tomatoes.) Boil for one hour and stir often.

Mrs. W. M. Garrard, Jr.
INDIANOLA, MS

Fudge Sauce

1/2 cup cocoa
3/4 cup sugar
1/8 teaspoon salt
1 cup corn syrup
1/2 cup hot water
2 tablespoons butter
1/2 teaspoon vanilla

Stir all ingredients until well mixed, except butter and vanilla. Cook over low heat, stirring occasionally until the mixture comes to boil. Cook without stirring 10-12 minutes. Take from heat and add butter and vanilla. Beat until slightly cooled and add 1/2 cup pecans if desired. The recipe makes two cups, enough for 8-10 sundaes. This sauce may be served either hot or cold over ice cream.

Mrs. Joe Hendon
JACKSON, MS

Mock Hollandaise Sauce

2 (3 ounce) packages
  Philadelphia cream
  cheese
2 egg yolks
2 tablespoons lemon juice
  (fresh)
Dash of salt and cayenne
Paprika

Soften the cream cheese and add the egg yolks, one at a time blending thoroughly after each addition. Add the lemon juice and salt. Place over hot water just until the sauce is heated through. Serve on hot cooked vegetable.

Mrs. Joe Baird
INVERNESS, MS

Quick Hollandaise Sauce

3 egg yolks
1 tablespoon lemon juice
1/4 teaspoon salt
Pinch cayenne pepper
1/2 cup (1 stick) oleo or
  butter

Heat the butter to bubbling in a small pan.

Place egg yolks, lemon juice, salt and pepper in the container of an electric blender. Cover and turn on low speed. Immediately remove cover or center cap and pour in the butter in a steady stream. When all the butter is added, turn off.

Mrs. Leslie R. Fletcher
INDIANOLA, MS

Jezebel Sauce

1 medium jar pineapple
  preserves
1 medium jar apple jelly
1 medium jar prepared
  mustard
1 medium jar horseradish
Salt to taste
Pepper to taste

Combine all ingredients in small bowl. Mix with electric mixer on lowest speed. Makes about 1 quart. This is delicious on baked ham, roast beef, and other meats. It keeps indefinitely in refrigerator.

Josephine W. Collier
YAZOO CITY, MS

Kum-back Sauce

1/4 cup salad oil
2 garlic cloves, chopped fine
1 cup mayonnaise
1/4 cup chili sauce
1/4 cup catsup
1 teaspoon Worcestershire sauce
1 teaspoon black pepper
Dash Tabasco sauce
Dash paprika
Juice of grated onion
2 tablespoons water
1 teaspoon prepared mustard

Put all ingredients in quart jar and shake well. Keep in refrigerator. Makes a full pint. This sauce is a delicious on vegetable salad or shrimp.

Miss Maurice Renfroe
INDIANOLA, MS

Lemon Sauce

1/2 cup sugar
1 tablespoon corn starch
1/8 teaspoon salt
1 cup boiling water
2 tablespoons butter
2 tablespoon lemon juice
1 egg yolk

Mix sugar, corn starch, and salt. Add boiling water slowly, stirring constantly. Boil 5 minutes. Remove from heat and add butter, lemon juice, and beaten egg yolk. Delicious on ginger bread.

Mrs. Peter Howard Rutledge
NEW YORK, NY

Barbecued Wine Sauce for Venison, Beef, Pork, or Lamb

1/2 cup Burgundy or other
   dry red wine
1/2 cup chili sauce
1/4 cup salad oil
3 tablespoons wine vinegar
2 cloves garlic
2 tablespoons chopped
   onion
1 tablespoon
   Worcestershire sauce
1 bay leaf
Salt and pepper

Combine all ingredients and pour over meat. Marinate (turning occasionally) from 3 hours to 3 days. Bake in sauce at 275 - 300°.

Also good when meat is chipped, frozen in sauce, reheated and served on buns.

Brigadier General Morgan Roseborough
FRANKFURT, GERMANY

Favorite Marinade

4 parts soy or teriyaki
   sauce (low sodium
   preferred)
1 part tequila (no kidding,
   do not omit, alcohol
   cooks out)
1/2 part liquid smoke
3 - 4 cloves fresh garlic,
   pressed
Juice of 1 - 2 limes
Favorite dry seasoning (We
   like D. L. Jardine's steak
   seasoning)
Fresh herbs minced

In lieu of store-bought seasoning mixture:
   1 tablespoon garlic powder
   1 tablespoon onion powder
   1/2 tablespoon chili powder
   1/2 tablespoon paprika
   1/2 tablespoon celery salt
   1/2 tablespoon coriander
   1/2 tablespoon oregano
   1/2 tablespoon dried lemon peel
   1/4 tablespoon allspice
Use on beef, pork or chicken.

Trish Berry
INDIANOLA, MS

Meuniere Sauce

1 tablespoon chopped
    parsley
1 tablespoon chopped
    green onions
1/2 cup butter
1/2 teaspoon salt
2 tablespoons lemon juice
1/2 teaspoon pepper
Dash of hot sauce
Dash of Worcestershire
    sauce

Mix ingredients. Stir over low heat and simmer a few minutes. Serve over fish.

Mrs. Edwin Bowman
BATON ROUGE, LA

Hot Cooked Mustard

1 cup dry mustard
1 cup tarragon vinegar
3 eggs, beaten
1 cup sugar

Mix mustard and vinegar in glass bowl. Chill overnight. Next day add sugar and eggs and cook until thick. Yield 1 pint.

Mrs. James H. Lear
INDIANOLA, MS

Rum Sauce

1/2 cup water
2 tablespoons sugar
1 teaspoon cornstarch
Pinch of salt
1 tablespoon rum
1 tablespoon butter

Heat ingredients to desired consistency. May roast nuts with this sauce and serve over ice cream. May be served over spiced cakes. Serves 4.

Mrs. R. E. Hutchins
STATE COLLEGE, MS

Salsa Fria

4 cups tomatoes, freshly peeled or canned. If canned, use Italian plum tomatoes
4 tablespoons green chilies
4 tablespoons wine vinegar
2 tablespoons oil
2 tablespoons finely chopped parsley
2 cloves garlic, finely chopped
1 teaspoon rubbed oregano
1 teaspoon fresh or one-quarter teaspoon dried thyme
2 teaspoons freshly chopped basil or half the amount dried
Salt and freshly ground black pepper.

Chop the tomatoes and combine the remaining ingredients. Chill until ready to serve. Yield: Eight servings.

Craig Claiborne
NEW YORK TIMES

Sweet Sour Basting Sauce

2 tablespoons salad oil
1 teaspoon salt
1/8 green pepper
1 (6 ounce) can pineapple juice concentrate
1/2 clove garlic
1/3 cup brown sugar
1/2 cup wine vinegar
1 teaspoon soy sauce
1/2 (2 ounce) jar pimiento
Pineapple chunks
Green pepper strips

Put all ingredients except pineapple and green pepper into blender; cover and mix. Brush on pork or chicken while it broils, roasts, or barbecues. Add the fruit and pepper strips for garnish.

Mrs. Lenore McLean
GREENWOOD, MS

Tartar Sauce

3/4 cup mayonnaise
3 tablespoons chopped
  pickle
2 tablespoons finely
  chopped olives or capers
1 tablespoon finely
  chopped parsley or
  chervil
1 tablespoon finely
  chopped chives or onion
1 teaspoon horseradish

Combine and blend all ingredients. Serve with fried fish or shell fish. Yield: 1 cup.

Mrs. Hudson Bell
CLARKSDALE, MS

Vegetable Wine Sauce

1/4 teaspoon curry powder
1 cup mayonnaise
1 teaspoon lemon juice
1/4 cup dry white wine

Stir curry powder into mayonnaise. Stir in lemon juice and wine. Heat, stirring constantly, but do not boil. Makes enough for 2 1/2 pounds of fresh vegetables or two (10-ounce) packages of frozen.
(Delicious on broccoli, asparagus, or green beans.)

Mrs. Harry C. Griffith
YAZOO CITY, MS

Salad and Salad Dressing

Spanish Proverb: to Make a Perfect Salad, There Should Be a spendthrift for oil, a miser for vinegar, a wise man for salt, and a madcap to stir the ingredients up and mix them well together.

Mrs. J. Stewart Frame
GREENVILLE, MS
FROM THE ST. JAMES' 1902
TWENTIETH CENTURY COOKBOOK

Anchovy-Tomato Salad or Hors D'oeuvre

Holland Rusk
Anchovy paste
Hard boiled eggs
Tomato (thinly sliced)
Cream (thick)
Mayonnaise (homemade)
Lemon juice

On a lettuce leaf, place a slice of Holland Rusk which has been lightly topped with anchovy paste. Top toast with a slice of tomato. Spread mayonnaise on this. Place a half hard boiled egg (split side down) on top of the tomato. Mix lemon juice, anchovy paste (7 tablespoons mayonnaise to 1 anchovy paste) mixed with mayonnaise. If consistency is not that of a thick gravy then add cream to sauce. Season with cayenne pepper, paprika or to taste. Caviar may be substituted for anchovy paste. Perfect for a first course dish.

Mrs. Hilliard Harper
GREENWOOD, MS

Apricot Salad and Dressing

1 package lemon jello
1 3/4 cup hot water
1 cup celery, chopped finely
1 small can crushed pineapple
1 tablespoon lemon juice
1 pinch salt
12 whole (seeded) apricots
1 small package cream cheese seasoned with mayonnaise, lemon and onion juice

Rub garlic around inside of mold. Place apricots, which have been stuffed with seasoned cream cheese, around mold. Pour the jello mixture over them and place in refrigerator. After congealing, unmold salad and fill center with above dressing. Can be unmolded in a plate size shredded lettuce nest with sauce in center.

Dressing:
3 egg yolks (beaten well)
4 tablespoons vinegar
12 chopped marshmallows
1 cup chopped pecans
1 cup whipped cream

Cook egg yolks and vinegar in double boiler until thick. Cool and add marshmallows, pecans, and whipping cream.

Mrs. Arthur Clark, Jr.
INDIANOLA, MS

Asparagus - Cheese Salad

1 package lime jello
1 cup boiling water
1/4 cup milk
1 tablespoon vinegar
1 cup mayonnaise
1 cup cut green asparagus
1/2 cup grated cheese
1 tablespoon grated onion
1/2 teaspoon salt
Dash of pepper

Prepare jello with boiling water. When cool add milk and vinegar. Mix all other ingredients with mayonnaise. Allow jello to thicken somewhat and then combine with mayonnaise mixture. Serves 6 to 8.

Mrs. J. W. Philley
INDIANOLA, MS

Asparagus Vinaigrette

1 teaspoon salt
1 teaspoon pepper
1 tablespoon parsley
1/2 tablespoon chives
1 tablespoon minced
  onions
Pimiento
1 tablespoon dill pickle
2 teaspoons capers
3 tablespoons wine vinegar
5 tablespoons olive oil
Bunch of fresh asparagus

Combine salt, pepper, chives, onion (minced), chopped dill, capers, and red wine vinegar and let stand 10 minutes. Then add and stir vigorously the olive oil.

Remove about 1/2 inch from each asparagus spear. Soak spears in cold water. Place spears in boiling water and boil for approximately 10 minutes. Drain and chill overnight. Into individual salad plates place the asparagus with thin pimiento strips laid over them. Stir well the vinaigrette sauce and pour over each serving. Serves 4.

W. W. Gresham, Jr.
INDIANOLA, MS

Avocado, Cantaloupe, and Grapefruit Salad

Lettuce
1 can drained grapefruit
  sections
2 medium cantaloupes
3 small ripe avocados
Celery seed dressing

Slice cantaloupe and avocado and arrange with grapefruit sections on lettuce. Pour celery seed dressing over fruit.

Celery Seed Dressing:

1 1/4 cups sugar
2 teaspoons salt
1 tablespoon onion juice or
  grated onion
2 teaspoons prepared
  mustard or dry mustard
2/3 cup vinegar
2 cups oil
2 tablespoons celery seed

Combine sugar, salt, onion juice, mustard and 1/2 of the vinegar and beat. Add remainder of vinegar alternately with oil until emulsion is formed. Then add celery seed.

Mrs. Ross Jones
TULSA, OK

Double Bean Salad

2/3 cup vinegar
3/4 cup brown sugar
1/3 cup salad oil
1/4 teaspoon
  Worcestershire sauce
1 pound tiny green lima
  beans, drained
1 (15 1/2 ounce) can small
  whole green beans,
  drained
1/2 cup sliced pitted ripe
  olives
1/4 cup finely chopped
  pimiento
1/4 cup finely chopped
  onion
Salt and freshly ground
  pepper to taste

Blend together the vinegar, brown sugar, oil and Worcestershire sauce. Mix together remaining ingredients. Pour marinade over bean mixture and chill thoroughly. Serves 8.

Mrs. Opie Little, Jr.
INDIANOLA, MS

Corned Beef Salad

1 package lemon jello
1 cup hot water
1 can beef consomme
1 medium onion, diced or
  grated
1/2 cup diced green pepper
1 cup diced celery
1 cup mayonnaise
1 can corned beef, minced
6 hard-boiled eggs,
  chopped

Dissolve jello in 1 cup hot water. Let it partially congeal. Then add remaining ingredients. Pour into 9 x 13" pan and let set overnight. Serves 12 to 14.

Mrs. Jimmy Lee
GREENVILLE, MS

Beet Salad

1 package lemon Jello
1 1/4 cup hot water
3 tablespoons vinegar
1/2 teaspoon salt
4 teaspoons horseradish
2 tablespoons grated onion
1 cup chopped cooked
  beets
1/2 cup grated cucumber

Dissolve Jello in water and add other ingredients and mold for 6 to 8 servings.

Adelaide W. Fletcher
INDIANOLA, MS

Black-eyed Pea Salad

1 can black eye peas rinsed
  and drained
1 green bell pepper,
  chopped
1 large tomato, chopped
1 small onion, chopped

Dressing:
1 tablespoon vegetable oil
1 tablespoon mayonnaise
1 tablespoon vinegar

Mix all ingredients and toss with dressing. Chill and serve. Great summer salad.

Mimi Alexander
INDIANOLA, MS

Blueberry Salad

1 large can blueberries
1 can Bing cherries (pitted)
1 large-sized package of
  raspberry or cherry jello
1 small package plain
  gelatin
1/2 cup nuts (chopped)
1 large can crushed
  pineapple
1/2 pint whipped cream or
  sour cream

Drain liquid from cherries and blueberries. Heat and pour over jellos. Dissolve. Add berries, nuts, fruit, juice and all. Refrigerate until lightly chilled. Add whipped cream and pour into desired mold. Refrigerate. Serves 10 to 12.

Mrs. Frank Tindall
INDIANOLA, MS

Cajun Salad

2 cans black eye peas
  drained
2 cans whole kernel corn
  drained
1 green pepper, diced
1 small onion, diced
2 or 3 tomatoes, diced
2 teaspoons creole seasoning
1 bottle spicy Italian
  dressing (small if you
  only like a little, large if
  you like more).

Drain the peas and corn, add diced pepper, onion and tomatoes, sprinkle with seasoning, gently stir in the dressing. The salad is best if left in
refrigerator for about 1 to 2 hours. Great for
picnic lunches, will last a long time without refrigeration.

Marty Vincent
INDIANOLA, MS

Cheese Balls in Aspic

Aspic:
1 can consomme
1 envelope gelatin
1 1/2 cups V8 juice
2 tablespoons cider vinegar
1 tablespoon sugar
2 teaspoons seasoning salt
1 teaspoon Worcestershire
  sauce
Dash hot sauce

Cheese Balls:
1/2 pound cream cheese
1/2 cup chopped pecans
3 teaspoons horseradish
8 stuffed olives, slivered

Soak gelatin in 1/4 cup consomme for about 5
minutes. While this is standing, heat the remaining can of consomme and pour over gelatin. Stir
until the gelatin is well dissolved. Add V8, vinegar, sugar, salt, Worcestershire sauce, and hot
sauce. Set bowl aside to cool until thick. Stir
gently every now and then to keep the mixture
from settling. Between stirs, mix cream cheese,
pecans, horseradish, and olives. Make into small
balls and chill a bit. Place three balls in each
individual mold and fill it with aspic. Serve on
salad greens and garnish with mayonnaise.

Zelda B. White
INDIANOLA, MS

Bing Cherry Salad

1 package (3 ounce) cherry jello
1 cup hot water
1 cup black cherry juice
1 large package cream cheese softened with cream or milk
1 package orange jello
1 cup hot water
1 small can crushed pineapple
1 can Bing cherries
1 cup chopped nuts

Dissolve cherry jello in 1 cup of hot water and add the cup of cherry juice. Set until firm in mold. Spread with cream cheese. Dissolve orange jello with 1 cup hot water. Add pineapple, Bing cherries, and nuts. Pour over cherry jello and cream cheese. Refrigerate overnight.
Variation: 1/2 Cup Stuffed Olives may be added.

Mrs. J. W. Askew, Jr.
HATTIESBURG, MS

Chicken Aspic

1 3/4 cups cooked, diced chicken
2 cups chicken stock
1 envelope gelatin
Salt and pepper to taste
1 small bottle stuffed olives, sliced

Curry Mayonnaise:
1 cup mayonnaise
1 tablespoon curry powder
1/8 teaspoon ginger
1 crushed garlic clove

If a hen is used, rub it well with salt and pepper before cooking. Boil in enough water to make several cups of stock. Chopped onion and celery tops added to water enhance the taste of the chicken.

Dissolve gelatin in 1/2 cup stock over low heat. Add to rest of stock and blend in chopped chicken. Pour into greased mold to congeal. Serve with curry mayonnaise.

Mrs. Marjorie M. Magruder
TUPELO, MS

Chicken Salad

4 cups cubed chicken
   breasts (4 whole breasts)
1 tablespoon grated onion
1 cup chopped celery
1/4 cup sour cream
2/3 cup mayonnaise
1/4 teaspoon pepper
1 tablespoon tarragon
   vinegar
4 hard boiled eggs
   (chopped)

Combine chicken, celery, onion. Mix sour cream, mayonnaise, salt, pepper and vinegar. Combine and refrigerate. Fold in hard boiled eggs.

Mary Tucker Myres
INDIANOLA, MS

Bess's Chicken Salad

3 large whole chicken
   breasts, cooked
Juice of 1 lemon
1 bottle capers, drained
2 full cups chopped celery
4 hard boiled eggs,
   chopped

Chop chicken, adding a little lemon and capers at a time until all chicken is chopped. Then fold in celery. I use my hands to do all of this. Then fold in mayonnaise and last add chopped eggs. Wrap in foil and refrigerate overnight.

Bess Campbell
INDIANOLA, MS

Chicken Salad Exotique

3 cups cooked chicken, diced
1 cup grapes, seedless, and halved
1 cup celery, diced
2 1/2 cups almonds, blanched, salted, and chopped
1 cup bell pepper, diced
1/2 cup sour cream
Fresh lemon juice
Pinch tarragon
Chervil
Nutmeg
1 cup home-made mayonnaise
6 cantaloupe rings

Combine ingredients and chill several hours. Serve on a cantaloupe ring cut 1/2" thick.

Mrs. Joseph Compton
VICKSBURG, MS

Chinese Salad

1 whole or more chicken breasts, boiled and shredded
3 tablespoons sesame seeds
3 tablespoons sliced almonds
1 head chinese nappa cabbage-sliced thinly (can use iceberg lettuce)
1 package uncooked chinese noodles - crumbled
3 tablespoons candied ginger - cut up
4 green onions, chopped

Dressing:
2 tablespoons sugar
1/2 cup salad oil
1 teaspoon salt
1/2 tablespoon black pepper
3 tablespoons vinegar

Toast sesame seeds and sliced almonds about 5 minutes. Mix and chill all ingredients.

Mix dressing ingredients and add over cabbage mixture. Serve with french bread. Serves 6 to 8.

Julia Lewis Miller
HOUSTON, TX

Cucumber Salad

1/2 onion
2 cucumbers
1/2 cup sour cream
1 tablespoon red wine
  vinegar
1 teaspoon chopped
  parsley
1 clove garlic, crushed
1 1/2 teaspoon salt
1 teaspoon sugar
1/2 teaspoon coarse
  ground pepper

Peel, grind and drain onion and cucumbers. Mix with other ingredients. Let ripen at least 6 hours. Serve with tossed mixed greens. Serves 12.

Kay Johnson
INDIANOLA, MS

Cool Cucumber Salad

2 small packages lemon
  Jello
1 1/2 cups boiling water
1 pint creamed cottage
  cheese
1 1/2 cups salad dressing
Green food color
1 cup celery (finely
  chopped)
1 cup spring onions (finely
  chopped)
1 cup grated cucumber
1 cup pecans (optional),
  finely chopped

Pour boiling water over Jello; dissolve; cool. Beat cottage cheese and salad dressing until smooth. Mix celery, onions, cucumber and nuts. Add coloring until pale green. Mix all together until cool and mold. Nuts may be sprinkled on top instead of included. Serves 8 to 10.

Mrs. J. S. Conner
SIOUX FALLS, SD

Egg Ring "Cheairs"

10 hard boiled eggs, grated
1/2 cup chili sauce
1/2 cup mayonnaise
1 tablespoon grated onion
Salt, red pepper, and black
   pepper to taste
1 cup chicken broth
2 tablespoons gelatin

Dissolve two tablespoons gelatin in little cold water add to warm chicken broth. Stir until dissolved. Pour this liquid over egg mixture and put in ring mold.

Fill the center of the ring with chicken salad, shrimp salad or crabmeat. Garnish the outside of the ring with tomato wedges, green pepper rings and sticks of green asparagus marinated in French dressing. Also, use pears or peaches stuffed with cream cheese. Makes a complete salad tray. Serve with french bread or "salad rolls."

Mrs. Honey Morris
INDIANOLA, MS

Grandmother Humber's Frozen Fruit Salad

1 can apricots
1 can pears
1 can Queen Ann cherries
1 bottle red cherries
1 can pineapple
4 oranges, sliced
2 bananas
1 cup pecans

Drain and chop fruits; do not use fruit syrup.

Dressing:

2 whole eggs
4 tablespoons vinegar
4 tablespoons sugar
1 small box marshmallows
   or 1 jar marshmallow
   cream
1 cup whipping cream

Beat eggs, add vinegar, sugar, and cook in double boiler until thick, stirring constantly. Remove from heat and add marshmallows. Stir until dissolved. When cool, add whipped cream. Fold into fruit mixture. Freeze for 24 hours. If more dressing is desired to top individual servings, double the dressing recipe.

Jan Robertson
GREENVILLE, MS

Orange Aspic

2 cans mandarin oranges, drained, reserve juice
2 cups orange juice
2 packages orange jello
1 pint orange sherbet

Drain oranges. Use juice and enough fresh orange juice to make 2 cups. Heat juice and dissolve into it the 2 packages of orange Jello. Beat orange sherbet into the 2 cups of liquid. Add orange slices. Pour into molds. Refrigerate until set.

Mrs. Jeptha Barbour
INDIANOLA, MS

Lemon Pineapple Mold

2 boxes lemon jello
2 cups water
Juice of one lemon
1 small can crushed pineapple and juice
3 ounces cream cheese
2 tablespoons mayonnaise
1 small can pimiento
1 cup chopped celery
1 cup chopped pecans, toasted
1 cup whipped cream

Dissolve Jello in 2 cups boiling water. Add lemon juice and pineapple juice. (Reserve pineapple). Chill. To cream cheese add mayonnaise, pimiento, and pineapple, celery and pecans. Fold whipped cream into Jello mixture. Will fill 12 molds.

Mrs. Guy Robinson
INDIANOLA, MS

Wilted Lettuce Salad

3 cups salad greens
4 slices bacon
1/2 cup buttermilk
1 egg
1 teaspoon salt
1 teaspoon sugar
1 teaspoon vinegar

Fry bacon until crisp, drain. Use teacup. Break egg in same. Fill 1/2 full of buttermilk. Add 1 teaspoon each of salt, sugar, and vinegar. Pour into hot bacon fat and then over fresh garden lettuce. Crumble bacon over the top. Serves four.

Mrs. Charles R. Harris
GREENWOOD, MS

Spiced Peach Salad in Wine Jelly

2 tablespoons plain gelatin
1/2 cup cold water
1 cup wine (sherry or port)
2 cups boiling water
3 tablespoons lemon juice
1 cup sugar
1/4 cup pecans, finely
   chopped
1 can spiced peaches
1 package Philadelphia
   cream cheese
1/4 cup cream as needed

Drain peaches and remove pits. Stuff with nuts and creamed cheese (softened with cream). Soften gelatin in cold water. Add boiling water and stir until dissolved. Add sugar, lemon juice and wine. Place thin layer of gelatin mixture in bottom of mold. When slightly set, put in peach and cover with rest of jelly. Serves 8.

Mrs. Waldemar Prichard
INVERNESS, MS

Tangy Spiced Pears

1 can (1 pound 13 ounce)
   Bartlett pear halves
1/4 cup vinegar
1 cup sugar
1 stick cinnamon
5 whole cloves
3 whole allspice

Drain pears, reserving 3/4 cup of syrup. Combine pear syrup, vinegar, sugar and spices in saucepan. Bring to boil and simmer 10 minutes. Add pears to hot syrup and bring to boil again. Cover and chill several hours or overnight. Makes 8 servings.

   Good with baked ham.

Martha Huston
INDIANOLA, MS

Potato Salad

5 good size potatoes
1/2 cup sauterne
1/3 cup Wishbone or
   Italian dressing
1 tablespoon capers
3 green onions, chopped
2/3 cup cauliflower, sliced
2 pimentos, chopped
1/2 teaspoon salt

Boil and slice potatoes. Marinate in sauterne for 2 hours. Toss lightly with other ingredients and chill.

Mrs. Lucy Fisher
INDIANOLA, MS

German Potato Salad

8 cooked potatoes, sliced
  and salted
1 onion, sliced
1 large bell pepper, sliced
  in rings
1 small jar sweet pickle
  relish
1 medium bottle stuffed
  green olives, sliced

Dressing:
1 cup Wesson oil
1/2 cup vinegar
3 tablespoons sugar
1 teaspoon dry mustard
1 teaspoon celery seed

Arrange ingredients in layers. Boil dressing ingredients and pour over top of layered dish. Chill before serving. Serves 10 to 12.

Mrs. M. S. Spiars
GREENVILLE, MS

Salmon Mousse De Beauzon

1 1/2 tablespoons
  unflavored gelatin
1/2 cup cold water
1/3 cup lemon juice
2 cups flaked, cold, cooked
  salmon
2 teaspoons grated onion
2 tablespoons capers
2 tablespoons
  Worcestershire sauce
1 cup mayonnaise
Tabasco to taste
Salt

Sauce verte:
1 cup mayonnaise
1 cup sour cream
1 teaspoon dry mustard
2 cucumbers, peeled and
  chopped
2 tablespoons chopped
  chives or parsley

Soften gelatin in water. Heat gently, stirring until gelatin is dissolved. Add lemon juice and set aside. Combine salmon, onions, capers, Worcestershire sauce, mayonnaise, Tabasco, and salt. Fold in the molded gelatin and turn into a 3-cup mold, rinsed with water. Chill until set. Serves 6. Serve with Sauce Verte.

Mrs. Richard Watson
TUNICA, MS

Cole Slaw

1 medium size cabbage
1 small onion
1 carrot
2 large dill pickles
3/4 cup mayonnaise
1 teaspoon salt
1/2 teaspoon pepper
2 tablespoons sugar
1/2 teaspoon prepared
  mustard
1 teaspoon lemon juice

Quarter cabbage. Wash and drain. Peel carrot. Grate cabbage, onion, and carrot. Chop and add pickles. Mix with dressing made from rest of ingredients.

Mrs. D. N. Magruder
TUPELO, MS

Italian Sweet–Sour Slaw

1 medium head of cabbage,
  shredded
2 Bermuda onions, sliced
  very thin
7/8 cup sugar
1 tablespoon salt
1 teaspoon dry mustard
1 teaspoon celery seed
2 teaspoons sugar
1 cup vinegar
3/4 cup salad oil

Alternate layers of cabbage and onions in bowl. Cover with 7/8 cup sugar

In saucepan, combine salt, mustard, celery seed and 2 teaspoons of sugar. Mix together well, then add vinegar, and salad oil. Heat and stir to rolling boil. Pour, while hot, over cabbage and onions. Refrigerate slaw at least four hours. This will keep indefinitely and improves in flavor. Very good with fish, chicken or roast.

Rachel Little
TOPEKA, KA

Tomato Soup Aspic

1 can tomato soup
9 ounces cream cheese or
  cottage cheese
1 cup chopped celery
1/2 cup chopped green
  peppers
1/2 cup chopped stuffed
  olives
2 tablespoons unflavored
  gelatin
1/2 cup cold water
2 tablespoons lemon juice
1 cup homemade mayon-
  naise
1 heaping tablespoon
  minced onion
1 tablespoon
  Worcestershire sauce
Salt to taste
1 or 2 teaspoons Tabasco

Soften gelatin in cold water. Heat soup in double boiler; add cream cheese. Whip with rotary egg beater and add gelatin. Stir until dissolved. Cool, then add other ingredients. Pour into oiled mold or molds. Chill. Serves 6-8.

Mrs. Robert Colemen, Jr.
BATON ROUGE, LA

Vermicelli Salad

1 (12 ounce) package
  vermicelli
1/2 cup olive oil
1 package Hidden Valley
  Dressing Mix
4 ounces chopped pimiento
2 (4 ounce) can ripe olives,
  chopped or sliced
3 tablespoons mayonnaise
1 tablespoon lemon pepper
4 or 5 chopped green
  onions
Greek seasoning to taste
Juice of one lemon

Cook vermicelli in boiling water 6 minutes. Immediately put in colander and wash under cold water (drain).

Mix remaining ingredients. Stir vermicelli into mixture, mixing well! Shrimp or chicken added makes a meal. 20 minute preparation time. Serves 10.

Maryem Fowlkes
GULFPORT, MS

Bleu Cheese Dressing with Capers

1 pint mayonnaise
1/2 cup buttermilk
4 ounces bleu cheese
Small pod garlic, pressed
Capers to suit
Pepper to taste

Blend 1/2 the bleu cheese into mayonnaise and buttermilk mixture. Add garlic, capers and pepper. Crumble remainder of cheese and add to mixture. This is delicious as a dip for vegetables, a dressing for cold artichokes or over lettuce.

Mrs. Sam Fowlkes
GULFPORT, MS

Cooked Dressing for Chicken Salad

3/4 cup milk
2 eggs yolks
1/4 cup mild vinegar
1 tablespoon butter
2 tablespoons sugar
1 teaspoon salt
2 tablespoons flour
1 teaspoon dry mustard
Dash cayenne pepper

Add milk to slightly beaten yolks and combine with mixed dry ingredients. Add vinegar and cook over hot water. Stir constantly until thick. Add butter and chill. Makes 1 1/2 cups dressing.

Mrs. Kent Lovelace
INDIANOLA, MS

Salad Dressing for Slaw

1 can tomato soup
3/4 cup vinegar
1/2 cup salad oil
1/4 cup sugar
1 tablespoon
  Worcestershire sauce
1 teaspoon salt
1 teaspoon paprika
1 teaspoon dry mustard
1 teaspoon onion juice

Put all ingredients in quart jar and shake well.

Mrs. James O. Eastland
DODDSVILLE, MS

Salad Dressing Eleanor

The fresh lemon juice is the secret.

1/2 cup fresh lemon juice
1 1/4 cup salad oil
2 1/2 teaspoon (rounded) salt
1/2 garlic pod, mashed

Blend in blender or shake in jar and refrigerate until chilled.

Mrs. Eleanor Steele Davis
INDIANOLA, MS

Salad Dressing a La Tom Barron

4 tablespoons olive oil
1 teaspoon mustard
1 clove garlic
1 1/2 tablespoon wine vinegar
Pinch salt and pepper
4 strips bacon

Mix well and chill first five ingredients. Fry 4 strips of bacon. Crumble in 1/8 inch squares. Tear fresh greens (lettuce or spinach). Chill. When ready to serve toss with above dressing. Add 2 teaspoons hot bacon fat and re-toss. Serve with garnishments of crumbled bacon.

Tom Barron
INDIANOLA, MS

Vinaigrette Salad Dressing

1 clove garlic
1 teaspoon salt
3 - 4 teaspoons red wine vinegar
1/2 teaspoon fine mustard
2 - 3 tablespoons olive oil
Cracked pepper to taste

Mash together garlic and salt until it forms a paste. Stir in vinegar with wire whisk. Add mustard. Gradually add oil, stirring with whisk. Add pepper. Toss with crisp romaine. Serves 4.

Marion Barnwell
JACKSON MS

Green Goddess Salad Dressing

1 clove garlic, crushed, or
1 teaspoon garlic salt
3 tablespoons chives, chopped
3 tablespoons anchovies, chopped
1 tablespoon lemon juice
1 tablespoon tarragon vinegar
1/2 cup parsley, finely chopped
1/2 cup sour cream
1 cup mayonnaise
Salt to taste
Pepper to taste

Mix all ingredients, except salt and pepper. Beat with electric mixer for 3 minutes at medium speed or whirl for 1 minute in blender. Add salt and pepper. Refrigerate for 24 hours. Serve on salad greens.

Mrs. J. C. Allen, Jr.
INDIANOLA, MS

Mayonnaise by Blender

1 large egg
1/2 teaspoon dry mustard
1/2 teaspoon salt
1 1/2 tablespoons lemon juice
1 cup salad oil, chilled
Dash of Tabasco
Dash of Worcestershire
1/4 teaspoon garlic powder, optional or 1 clove garlic

Combine egg, mustard, salt, lemon juice, tabasco, Worcestershire, garlic and 1/4 cup oil in blender. Blend on low speed for 1 minute. Uncover immediately and pour in remaining oil in a steady, slow stream. Takes 5 minutes to complete.

Mrs. Robert (Anne) Lake
GREENVILLE, MS

Poppy Seed Dressing

1/2 cup sugar
1 teaspoon dry mustard
1 teaspoon salt
1 cup Wesson oil
1/3 cup vinegar
1/3 medium onion, grated
1 1/3 teaspoons poppy seed

Mix sugar, mustard, salt, oil, and vinegar in electric mixer. Add onion and poppy seed last.

Mrs. John C. Lake
INDIANOLA, MS

Roquefort Cheese Dressing

2 tablespoons paprika
2 tablespoons sugar
1/2 teaspoon salt
1/4 cup vinegar
2 egg yolks
3/4 pint salad oil
2 cubes Roquefort or bleu
  cheese
V8 Cocktail Juice

Mix dry ingredients with egg yolks. Add oil and vinegar as if making mayonnaise. Thin down with V8 Cocktail juice to desired consistency. Small piece of garlic can be added or bowl rubbed.

Mrs. Katie Gooch.
INDIANOLA, MS

Thousand Island Dressing

1 teaspoon sugar, rounded
3/4 teaspoon salt
1 teaspoon prepared
  mustard
1 tablespoon
  Worcestershire sauce
3 tablespoons catsup,
  rounded
3 tablespoons vinegar
3 tablespoons chili sauce,
  rounded
1 small jar chopped
  pimiento
6 hard boiled eggs,
  chopped
1 small onion, minced
1 pint mayonnaise
Little black pepper
Little Red Hot sauce

Mix in the order of listing, adding the mayonnaise last.

If not counting calories, you can add 1 cup whipped cream.

Mrs. Robert M. Donald
MOORHEAD, MS

Birthplace of Kermit the Frog.
Washington County Tourist and Information
Center, Leland, Mississippi

Meat

Beef Bordelaise Style

3 pounds eye of round
1 1/2 cup dry white wine
1/2 cup olive oil
2 onions sliced
2 teaspoons salt
1/2 teaspoon ground
  pepper
1 bay leaf
3 tablespoons butter
2 tablespoons parsley,
  minced

Trim fat off meat. Cut in 6 slices. In a bowl (not metal) combine wine, oil, onions, salt, pepper and bay leaf. Marinate the meat in mixture over night or longer. Drain. Reserve marinade. Melt butter in shallow casserole and brown meat. Add half the marinade. Cook 350° for 1 hour. Add remaining marinade after 1/2 hour. Baste frequently. Serve with parsley.

Mrs. Bill McKamy
LAKE WASHINGTON, MS

Brisket Roast

1 beef brisket
Salt
Pepper
1/2 can beer
1 package dry onion soup
1/2 jar chili sauce

Season roast with salt and pepper. Place in roasting pan. Cover roast with dry onion soup, chili sauce, and beer. Cover and cook at 325° for 3 to 4 hours or until tender. Baste roast while cooking.

Julia Lewis Miller
HOUSTON, TX

Beef Stroganoff

1 1/2 pounds beef tender-
loin, cut in strips
3 tablespoons butter
1 clove garlic, chopped
3/4 cup onions, chopped
3/4 cup mushrooms, sliced
2 tablespoons flour
2 cups bouillon
3 tablespoons sherry
1 tablespoon dry mustard
2 tablespoons tomato paste
2/3 cup sour cream

Salt and pepper beef and let stand at room temperature. Sauté onions, mushrooms, and garlic in butter. Remove from skillet and add another tablespoon butter and sear beef. Add flour and brown. Slowly add bouillon, sherry, mustard, and tomato paste. Return vegetables to skillet and cook until thick, stirring constantly. Five minutes before serving, add sour cream. Heat, but do not boil. Serve over rice or noodles. Serves 6.

Mrs. M. M. Pace
GREENVILLE, MS

Variation: Substitute wild rice. Add 3 tablespoons lemon juice, paprika, chopped parsley. Serve with dry red wine.

Mrs. Fincher Word
INDIANOLA, MS

Chuck Wagon Roast

3-4 pounds chuck roast
2 tablespoons unseasoned
meat tenderizer

Marinade:
2 tablespoons instant
minced onion
2 teaspoons thyme
1 teaspoon marjoram
1 bay leaf, crushed
1 cup wine vinegar
1/2 cup salad oil
3 tablespoons lemon juice
1/4 cup pepper corns,
cracked

Sprinkle meat with tenderizer—no salt. Place in shallow pan. Let stand 2–3 hours in marinade. Cook to desired doneness over charcoal fire—approximately six inches from coals. Baste with marinade.

Mrs. Fred Jepson
INDIANOLA, MS

Sirloin Roast Casserole

3 pounds sirloin roast, cubed
6-8 slices bacon, cooked
2 onions, chopped
1 clove garlic, minced
1 cup raw rice
1 cup red dry wine
2 cups beef consommé
1/2 teaspoons thyme
1 teaspoon dry parsley
1 1/2 cups fresh tomatoes, diced
1 cup Parmesan cheese, grated

Place drained bacon in casserole; brown beef in part of bacon fat—sauté onion and garlic in remaining fat. Brown rice in fat; set aside. Mix beef with onion and garlic; put over bacon. Combine wine, consommé, thyme, parsley; pour 1 1/2 cups over beef in casserole. Cover and cook 1 hour at 325°. Add tomatoes, rice, and remaining consomme mix. Bake 1 hour at 325°. If it gets too dry, add more consomme or water while cooking. When done, stir in cheese. Serves 8-10.

Mrs. Shelby Goza
ROSEDALE, MS

London Broil

Marinade:
2 tablespoons sherry
2 tablespoons soy sauce
2 tablespoons sugar
1/2 teaspoon cinnamon

Buy a flank steak (1/3 pound per serving). Score slightly across grain both ways. Marinate for at least one hour in marinade.

Broil 4 inches from heat for 4 minutes per side. Cut in thin slices diagonally across the grain of the meat.

J. Wesley Watkins
WASHINGTON, D.C.

Beef and Green Bean Casserole

2 pounds ground chuck
1 can (14 1/2 ounces) cut
  green beans, drained
1 can (12 ounces) tomato
  paste
Small amount of onion,
  chopped
1 cup water
Salt and pepper, to taste
1/2 cup shredded cheddar
  cheese
1 can (10 count) biscuits

Brown chuck; drain. Return to skillet and add beans, tomato paste, and onion. Mix well, adding water gradually to thin the mixture. Add salt and pepper. Pour into large, square casserole. Sprinkle cheese and then top mixture with 1 layer of uncooked biscuits. Bake uncovered in pre-heated oven at 375° for 30 - 45 minutes or until biscuits are done.

Myrtis Woods
GREENVILLE, MS

Bobette's Stew

2 pounds stew meat
1 can Golden Mushroom
  soup
1 can onion soup
2 cloves garlic
1 can tomatoes
6 small potatoes, cubed
1/2 teaspoon oregano
Salad oil
1 pint Brussels sprouts,
  optional
1 pint pearl onions,
  optional

Brown stew meat in salad oil. Add both cans of soup and garlic. Cook 1 1/2 hours. Add potatoes, tomatoes, and oregano and cook 45 minutes more or until tender. Serves 3 or 4. Serve over rice.

Mrs. W. E. Howard, Jr.
LAUREL, MS

Rouladen

1 1/2 pounds sirloin
1/2 teaspoon salt
1/8 teaspoon pepper
3 tablespoons chopped onion
Sliced bacon, cut into squares
1/4 cup shortening
3 tablespoons flour
2 cups water
1 can mushrooms, (optional)

Have butcher cut beef into a 10 x 4" piece about 1/4" thick. Sprinkle with salt and pepper. Cover with onion. Distribute bacon squares over meat surface. Roll up as for jellyroll. Secure with toothpicks or string. Brown in shortening on all sides. Remove meat. Add flour to pan and blend well. Stir in water. Cook, stirring, until slightly thickened. Add browned meat. Cover. Cook for 1 1/2 hours or until meat is tender. Season gravy to taste. Yield: 4 to 6 portions. You may add 1 can of mushrooms to the gravy, if desired.

Mrs. Fritz Berge
INDIANOLA, MS

Black-eyed Pea Jambalaya

1 pound bag dried black-eyed peas
1 pound mild bulk pork sausage (you can use regular, mild, or hot)
2 large onions, chopped fine
2 cloves garlic
1 can tomato sauce
1/2 teaspoon thyme
1/2 teaspoon parsley
Water
2 cups uncooked rice

Boil black-eyed peas in salty water until soft and tender. Drain peas and set aside. Fry pork sausage, chopping up as it cooks. To the sausage, add onions and garlic. After the onions and garlic are done, add tomato sauce. Stir constantly to prevent sticking. Add a little water so the gravy can fry well. As the water fries out, add a little more, do this several times. When gravy looks a rich red, add 1 cup of water, thyme, and parsley. Cook slowly until gravy gets thick. In a separate pot, cook rice until done. Mix thoroughly black-eyed peas, gravy, and rice.

Lynne Monju Kwitzky
SALEM, OR

Chasen's Chili

1/2 lb. (1 cup) pinto beans
5 cups canned tomatoes
1 pounds (3 cups) chopped
   green pepper
1 1/2 pound (4 cups)
   chopped onions
1 1/2 tablespoon salad oil
2 cloves garlic crushed
1/2 chop chopped parsley
1/2 cup butter
2 1/2 pounds coarse
   ground chuck
1 pound ground lean pork
1/3 cup chili powder
2 tablespoons salt
1 1/2 teaspoon pepper
1 1/2 teaspoon cumin seed
1 1/2 teaspoon Accent

Wash beans; soak overnight in water. Simmer, covered, in same water until tender. Add tomatoes and simmer five minutes. Sauté green peppers in salad oil five minutes; add onions; cook until tender, stirring often. Add garlic and parsley. Melt butter and sauté meat for fifteen minutes. Add meat to onion mixture. Stir in chili powder and cook for ten minutes. Add this to bean mixture along with the spices. Simmer covered for one hour. Cook, uncovered, for thirty minutes. Skim fat from top. Serves 8 to 10 generously.

Mrs. Mort Hardwicke, Jr.
PARIS, AR

Hamburger Cornpone Pie

1 pound ground beef
1/3 cup chopped onion
1 tablespoon shortening
2 teaspoons chili powder
3/4 teaspoon salt
1 teaspoon Worcestershire
   sauce
1 cup canned tomatoes
1 cup drained kidney
   beans
1 cup cornbread batter

Brown meat and chopped onions in melted shortening. Add seasonings and tomatoes. Cover and simmer over low heat for 15 minutes; then add kidney beans. Pour meat mixture into greased one or one and a half quart casserole. Top with corn bread batter, spreading carefully with a wet knife. Bake in hot oven (425°) for twenty minutes.

Marjorie Hopkins West
HATTIESBURG, MS

Hamburger Stroganoff

1/4 cup butter
1/4 cup green onions and
  tops
1 pod minced garlic
1/2 pound sliced mush-
  rooms
1 pound ground chuck
1/2 - 3/4 cup sherry
3 tablespoons lemon juice
1 can consommé
1 teaspoon salt
1 teaspoon pepper
1/4 pound medium noodles
1 cup sour cream

Brown onion, garlic, and mushrooms in butter. Add meat and brown. Add liquids, salt, and pepper. Simmer 15 minutes. Add uncooked noodles, cover, and cook until tender about 7 minutes. Add sour cream; stir gently. Sprinkle parsley on top. Serves 4. (Freezes well).

Mrs. Burrell McGee
LELAND, MS

Johnnie Mazzetti Casserole

1 pound chopped onions
1 pound chopped bell
  pepper
1 large bunch celery
  (include tops), chopped
2 pounds ground chuck or
  round steak
1 can tomato soup
1 can tomato paste
1 can tomato sauce
1 can Franco-American
  spaghetti sauce with
  mushrooms
1 large can mushrooms
  (stems and pieces)
1 large jar salad olives,
  sliced
1 (12 ounce) package wide
  egg noodles
1 (10 ounce) package sharp
  cheese, grated (not fine)
Salt, pepper and oregano
  to taste

Sauté onions and celery in greased pot. Add meat and cook until meat loses redness. Add bell pepper, tomato sauce, soup and paste. Cook on simmer for 1 hour. Add mushrooms and olives and simmer for another hour. Parboil noodles in salted water (usually 5 to 6 minutes). Add noodles to meat mixture and cook 20–25 minutes. Add cheese, and cook 5 minutes. Add salt, pepper and oregano. For variation you may add cumin, chili powder, and crushed red pepper. Serves 10–12 adults.

Mrs. Clarke Johnson
INDIANOLA, MS

Lasagna

1 1/2 teaspoon dried
  oregano
1/8 teaspoon black pepper
1 teaspoon onion salt
1 cup minced onion
1 minced garlic clove
1/3 cup salad oil
1 pound ground meat
1 teaspoon Accent
1 teaspoon salt
1/2 pound lasagna
1/2 pound mozzarella
  cheese
1/4 cup grated Parmesan
  cheese
3/4 pound Ricotto or
  cottage cheese
1 no. 2 1/2 can Italian
  peeled tomatoes
2 (8 ounce) cans tomato
  sauce
1 teaspoon salt

In a large saucepan, combine tomatoes, tomato sauce, salt, dried oregano, pepper, and onion salt. Simmer. In skillet, sauté onion and garlic in oil. Add meat, Accent, and salt. Sauté until meat is no longer red. Add sautéed ingredients to large saucepan. Cook sauce for 2 1/2 hours. Cook lasagna as directed on package. In casserole, layer meat sauce, lasagna (crisscrossed), cottage cheese, mozzarella cheese, and Parmesan cheese. Make two or three layers. Cook at 350° for 50 minutes. Cool 10 minutes before serving. Serves 8.

Mrs. Lawrence W. Long, III
HOLLY RIDGE, MS

Meat Balls in Caper Sauce (Klopse)

4 tablespoons butter,
 divided
3 onions, chopped
6 slices white bread
1 cup light cream
1 1/2 pounds beef, ground
1/2 pounds veal, ground
1/2 pounds pork, ground
4 anchovy fillets
3 eggs
2 teaspoons salt, divided
1 teaspoon pepper, divided
1/2 cup ice water
3 cups boiling water
1/4 teaspoon marjoram
3 sprigs parsley
3 stalks celery
2 tablespoons flour
2 tablespoons lemon juice
1/4 cup capers, drained
Dash of nutmeg

Melt 2 tablespoons of butter in a skillet and add onions. Sauté for 10 minutes, stirring occasionally. Soak the bread in cream for 10 minutes. Press excess liquid from it. Grind bread with the sautéed onions, ground beef, veal, pork, and anchovies in a food chopper. Add the eggs, 1 teaspoon of salt, 1/2 teaspoon of pepper, and ice water. Mix together and shape into 2" balls. Combine in a deep saucepan, the boiling water, remaining salt and pepper, marjoram, parsley, and celery. Drop meat balls into it and boil for 20 minutes.

Add nutmeg to the gravy. Melt the remaining butter in a saucepan. Add the flour and mix to a smooth paste. Strain the liquid in which the meat balls were cooked, and add, stirring constantly until the boiling point is reached. Cook over low heat for 5 minutes. Add the lemon juice and capers and stir well. Place meat balls on a platter and pour sauce over them.

Mrs. Fritz Berge
INDIANOLA, MS

"The Filet Mignon of Meatloaves"

1 pound ground chuck
1 pound ground pork
1/2 cup dry bread crumbs
1/2 cup oatmeal
2 eggs
2 medium onions, chopped
2 tablespoons butter
1 cup strong beef stock, or
  bouillon
2 teaspoons salt
Coarse ground pepper to
  taste
Good pinch of cayenne
  (optional)
1/2 cup fresh parsley,
  coarsely chopped
1/4 teaspoon cinnamon
1/4 teaspoon nutmeg
1/4 teaspoon ground cloves
1/4 teaspoon ground
  coriander
1/4 teaspoon ground
  allspice
2 tablespoons catsup

Crumble meats together in a large bowl. Add crumbs, oatmeal, and eggs. Let sit to warm a bit while you sauté onions. Sauté onions in butter until they caramelize. Remove from heat and add stock or bouillon to pan to loosen all the browned crusty bits. Dump onions, stock, salt, pepper(s), parsley, spices, and catsup into meat mixture. Get your hands in there and mix well!

Preheat oven to 350° (325° for Pyrex). Bake in a loaf pan until browned on top, and a metal skewer inserted in the middle comes out clean and hot, about 1 hour.

If possible, let loaf cool in its pan with another loaf pan placed on top and weighted down with some canned goods. This ensures a dense moist loaf that slices well. Serve slightly warm or, even better, cold.

Kate Failing
INDIANOLA, MS

Sausage Casserole

1 pound bulk sausage
1/4 cup onion, chopped
1 cup celery, sliced
1 1/2 cups rice, uncooked
2 cans chicken broth, (14 ounce)
1/2 cup almonds, slivered
1 tablespoon soy sauce

Fry sausage, stirring; do not brown. Sauté celery and onions in small amount of sausage grease. Drain sausage well and add to rice, celery, and onions. Pour in chicken broth. Add almonds and soy sauce. Bake in large covered casserole (3 quarts) about one hour at 350°. Stir before serving.

Mrs. Thomas H. Campbell, Jr.
YAZOO CITY, MS

Sausage Beef Casserole

1/2 pound bulk sausage
1/2 pound ground beef
1 medium onion, chopped
1/4 cup green pepper, chopped
2 tablespoons parsley, chopped
2 cups tomato juice
1 can cream of mushroom soup
1/2 teaspoon salt
1 tablespoon Worcestershire sauce
Pinch of oregano
1/4 teaspoon seasoned salt
1 (5 ounce) package elbow macaroni
1 cup grated cheese

Brown sausage in skillet; stir to break up; remove from fat. Cook onion, pepper, and ground beef in fat until meat turns white. Add all other ingredients except macaroni and grated cheese.

Cook macaroni as directed on package. Drain and mix with sausage mixture and pour in 2 quart casserole dish. Bake in 350° oven for 30 minutes. Put grated cheese on top and bake additional 10 minutes. Yield 6-8 servings.

Mrs. Henry Crowell
INDIANOLA, MS

Spaghetti Sauce

1 pound ground chuck
1/2 cup chopped onion
1 large crushed garlic clove
2 tablespoons minced
  parsley
2 cups water
1 teaspoon monosodium
  glutamate
1 bay leaf
2 teaspoons sugar
1/8 teaspoon pepper
1 teaspoon salt
1/2 teaspoon basil
1/2 teaspoon oregano
3 1/2 cups Contadina pear
  shaped tomatoes
1 1/3 cups Contadina
  tomato paste
Mushrooms
Parsley

Brown ground chuck and onion in large saucepan. Add garlic, parsley; sauté 1 minute. Add water, monosodium glutamate, bay leaf, sugar, pepper, salt, basil, oregano, tomatoes, tomato paste. Simmer 1 hour uncovered; stir occasionally. Remove bay leaf; serve over cooked spaghetti. Garnish with sautéed mushrooms topped with sauce and parsley. Serves 6 - 8.

E. M. Hall
BELZONI, MS

Ham 'N Red-eye Gravy

Ham
Milk
Gravy
1 cup black coffee, strained
Dash of pepper

Slice ham, preferably well aged, into 1/4" steaks. Soak in milk overnight. Put just enough ham fat into skillet to keep ham from sticking. Have skillet hot. Slowly brown ham evenly on both sides. When done, remove to hot platter. For the gravy, add 1 cup strong black coffee to ham drippings in skillet. Sprinkle with a bit of pepper and let come to a boil. Stir well and serve piping hot. Fine over hot biscuits or grits.

Mrs. Eva Neill
INDIANOLA, MS

Lily's Ham Puff

1 cup ground cooked ham
2 cups milk
1 tablespoon butter
3/4 cup meal
3 eggs, separated
1 cup sharp cheese, grated
Salt and pepper

Heat milk and butter to boiling point. Slowly add meal, stirring all the time. Cook until thick and add cheese. Remove from fire. Add beaten egg yolks, salt, pepper, and ham. Fold in stiffly beaten egg whites. Pour into greased casserole. Bake 325° for 40 minutes. Serve immediately.

This recipe used by my family in Jacksonville, Florida, and in my home, originally came from cousin (Lily) who lived in North Carolina in 1875.

Mrs. F. C. Ewing
GREENWOOD, MS

Liver in Wine

1 1/2 pounds liver
Flour, salt and pepper
3 tablespoons butter
1 cup consommé
1 cup sherry
1 cup water
2 tablespoons parsley

Coat liver with flour, salt, and pepper and brown in butter. Add all other ingredients. Cover and put in 350° oven for 45 minutes.

Susie Calvert
WEST POINT, MS

HOLT COLLIER

Born a slave in 1846, Collier served as a Confederate sharpshooter and cavalryman. Famed as a bear hunter, he guided Pres. Theodore Roosevelt on a hunt near Onward, MS, in 1902. When Roosevelt refused to shoot a bear Collier had roped, cartoonists coined the term "Teddy Bear." Collier was buried here in Live Oak Cemetery in 1936.

Sign at Onward

Mock Sukiyaki

1 pound thinly sliced
   round steak
2 tablespoons oil
1 1/2 cups sliced celery
1 green pepper, sliced
1 onion, sliced
1 1/2 cups sliced fresh
   mushrooms (or 6 ounce
   can drained)
1/2 cup green onion, sliced
1 can beef broth
1 tablespoon soy sauce
1/4 cup water
2 tablespoons cornstarch
4 cups cooked rice

Brown meat in salad oil. Add vegetables, broth, and soy sauce. Cover and cook over low heat 10 minutes or until vegetables are near tender. Stir often. Combine water and cornstarch; add meat mixture; stir until thick. Serve over hot rice. Serves 4.

Lucy Fisher
INDIANOLA, MS

California Pork Chops

6 thick pork chops
1 teaspoon poultry seasoning
1 teaspoon salt
1 tablespoon oil
1 can artichoke hearts
1 can Cheddar cheese soup

Sprinkle pork chops with poultry seasoning and salt. Brown in oil in large skillet over medium heat. In casserole dish, arrange pork chops and artichoke hearts (sliced in half). Spoon soup over top. Cover and bake at 325° for 1 hour. Serve over noodles or rice.

Jackie Brocato
INDIANOLA, MS

Perfect Pork Chops

4 pork chops, 1" thick
Salt and pepper
4 slices onion, 1/4 inch
4 rings green pepper
1/4 cup rice
1 large can tomatoes
1 cup chopped celery

Brown seasoned chops in large skillet. Place onion and pepper on each chop, with 1 table-spoon rice in center. Pour tomatoes and celery around. Cover. Simmer 1 hour. Serves 4.

Elizabeth Nabors Bailey
HUNTINGTON, WV

Veal Parmesan

1 1/2 pounds veal cutlet, 1/2 inch thick
Salt and pepper
1 cup saltine cracker crumbs
1 tablespoon parsley, minced
1 clove garlic, minced
1 1/2 tablespoons grated Parmesan cheese
2 eggs, beaten
Salad oil

Cut cutlets into serving pieces and sprinkle with salt and pepper; combine cracker crumbs with parsley, garlic and Parmesan cheese. Coat cutlets with crumb mixture. Then dip in egg-again in crumbs. With fingers pat crumb mixture firmly into the meat. Brown meat slowly-evenly in hot oil in heavy skillet; reduce heat. Continue cooking until meat is tender. Serve with lemon slices. Serves 4.

Mrs. Henry Mura
INDIANOLA, MS

Veal Roulu

6 veal cutlets, cut 3 per pound
1/2 cup fine bread crumbs
1/4 pound pork sausage
1/4 cup chopped onion
1/2 clove garlic, minced
2 slices bacon, cook and chop
6 lemon slices
1 tablespoon minced parsley
1 egg yolk
2 tablespoons oil, or more
2 cups consomme
1 tablespoon flour
Parsley

Pound veal until it is 1/4 inch thick. Combine crumbs with milk. Mix together the sausage, crumbs, onion, garlic, bacon, parsley, and egg yolk. Lay 1 to 2 tablespoons of this filling across the center of each piece of veal; roll up, securing with wooden pick. Heat fat in skillet and sauté roll until brown. Add meat stock and simmer until done, 45 minutes to 1 hour. Thicken the liquid with flour to make sauce. Place rolls on platter, pour sauce over. Garnish with parsley and lemon slices. Serves 4 to 6.

Eleanor N. Failing
INDIANOLA, MS

Cheese Soufflé

5 slices white bread
5 teaspoons melted butter
1/2 pound grated cheese
4 eggs
2 1/2 cups milk
1 teaspoon salt
1 teaspoon dry mustard

Trim bread and butter slices well. Lay in the bottom of the baking dish. Sprinkle with cheese. Beat eggs; add milk, salt and mustard. Pour over bread and cheese. Let stand 4 hours or in refrigerator overnight. Bake 45 minutes in 350° oven.

Mrs. John M. Allin
JACKSON, MS

Variation Mock Cheese Souffle: Add 1/4 teaspoon cayenne pepper, 3/4 cup flaked lump white crabmeat.

Hebe Smythe Crittenden
GREENVILLE, MS

Cheese Casserole

1 pound Velveeta
8 ounces sharp cheese (grated)
8 ounces cottage cheese
1 stick butter, melted
4 eggs
1 tablespoon flour

Mix cottage cheese, butter, eggs and flour. Pour over Velveeta and sharp cheese. Bake 350° for 30 minutes.

Laura Gresham
INDIANOLA, MS

Cheese Soufflé

1 cup sweet milk
2 tablespoons butter, level
3 tablespoons flour, level
1 cup grated Cheddar
  cheese
3 eggs, beaten separately
1/2 teaspoon salt
Dash of red pepper

Melt butter. Add flour and blend well. Add milk gradually. Cook in double boiler until thick. Add grated cheese and stir until cheese is melted. Let cool. Add salt, pepper and egg yolks, beaten until light, to cheese sauce. Fold in stiffly beaten egg whites. Pour into a 2 quart baking dish which has been set in a shallow pan of water and cook in 350° oven until set through and browned. Serve at once. Use this as a base for Oriental chicken.

Mrs. D. N. Magruder
TUPELO, MS

Fish and Seafood

Bayou Baked Bass Superb

2 1/2 - 3 pound bass or
 other fish
2 cans crab, drained
1/2 cup bread crumbs
1/3 cup mayonnaise
2 tablespoon lemon juice
1/4 cup capers drained
1 tablespoon
 Worcestershire sauce
1 teaspoon dry mustard
1/2 teaspoon salt
1 egg white, beaten
1 teaspoon salt
1/4 cup butter
2 tablespoons lemon juice

Make large cavity in fish. Combine next 9 ingredients for stuffing. Stuff fish. Make sauce with remaining ingredients. Baste fish. Bake at 350° 20 minutes. Baste again and bake 20–30 minutes. Garnish with parsley. Serve with quick hollandaise sauce. Serves 4 to 6.

Eleanor N. Failing
INDIANOLA, MS

Catfish Cakes

5 small catfish fillets,
  poached in 1/4 cup white
  wine, water, parsley,
  basil, dill for flavor
  while poaching
1/4 cup onion, chopped
1/2 cup red bell pepper
1/2 cup mayonnaise
1 teaspoon creole season-
  ing
1/4 teaspoon garlic powder
1/2 teaspoon black pepper
2 tablespoons parsley
1 tablespoon Creole
  mustard
1/2 tablespoon
  Worcestershire sauce
2 eggs, beaten
Tabasco to taste
2 cups bread crumbs,
  divided
1/2 cup oil

Poach fish in herbs and wine for 20 minutes. Drain, cool, and chop coarsely. Mix all ingredients except bread crumbs. Add 1 1/2 cups bread crumbs to mixture and use 1/2 cup for breading cakes before frying. Shape into patties and fry.

Serve with Peppy Tomato "Tartar" sauce. Serves 6.

Peppy Tomato "Tartar" Sauce

1 fresh tomato, chopped
1 cup mayonnaise (or 1/2
  cup sour cream)
1/4 cup onion, finely
  chopped
Juice of one lemon
1 green jalapeno, chopped
1 roasted pepper, chopped
1/2 bell pepper, chopped

Mix well. Serve over catfish cakes or other seafood.

Claiborne Barnwell
JACKSON, MS

Catfish Caper

1 stick oleo
2 tablespoons lemon juice
1 teaspoon salt
1 clove garlic, crushed
1/4 teaspoon pepper
1 (4 ounce) jar mushrooms
  with juice
1 tablespoon capers
4 (3–5 ounce) catfish filets,
  cut in bite size pieces
Parsley
Paprika

Put all ingredients except fish in skillet and bring to a boil. Add fish. When sauce boils again, turn fish over. Reduce heat to low until fish is done - about 6 to 8 minutes. Sprinkle with parsley and paprika and serve over rice, Chinese noodles or pasta. Serves 4.

Elizabeth Lear McCarty
INDIANOLA, MS

Catfish and Collards (Portuguese Fisherman's Stew)

1/4 cup olive oil
2 pounds catfish fillets
3 pounds potatoes, cut in
  1/2" dice
8 cloves garlic, sliced
1 pound collards (or
  spinach, kale, mustard
  greens), chopped in 1/2"
  strips
Salt and pepper
1/4 pound smoked ham,
  cut in slivers
1 cup dry white wine

Heat olive oil in a large dutch oven. Toss garlic and greens in oil and cook 2 - 3 minutes until greens start to wilt. Toss in potatoes and ham; sprinkle with salt and pepper. Arrange fish on top of greens. Pour in wine and enough water to barely reach top of greens. Cover and simmer 35 minutes, shaking pan occasionally. Serve in soup plates.

Kate Failing
INDIANOLA, MS

Grilled Catfish With Clam Sauce

4 - 6 catfish fillets, grilled
1 cup milk
1 teaspoon celery salt
Salt, pepper
3 tablespoons margarine, melted
1 can New England clam chowder
1/2 cup mayonnaise
1 teaspoon Cajun seasoning
3/4 cup Monterrey Jack cheese

Rub fillets with salt, pepper, and margarine. Grill until flaky. Meanwhile, combine clam chowder, milk, celery salt, Cajun seasoning, mayonnaise, salt and pepper. Heat in microwave until bubbly. (If sauce is too thin, thicken with instant potato flakes.) Arrange fish in casserole, top with grated cheese, pour sauce over fish and bake, uncovered, at 300° for 30 minutes. Serve over rice.

Jackie Brocato
INDIANOLA, MS

Baked Fish With Tomato Sauce

1 snapper or
1 pound box filets of fish
1 tablespoon olive oil
1 medium onion, chopped
1 small green pepper, chopped
1 lemon
2 1/2 cups of canned tomatoes
2 celery stalks (leaves included), chopped
2 tablespoons parsley, chopped
Salt and Pepper

Clean fish thoroughly. Sprinkle with lemon juice and salt and let stand, while you prepare the sauce. To prevent the fish from sticking to the bottom of pan, line it with foil and arrange the fish in the pan. Sauté the onions, celery, green pepper in large skillet with the olive oil. When tender add tomatoes, parsley and salt and pepper to taste. Cover and cook over medium heat for 20 minutes. If needed add a little water. Stir occasionally. Pour over fish and bake in 400° oven for 35 minutes, basting. Serves 6.

Mrs. Robert M. Randall
INDIANOLA, MS

Fish in Caper Sauce

4 medium tomatoes,
  peeled and chopped
1 medium onion, chopped
1 teaspoon dried oregano
1 teaspoon dried basil
1/4 teaspoon garlic powder
Salt to taste
1 to 2 tablespoons capers
1 1/2 teaspoons dry sherry
1 3/4 pounds orange
  roughy fillets, catfish,
  redfish or trout fillets

Combine first 5 ingredients in a large skillet. Cook over medium heat 5 minutes or until onion is tender. Add capers and sherry; cook 1 to 2 minutes. Remove mixture from skillet, set aside. Add fish to skillet; top with vegetable mixture. Cover and cook 10 to 12 minutes or until fish flakes easily when tested with a fork. Yields 4 to 6 servings.

Lynn Eastland
INDIANOLA, MS

Courtbouillon Creole Style

Fresh water fish
1 large green pepper,
  chopped fine
1 large onion, chopped fine
2 tablespoons celery leaves,
  chopped
1 tablespoon oil
1 bay leaf
1 small piece lemon peel
2 1/2 cups canned toma-
  toes
Juice of 1/2 small lemon

In broiler, add pepper, onion, celery, oil, bay leaf, and lemon peel and cook slowly until nearly done. Remove bay leaf and lemon peel; add tomatoes and lemon juice reducing heat as low as possible. The flavors blend with long cooking. Add fish as desired and cook 15 minutes or until done; remove and debone. Return to sauce; heat thoroughly. Serve over rice with pat of butter and fresh ground pepper. Garnish with chopped green onion tops and chopped parsley.

Jessie P. Lee
INDIANOLA, MS

Stuffed Flounder

4 flounders (3/4 pound
  each)
2 eggs
2 cups cooked shrimp or
  crabmeat
1 cup cream
2 tablespoons butter
1/2 cup mushrooms
2 teaspoons chives,
  chopped
1 tablespoon flour
4 tablespoons sherry

Mix the shrimp, egg, and cream together. Melt butter, add mushrooms and chives and sauté until soft; add flour and cook until bubbly. Add shrimp mixture and sherry and cook until thick. Slit the flounder along the back bone and cut the flesh of the fish away from the bone, leaving intact. Spoon as much stuffing into the slit as possible. Top with butter and bake in 300° oven until done, about 30 minutes.

Tom Barron
INDIANOLA, MS

Pescada En Salsa Verde (Trout in Green Sauce)

4 fillets trout (or catfish)
1 clove garlic
1/2 cup olive oil
1 cup finely chopped
  parsley
1 teaspoon flour
1/2 cup water

Put enough olive oil in heavy pan to cover the bottom well. Put clove of garlic into oil and cook gently until garlic flavor has permeated the oil. Remove garlic. Then put in 1 cup finely chopped parsley, flour and water. Cook gently until well blended. Put fish fillets in sauce. Let cook 10 minutes. Salt and pepper to taste. Serves 2.

Mrs. J. C. Allen, Jr.
INDIANOLA, MS

Coquilles St. Jacques

1 cup dry white wine
1/2 teaspoon salt
Pinch of white pepper
1/2 bay leaf
2 tablespoons minced
  green onions and tops
1 pound fresh scallops,
  sliced
1/2 pound fresh mush-
  rooms, sliced

Roux:

3 tablespoons butter
4 tablespoons flour
3/4 cup milk
2 egg yolks
1/2 cup heavy cream
Salt and white pepper
1 tablespoon lemon juice
Grated Swiss cheese

Simmer 5 minutes wine, salt, pepper, bay leaf, and onions. Add thawed washed scallops, mushrooms, and enough water to cover. Again simmer for 5 minutes. Remove only scallops and mushrooms and continue to boil until only 1 cup liquid remains.

In skillet melt butter and add flour to make Roux; reduce heat and add above wine with milk added, and boil 1 minute. To beaten yolks to which cream has been added, slowly beat in hot sauce mixture and boil another minute. Season to taste with salt, pepper and lemon juice. Strain. Combine sauce, scallops, mushrooms in buttered casserole and sprinkle with grated Swiss cheese, paprika, and dots of butter. Bake in 400° oven until brown and bubbly. (May use individual shells if prefer.)

Mrs. Jo Prichard
Mrs. Walter Jones
INVERNESS, MS

Jackie Kennedy Crabmeat Casserole

1 pound lump crabmeat
1 large onion
1 bell pepper
1 clove garlic
3 ribs celery
1 stick butter or oelo
3 eggs
8 pieces bread
1/4 pound cheese
2 tablespoons
  Worcestershire sauce
Salt
Pepper

Chop vegetables fine and sauté in butter or oleo. Crumble 8 pieces of white bread and soak in 1 cup water. Grate 1/4 pound cracker barrel cheese. Add Worcestershire sauce and red pepper to taste. Mix sautéed greens with 3 raw eggs and crab meat. Mix all together. Add salt and pepper to taste. Place in baking dish and sprinkle with cracker crumbs and dot with butter. Bake 20 minutes at 450°. Serves 6.

Mrs. Ann Gresham
INDIANOLA, MS

Deviled Crab

1 cup fresh crab meat
1/3 cup vinegar
2/3 cup water
1 tablespoon
    Worcestershire sauce
1 teaspoon mustard
3 eggs
1/2 teaspoon celery seed
1 tablespoon butter
1 cup crackers, crushed
Salt
Pepper
1 tablespoon flour

Mix water and vinegar. Beat eggs lightly and add to the liquid. Mix Worcestershire and mustard, then add to the liquid. Add celery seed, salt, and pepper and cook until mixture thickens. Add flour mixed with a little water. Cook until thick. Add crab meat and cracker crumbs. Heat in individual shells. Serves 6.

Mrs. Ernie Baker
INDIANOLA, MS

Crab Louie

1 1/2 pounds lump crab
    meat (shrimp or lobster)
1 cup chopped celery
1/2 cup mayonnaise (fresh)
Lemon juice
White pepper
Lettuce
4 medium fresh garden
    tomatoes
4 hard-boiled eggs
Louie dressing (same as
    1000 Island Dressing)
Lemon wedges
Ripe olives
Avocado slices
4 Crab legs

Pick over crab meat removing any bits of shell. Flake and mix gently with celery and enough mayonnaise to moisten. Season with lemon juice and a little white pepper. Arrange lettuce on 4 large salad plates and heap with mounds of crab. Top each with crab leg and surround with quartered tomatoes, avocado slices (squeeze lemon juice over to keep from turning black), and ripe olives. Cover with saran wrap and chill. Serve with Louie dressing. Chilled dry white wine is excellent addition to luncheon!

Arthur Clark, Jr.
INDIANOLA, MS

Crabmeat a La Mornay

1 stick butter
1 small bunch green
  onions, chopped
1/2 cup finely chopped
  parsley
2 tablespoons flour
1 pint light cream
1/2 pound grated Swiss
  cheese
1 tablespoon sherry
Red pepper and salt to
  taste
1 pound fresh white crab
  meat

Melt butter in heavy pot and sauté onions. Blend in flour, cream, and cheese until cheese is melted. Add other ingredients and gently fold in crabmeat. This may be served in a chafing dish with Melba rounds as a dip or in patty shells.

Mrs. Edgar Eaton
PORT GIBSON, MS

Deviled Oysters

1 quart oysters
2 cups celery, diced
1 cup onions, diced
1 stick butter
1 teaspoon black pepper
2 tablespoons Lea and
  Perrins
Cracker crumbs

Cut oysters in halves; use just juice that sticks to oysters. Cook until oysters begin to curl. Sauté onions and celery in butter, until onions begin to turn yellow. Mix oysters, onions, celery, and cracker crumbs with other ingredients. Bake in 500° oven about 20 minutes. Use just enough crackers to hold together.

Ina May Heathman
INDIANOLA, MS

Oysters "Johnny Reb"

2 quarts oysters, drained
1/2 cup finely chopped
  parsley
1/2 cup finely chopped
  shallots or onions
Salt and pepper
Tabasco
1 tablespoon
  Worcestershire sauce
2 tablespoons lemon juice
1/2 cup melted butter
2 cups fine cracker crumbs
Paprika
3/4 cup milk, half and half

Place a layer of oysters in bottom of greased shallow two-quart baking dish. Sprinkle with half of parsley, shallots, seasonings, lemon juice, butter and crumbs. Make another layer of the same. Sprinkle with paprika. Just before baking, pour the milk into evenly spaced holes, being very careful not to moisten crumb topping all over. Bake at 375° for about 30 minutes, or until firm. Yield: 12 to 15 portions.

Originated at the Old Southern Tea Room
VICKSBURG, MS.

Baked Oyster Loaf

This is delicious and a "cross" between oyster stew and scalloped oysters.

3 pints milk
3 dozen oysters
2 tablespoons butter
2 stalks celery
12 saltine crackers,
  coarsely rolled
Salt and pepper

Bring the milk to the boiling point and pour into a deep baking dish; add all the remaining ingredients except the oysters. Place in 450° oven and let a light brown crust form on top. Turn thin crust under with a spoon and allow another to form on top. Remove the celery, season with salt and pepper, and serve in the baking dish in which it has cooked. Put oysters in after the soup has been turned twice; after oysters have been put in turn once more. (This will be three turns in all.) Serves 6.

Katherine Haxton
GREENVILLE, MS

Oyster Ragout-1896

3 dozens large oysters
Cracker crumbs to equal
   volume of oysters
Juice of lemon
Salt and pepper to taste
2 egg yolks
2 hard boiled eggs, finely
   mashed
1 small onion, grated
1 lump butter

Mix together chopped oysters and rolled cracker crumbs, lemon juice, egg yolks, hard boiled eggs, grated onion, melted butter, and salt and pepper. Bake in a pan 1/2 hour, then put mixture in shells, sprinkling over the top with cracker crumbs. Pour over each a little melted butter. Return to oven and brown.

Mrs. W. B. Walker
INDIANOLA, MS

Scalloped Oysters and Chicken

1 (6 pound) chicken
1 tablespoon Accent
2 tablespoons salt
2 pounds fresh mush-
   rooms
Butter
4 1/4 dozen large oysters
Soda crackers
Milk (half and half)

Cook roasting chicken in sufficient water plus Accent and salt. Let cool in broth before cutting meat into bite-size pieces. Strain broth, remove fat from the top. Reserve liquid. (You could freeze all this ahead.) In bottom of casserole alternate: crackers. coarsely broken; dot with butter, salt and pepper, layer of chicken pieces, layer of sliced mushrooms. Sprinkle with salt and pepper, more crackers and butter. Add a mixture of chicken broth and milk. Pour in only enough so that you can see if you tip the casserole to the side. You can add more as it is cooking at 400°. Turn up to 500° for final browning (5 minutes). Serves 10.

Add raw cauliflower to your tossed salad for the change of texture you need with this dish. It's really delicious!

Mrs. Johnson Garrott
OXFORD, MS

Oyster Stew With Mace

1 quart large plump
   oysters
1 cup liquor with oysters
1 tablespoon butter
1 tablespoon flour
2 cups cream
4 tablespoons milk
2 blades mace
Salt and pepper

Scald oysters in their own liquor. As soon as they are plump, remove them to another dish. Mix well butter, flour, and milk, and add to liquor. Then pour in cream, season to taste with salt and pepper, and add mace. Let this become very hot but do not boil. Then add oysters. As soon as soup nears boiling point, remove mace from stew and serve. Serves 8.

Mary R. Wall
INDIANOLA, MS

Baked Stuffed Oysters

3 dozen oysters
2 cups oyster liquor
1 large onion
1 large pod garlic
1 green pepper
1 stalk celery
2 teaspoons lemon juice
2 dashes Tabasco
1 teaspoon paprika
1/2 teaspoon
   Worcestershire sauce
1/2 cup cooking oil
4 tablespoons butter
1/2 cup mushrooms
1 1/4 cup bread crumbs
1/2 cup flour

Drain oysters and chop into coarse pieces. Chop onion, garlic, green pepper and celery. Heat oil, add flour, stir until light brown. Then add onion, garlic, celery and green pepper and cook slowly until brown. Then add the oysters, chopped mushrooms, oyster liquor and all other ingredients except bread crumbs. Cook for 10 minutes. Add 1 cup of bread crumbs. Stir, and remove from heat. Fill shells, sprinkle with bread crumbs. Bake in moderate oven 15 minutes.

This is a traditional Creole recipe from New Orleans used by my mother Mrs. Carré.

Janie Dale
GREENWOOD, MS

Saucy Salmon Supreme

1 pound can salmon
1 can cream of celery soup
1/4 cup grated onion
1/4 cup chopped parsley
Juice of 1 lemon
Dash Worcestershire
Dash Tabasco
Salt and pepper to taste
2 eggs, beaten

Mix all ingredients together and put buttered crumbs or cracker crumbs on top. Bake in 350° oven for 20–30 minutes. Serves 6.

Ruth Morris
INDIANOLA, MS

Aunt Elise's Seafood Casserole

2 cans crab meat
2 cans lobster
2 pounds fresh cooked shrimp
3 cups white cream sauce
4 tablespoons minced celery
1 small onion grated
2 jiggers of sherry
1 pound New York cheese

Make 3 cups cream sauce, seasoned with celery and onion. Add Tabasco, Worcestershire sauce, and paprika. Add 1/2 pound grated cheese and stir until it melts. Add sherry, lobster, and shrimp. Top with another 1/2 pound grated cheese. Delicious served in buttered toast ramekins or in shell ramekins as for main dish - especially for ladies luncheon.

Mrs. R. J. Allen, Jr.
INDIANOLA, MS

Belmont Seafood

1 can hearts of artichokes
1 pound shrimp (after
 being cleaned and
 cooked)
1 pound lump crabmeat

Sauce:
2 tablespoons butter
3 tablespoons flour
Red pepper, paprika
Salt to taste
1 pint half and half cream
1 teaspoon Worcestershire
 sauce
1 tablespoon tomato
 catsup
1 tablespoon lemon juice
2 tablespoons sherry wine
1 cup grated cheese

Slice artichokes thin and drain for one hour. Place layer of seafood and layer of artichokes in casserole until dish is almost full. Pour sauce over it. Cook long enough to heat well. Put buttered crumbs on top.

Mix flour, butter, pepper, salt, and paprika. Add half and half. Cook slowly until it thickens and is well blended. Then add: Worcestershire sauce, tomato catsup, lemon juice, sherry wine and sharp cheese. (Can be frozen) Serves 8.

Mrs. Ross Jones
TULSA, OK

Seafood Casserole

1/2 pound shrimp or 2
 (5 ounce) cans
1/2 pound crab meat or
 1 (7 1/2 ounce can)
1 pint half and half
2 cups mayonnaise
2 cups plus 2 slices soft
 bread crumbs
2 tablespoons fresh
 chopped parsley or 1
 tablespoon dried parsley
 flakes
1 tablespoon instant dried
 onion
1 teaspoon season salt
1 teaspoon freshly cracked
 pepper
4 hard boiled eggs,
 chopped

Mix all ingredients and arrange in a 2 quart casserole, several smaller ones, or in shells. Bake at 350° until solid or browned. Can be prepared the day before, and baked when ready to serve.

Nancy Lloyd Conner
BERKELY, CA

Seafood Pasta With Basil Cream

1/2 cup white wine
  vinegar
3 tablespoons dry sherry
2 cloves garlic, crushed
1 teaspoon salt
2/3 cup olive oil
2 cups broccoli florets
2 pounds catfish filets or
  shrimp
1 bunch green onions
1 cup cherry tomatoes,
  halved
8 ounces thin pasta

Basil cream:

3 tablespoons white wine
  vinegar
1 tablespoon Dijon mus-
  tard
6 tablespoons fresh basil or
  2 tablespoons dried
1 large clove garlic, minced
3 tablespoons olive oil
1/2 cup sour cream
4 tablespoons chopped
  parsley

Combine first 5 ingredients and set dressing aside. Steam broccoli florets and refrigerate. Poach catfish filets or shrimp. Mince green onions. Half cherry tomatoes. Cook pasta. Toss pasta and spring onions with half of dressing. Season with salt and pepper. Toss flaked catfish with remaining dressing.

Toss pasta, seafood, broccoli, and tomatoes together. Add basil cream sauce and toss again. Best when made at least a day in advance. Serves 6 - 8.

Joanne Lear
INDIANOLA, MS

Cajun Shrimp

1 pound jumbo shrimp, raw, peeled
1 to 2 sticks butter or margarine
2 - 3 cloves garlic, pressed
1 tablespoon cajun spices (or more to taste)
1/4 cup white wine
2 - 3 tablespoons fresh herbs, if available (basil, parsley, cilantro, etc. if fresh not available 1 1/2 tablespoons dried herbs)
1 - 2 cups heavy whipping cream (optional)

Sauté shrimp in butter 1 - 2 minutes on each side, or until they are white and opaque. Remove shrimp. To skillet, add wine, spices and herbs. 1 - 2 cups cream can be added at this point if desired. Simmer until cream reached the desired thickness. Return shrimp to skillet. Taste and adjust seasonings. Excellent served over fresh pasta, rice or in pastry shells.

Trish Berry
INDIANOLA, MS

Scampi Bayou

1 cup soft butter
4 shallots, finely chopped
4 garlic cloves, crushed
2 tablespoons lemon juice
3 tablespoons bottled steak sauce
1/2 teaspoon salt
1/2 teaspoon pepper
1 pound large raw shrimp

Beat together until creamy or purée in a blender butter, shallots, garlic cloves, steak sauce, lemon juice, salt and freshly ground pepper. Peel and devein shrimp, leaving the tails attached. Split the shrimp lengthwise being careful not to cut them through and spread them open. Put them in an oiled, shallow baking dish and broil them five minutes or until they are cooked through. Arrange the shrimp on a serving dish. Heat the seasoned butter until it is bubbling but not browned and pour it over the shrimp. Serve at once with hot French bread for mopping up purposes.

Mrs. Anheuser Rombauer
FORT LAUDERDALE, FL

Shrimp Creole

3 strips bacon
1 green pepper, chopped fine
1 cup okra, cut (frozen or fresh)
3 tablespoons flour
1 1/2 cup hot water
1 8 ounce can tomato sauce
1 1/2 pound shrimp, boiled and peeled
Garlic
Chili powder
Black pepper
Red pepper
Worcestershire sauce to taste

Fry bacon and drain. In bacon grease brown onions over low heat. Add chopped pepper and okra. Thicken with flour. Add water, stirring constantly to keep lumps out. Cook about 15 minutes. Add other ingredients and cook slowly 15 or 20 minutes. Add more water if needed. Add boiled shrimp and crumbled bacon. Serve on hot rice. Makes about six average servings.

Tottie T. Bishop
GREENWOOD, MS

Shrimp Creole (Cajun)

5 pounds cleaned, boiled shrimp
2 sticks butter (2 cups cooking oil)
3 green peppers, chopped fine
4 onions, chopped fine
2 cloves, garlic, chopped fine
3 cans tomatoes
1/2 stalk celery chopped fine
1/2 teaspoon black pepper
1 teaspoon salt
1 teaspoon curry powder
1 teaspoon thyme
1/2 teaspoon cayenne pepper

Sauté chopped peppers, onions, garlic and celery in butter. Add tomatoes and seasonings. Cook slowly for several hours. Add shrimp and cook 30 minutes more. Serve over rice. Serves 8-10 generously. Freezes well.

Mary Anne Ross
INDIANOLA, MS

Shrimp or Crabmeat au Gratin

4 tablespoons butter
5 tablespoons flour
1/2 teaspoon salt
2 cups milk
Red and white pepper to
taste
2 tablespoons sherry
1/2 pound extra sharp
cheddar cheese, cubed
2 pounds cooked shrimp or
crabmeat
1 pound fresh mushrooms,
sliced and sautéed or 2
cans large mushrooms,
sliced
Toasted fresh bread
crumbs

Make a béchamel sauce of first five ingredients. In heavy bottomed saucepan, combine butter and flour over low heat. Stirring constantly, slowly add milk. Cook for 3 - 5 minutes or until "floury" taste is gone. Add salt and white pepper to taste. Add sherry and cheese. Stir in seafood and mushrooms. Pour into buttered 9 x 12 casserole and top with toasted crumbs. Bake at 400° for about 25 minutes. Serves 12.

Mrs. Carl Megehee
PASCAGOULA, MS

Shrimp Floridian

2 pounds shrimp
1/2 pound bleu cheese,
Roquefort or
Gorgonzola
8 ounce package cream
cheese
1 tablespoon chopped
chives
1 tablespoon chopped
parsley
1 clove garlic, chopped
finely
3/4 cup dry white wine

Mash cheese and cream cheese and add parsley, chives, garlic, and wine to make sauce. Pour over raw, cleaned and shelled shrimp. Bake in a covered baking dish at 400° for 30 minutes. Serves 4.

Mrs. Arthur B. Clark, Jr.
INDIANOLA, MS

Shrimp and Grits

Grits:

1 cup Quaker quick grits
4 tablespoons unsalted
  butter
3/4 cup extra sharp
  cheddar cheese (white)
1/2 cup grated parmesan
  cheese
1 teaspoon cayenne pepper
1 1/4 tablespoons paprika
1 teaspoon Tabasco
Salt and pepper to taste

Shrimp:

2 cups chopped smoked
  bacon
3 tablespoons olive oil
1 1/2 pounds 26–30 count
  shrimp
Salt and black pepper
3 teaspoons minced garlic
3 cups sliced white mush-
  rooms
4 tablespoons white wine
2 tablespoons lemon juice
2 cups sliced scallions

Cook grits according to instructions on package. As grits are finishing whisk in butter, cheddar, parmesan, cayenne, paprika and tabasco. After all ingredients are incorporated season with salt and pepper. Set aside.

Cook bacon until it begins to brown, remove from heat, strain and reserve bacon grease and bacon bits. Heat large skillet until very hot, add olive oil and 2 tablespoons bacon fat. As oils begin to smoke, toss in shrimp to cover bottom of pan. Before stirring, season with salt and pepper (this will season shrimp in particular, but the rest of the dish as well). Stir until shrimp begin to turn pink all over (let pan return original hot temperature). Stir in minced garlic and bacon bits (be careful not to burn the garlic). Toss in mushrooms and coat with oil briefly. Add lemon juice and wine, stir for 30 seconds or so until everything is well coated. Toss in sliced scallions and stir for about 20 seconds. Serve over cheese grits. Serves 3 or 4.

Elizabeth Belk
BIRMINGHAM, AL

Shrimp Baked with Feta Cheese

3 cups imported canned
   Italian plum tomatoes
1 pound (about 24) shrimp
1/4 cup olive oil
1 teaspoon finely chopped
   garlic
1/4 cup fresh fish broth or
   bottled clam juice
1 teaspoon crushed dried
   oregano
1 teaspoon dried hot red
   pepper flakes
2 tablespoons drained
   capers
Salt and freshly ground
   pepper
3 tablespoons butter
1/4 pound feta cheese
1/4 cup ouzo, optional, a
   Greek anise-flavored
   liqueur widely available
   in wine and spirits shops

Preheat the oven to 350°. Put the tomatoes in a saucepan and cook until reduced to about 2 cups. Stir often to prevent burning and sticking. Shell and devein the shrimp and set aside. Heat the olive oil in another saucepan or deep skillet and add the garlic, stirring. Add the tomatoes, using a rubber spatula to scrape them out. Add the fish broth, oregano, pepper flakes, capers, and salt and pepper to taste. Heat the butter in a heavy saucepan or skillet and cook the shrimp briefly, less than 1 minute, stirring and turning them until they turn pink. Spoon equal portions of half the sauce into four individual baking dishes and arrange 6 shrimp plus equal amounts of the butter in which they cooked in each dish. Spoon remaining sauce over the shrimp. Crumble the cheese and scatter it over all. Place the dishes in the oven and bake for 10 to 15 minutes, or until bubbling hot. Remove the dishes from the oven and sprinkle each dish with 1 tablespoon ouzo, if desired, and ignite it. Serve immediately. Yield: 4 servings.

Craig Claiborne
EAST HAMPTON, NY

Shrimp Jambalaya

4 tablespoons fat (preferably bacon or ham)
1 large onion, chopped fine
2 cloves garlic
2 pounds uncooked shrimp, peeled
1 (28-ounce) can diced tomatoes with juice
1 tablespoons salt
2 bay leaves
1 teaspoon thyme
1 teaspoons pepper
1 1/2 cups uncooked rice
1 teaspoon sugar
1 tablespoon parsley

Must cook in iron pot. Fry onions and garlic lightly in fat; add shrimp and cook five minutes. Add tomatoes and seasonings. Bring to a good boil. Add rice, boil for five minutes, then cover pot tightly, and reduce heat to very low. Cook 1 hour. Do not stir.

Lynne Monju Kwitzky
SALEM, OR

Shrimp De Jonghe

1 garlic clove, mashed
1/3 teaspoon chopped
  tarragon
1/3 teaspoon chervil
1/3 teaspoon chopped
  parsley
1/3 teaspoon chopped
  onion
1 cup melted butter, mixed
  with
3/4 cup finely sifted dry
  bread crumbs
2 3/4 pounds cooked
  shrimp

Arrange 2 3/4 pounds of freshly cleaned, cooked shrimp in layers in a fairly large baking dish, alternating with half of herbs, spices, crumbs, and sherry mixture. Sprinkle the top with the other half of the mixture and an additional sprinkle of parsley. Place in hot oven 400° and let cook about 20 to 25 minutes.

Willie Morris
JACKSON, MS

Sherry Mixture:
1/4 teaspoon salt
1/16 teaspoon thyme
1/16 teaspoon mace
1/16 teaspoon nutmeg
1/4 teaspoon pepper
1 cup sherry

Shrimp New Orleans

2 tablespoons butter
1/2 cup chopped green
  pepper
1/2 cup chopped onion
3 cups cleaned cooked
  shrimp
1 tablespoon fresh lemon
  juice
2 cups cooked rice
1 can condensed tomato
  soup
3/4 cup light cream
1/4 cup sherry
3/4 teaspoon salt
1/4 teaspoon nutmeg
1/4 cup sliced toasted
  almonds (optional)

Cook green peppers and onion in butter until tender - not brown. Stir in other ingredients. Pour into 2 quart casserole. Bake at 350° for 30 minutes. Top with 1/4 cup toasted slivered almonds.

Mrs. Joel Hill, Jr.
GREENVILLE, MS

Stuffed Shrimp

16 large shrimp
2 tablespoons chopped parsley
2 tablespoons chopped green onions
1/2 stick butter
3/4 cup bread crumbs
1 egg, beaten
Salt
White pepper
Tarragon
1 can evaporated milk
Seasoned bread crumbs

Peel 12 raw shrimp and split down back. Soak shrimp in 1 can evaporated milk. Sauté in butter the parsley, onions, 4 chopped shrimp (crabmeat may be used) and seasonings. When done remove from heat, add bread crumbs and cool mixture. When cool, add one beaten egg. Fill shrimp cavity with stuffing, dip in milk again and roll in bread crumbs. Cook in hot fat until golden brown.

Burton Moore
INDIANOLA, MS

Sunday Night "Show-off"

2 packages (8 ounce) Vermicelli or thin spaghetti
1/2 cup butter or margarine
1/2 cup flour
1 cup chicken broth
1 cup heavy cream
1 cup shredded Swiss cheese
4 tablespoons sherry
White pepper to taste
1 large (16 ounces) can mushrooms sliced
3 pounds shrimp, cooked and peeled
1/2 cup fresh grated Parmesan
1/4 cup slivered almonds

Cook pasta and drain. Make cream sauce out of butter, flour, broth, and cream over low heat, stirring constantly until sauce thickens. Blend in cheese, sherry, and white pepper; heat and stir until cheese melts; add mushrooms. Remove from heat. Add shrimp. Add spaghetti to sauce. Turn into large shallow casserole. Sprinkle with Parmesan cheese and slivered almonds. Heat under broiler (5 to 7 inches) until lightly brown. Serve immediately. 12 servings Meal in one.

Mrs. Edward S. T. Hale
BROOKHAVEN, MS

Poultry and Game

Chicken Ambassador

6-8 large chicken breasts
1 tablespoon salt
1 teaspoon poultry seasoning
Paprika
1/2 cup melted butter
1 can beef consomme
1/2 cup sherry
1/2 pound mushrooms
(fresh or 1 large can
button mushrooms)
20 ounces canned arti-
choke hearts

Season chicken with salt and poultry seasoning. Sprinkle with paprika to give them a good color. Spread out in roasting pan, skin side up. Baste with combined melted butter and consomme. Bake at 325° in oven for one hour, basting every 20 minutes. Add the sherry to pan drippings and keep on baking and basting 1/2 hour longer. Sauté the sliced fresh mushrooms. When ready to serve, remove chicken breasts to heated platter and combine drippings in pan with mushrooms and artichoke hearts. Heat thoroughly and pour sauce over chicken. Serve at once.

Mrs. Rodgers Brashier
INDIANOLA, MS

Chicken Artichoke And Mushroom Casserole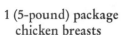

1 (5-pound) package
  chicken breasts
1 cup butter
3/4 cup flour
2 cups milk
2 cups chicken stock
1 teaspoon salt
1 bay leaf
1 teaspoon seasoned salt
1/2 teaspoon cayenne
  pepper
2 cloves garlic, pressed
6 ounces swiss cheese,
  grated
6 ounces sharp cheddar
  cheese, grated
3 (14 ounce) artichoke
  hearts, cut up
3 (4 1/2 ounce) mushrooms,
  sliced

Simmer chicken in water seasoned with celery, onion, 1 teaspoon salt, and 1 bay leaf. Remove chicken from bones and cut into chunks. Make a cream sauce of butter, flour, milk, chicken stock and seasonings. When thickened, stir in cheese until melted. Add artichokes, chicken, and mushrooms and mix well. Pour into a shallow 3-quart casserole. Top with additional grated cheese. Bake at 350° for 35 minutes. Serves 15. Freezes very well before cooking.

Susan Robertson Allen
INDIANOLA, MS

Southern Barbecued Chicken

Sauce:
1 bottle Heinz ketchup
2 tablespoons sugar
3 tablespoons flour
3 tablespoons vinegar
2 tablespoons
  Worcestershire sauce
  (Lea & Perrins)
1 tablespoon dry mustard
2 or 3 green peppers,
  chopped fine
1/3 stick butter

Use chickens weighing 2 1/2 to 3 pounds. Split down the back. Put in flat roaster, skin side down. Sprinkle with salt and pepper. On each half chicken, use 1/3 stick of butter. Add 2 or 3 cups of water and cook uncovered in oven at 400° until about half done. Baste with sauce once, turn and cover other side with sauce and cook until done. Do not overcook. Have gravy thick.

Cut up liver and gizzard in sauce. Mix well. Salt and pepper to taste. Serve 1/2 chicken to each person with rice, candied yams and hot buttermilk biscuits.

Mrs. H. J. Munnerlyn
BENNETTSVILLE, SC

Boneless Chicken Breasts

1/2 cup Parmesan cheese
1/4 cup chopped parsley
1 garlic button crushed
2 teaspoons salt
Red pepper to taste
Melted butter
1 cup bread crumbs or
    cornflakes
4 chicken breasts, deboned
Celery and onions

Mix cheese, parsley, garlic, salt, red pepper. Dip deboned chicken in melted butter, cover completely with above mix, and then bread crumbs. Roll each chicken breast and bake for 1 hour at 350°. Boil chicken bones, salt, pepper, celery, onions in small amount of water to make chicken broth. Use this to baste chicken breasts several times during the hour. Serves 4.

A marvelous and unusual dish for company.

Mrs. John Fair Lucas
GREENWOOD, MS

Chicken Breasts With Tarragon

3 whole chicken breasts,
    boned and halved
Salt and freshly ground
    pepper
1/4 cup flour
1/4 cup butter
1 tablespoon chopped
    shallots or onion
1/4 cup dry white Bordeaux wine
1 teaspoon freshly chopped
    tarragon or 1/2 teaspoon
    dried tarragon
1/4 cup chicken broth
1/4 cup heavy cream

Skin the chicken breasts. Sprinkle with salt and pepper and dredge with flour. Reserve the remaining flour. In a large skillet heat three tablespoons of the butter, add the chicken and brown on both sides. Transfer to a heated platter. Add the shallots to the skillet and sauté briefly. Add the wine. Cook the liquid over high heat until it is nearly evaporated, while scraping loose all the brown particles. Add the reserved flour and stir to make a thick paste. Sprinkle with the tarragon and stir in the chicken broth. Return the chicken to the skillet, cover and cook until tender, about twenty-five minutes. Transfer the chicken to a heated platter and keep hot. Add the remaining butter and the cream to the skillet; heat, stirring, and pour the sauce over the chicken.

(From Craig Claiborne)

Mrs. M. W. Swartz
INDIANOLA, MS

Oven Broiled Chicken

2 chickens, halved
1 tablespoon
   Worcestershire sauce
1 tablespoon lemon juice
1 bay leaf
1 stick margarine
Salt and pepper
Flour

Salt, pepper and flour chicken and brown in bacon grease. Place in flat pan and cover with sauce made of Worcestershire, lemon juice, bay leaf and margarine. Cover and bake in 250° oven at least 2 hours. Baste with sauce every 1/2 hour.

Mrs. Wallace Carter, Jr.
ROLLING FORK, MS

Chicken Cacciatore

3 pound frying chicken
1/2 cup salad oil
1 tablespoon chopped
   parsley
1/2 clove garlic, chopped
1/2 green pepper, cut up
2 stalks celery, cut up
1/2 onion, chopped
1/2 teaspoon oregano
1 small can tomato sauce
Salt and pepper to taste
1 1/2 cups water
1/4 cup dry white wine

Cut chicken into serving pieces and brown quickly in hot oil. Add remaining ingredients except wine and enough water to cover chicken. Cover pan and cook over low heat for 45 minutes or until chicken is done. Add wine and cook 15 minutes more. Serves 5.

Mrs. Henry Mura
INDIANOLA, MS

Chinese Chop Suey

Wesson oil
1/2 pound lean pork, chopped
2 whole chicken breasts, chopped
Salt
1/2 cup diced celery
1/2 cup chopped onion
1/2 pound bean sprouts or 1 (no. 2 can)
2 ounce can sliced mush-rooms
Soy sauce
Corn starch

Brown pork in Wesson oil. Add chicken and salt. When pork and chicken are done, remove from pan. Add small amount of Wesson oil and cook celery. When celery is almost done, add onions. Simmer a few minutes, then add bean sprouts and simmer about two minutes, stirring constantly. Add cooked pork and chicken breasts continually stirring. When almost done, add soy sauce, mushrooms, and salt. In a separate container make corn starch thickening and add to chop suey. Cover and simmer for two or three minutes. Uncover, stir, and serve hot. Serves 4.

Ray W. Joe
GREENWOOD, MS

Creole Chicken

2 cups diced cooked chicken meat
3 tablespoons chicken fat or butter
2 tablespoons chopped onion
2 tablespoons green pepper (chopped)
3 tablespoons flour
1/4 teaspoon salt
1/2 teaspoon paprika
1/2 cup strained tomatoes
1 cup chicken broth
1 tablespoon lemon juice
1 teaspoon horseradish
1/2 cup sautéed mush rooms, sliced
Pepper to taste
Rice

Melt chicken fat or butter; sauté onion, and green pepper in the fat. Stir in flour, salt, pep-per, and paprika Add tomatoes, mushrooms and chicken broth. Stir and bring to a low boil. Add lemon juice, horseradish, chicken, and mushrooms. Serve on rice ring or bed of rice. Serves 4.

Mary Speer
INDIANOLA, MS

Chicken Divan

4 bunches cooked broccoli
Slices of one boiled chicken
1/2 cup melted butter
1/2 cup flour
1 pint scalded milk
1 cup heavy cream,
    whipped
1/2 teaspoon
    Worcestershire sauce
1 1/2 tablespoon grated
    Parmesan cheese
1 jigger sherry
1/2 cup Hollandaise sauce
Salt and Pepper to taste

Arrange a layer of broccoli in casserole and cover with chicken slices. Combine butter, flour, and milk in a sauce pan over low heat and stir until thickened. Add cream, Worcestershire, cheese and wine. Mix until blended. Add Hollandaise. Season to taste. Pour over broccoli and chicken layers and sprinkle with Parmesan cheese. Brown under broiler. Serves 8-10.

Mrs. Joe S. Green
INDIANOLA, MS

Arwin's Chicken and Dumplings

1 whole chicken breast
1/4 cup shortening
2 cups self-rising flour
3/4 cup broth or water,
    (boiling)
2 quarts chicken broth
Salt
Pepper

Cook chicken breast seasoned with salt and pepper. Chop chicken. Mix shortening with flour until well blended. Gradually add boiling water to flour mixture. Separate dough into two balls and roll out as thin as possible. Cut in long strips and pinch each into small pieces. Drop in boiling broth, then turn heat to low and cook about 10 minutes or until dumplings are tender. Add chicken last. Serves 6. Lick your lips and enjoy!

Mrs. James Corder
INDIANOLA, MS

Enchiladas With Chicken And Spinach

1/2 pound chicken, boiled, drained and shredded
1 package chopped spinach, cooked and drained
1/4 cup green onion, chopped
8 ounces sour cream
1/4 cup plain yogurt
1/2 cup milk
2 tablespoons flour
1/4 teaspoon cumin
1/4 teaspoon salt
4 ounces green chilies - drained, (optional)
Flour tortillas
Salsa
Monterey Jack cheese - shredded

Mix chicken, spinach and onion. Mix sour cream, yogurt, milk, flour, cumin, salt and chilies. Divide in half. Mix half of sauce with chicken mixture. Spread some in center of each tortilla and roll up. Place seam side down in baking dish. Pour remaining sauce over top. Bake at 350° for 25 minutes. Top with cheese and salsa.

Mimi Alexander
INDIANOLA, MS

Mississippi Fried Chicken

6 chicken breast halves
Salt and pepper
Cooking oil
1 cup flour
1/2 teaspoon salt
1/2 teaspoon black pepper
1 teaspoon baking powder

In colander rinse chicken breasts. Salt and pepper. Let stand to drain. In plastic sack, combine flour, salt, pepper and baking powder. Shake chicken in this mixture until well coated. Put chicken in refrigerator for 1/2 to 6 hours. Put 1 inch cooking oil in large skillet. Heat to medium high. Place chicken pieces in skillet. When they are hot and cooking well, turn heat to medium low. Cook 7 to 10 minutes each side or until well browned.

Vera Gwin
INDIANOLA, MS

Grilled Chicken Pasta

1 (1 1/2 pound) chicken breasts, boneless and skinless
1/4 cup butter
2 tablespoons olive oil
1 (14 ounce) artichoke hearts, sliced
1 bunch green onions, chopped
1/2 teaspoon salt
1/4 teaspoon white pepper
1/4 teaspoon cayenne pepper
2 tablespoons flour
5 cloves garlic, minced
1 cup lite cream
1 cup chicken broth
10 ounces fettuccine noodles
1/2 cup freshly grated Parmesan cheese

Grill chicken, cut into chunks, reserve. In a heavy skillet heat butter and olive oil over medium high heat. Add artichoke hearts and onions and cook 1 minute. Reduce heat to low. Add seasonings, flour, and garlic. Mix well. Add cream and broth. Simmer for 20 minutes, stirring occasionally. Add more cream if necessary to thin. Add chicken. Meanwhile in large stockpot, cook fettuccine until tender but still firm. Drain. Pour sauce over pasta and toss. Mix in parmesan cheese and serve immediately. Makes 4 to 6 main dish servings.

Susan Robertson Allen
INDIANOLA, MS

Italian Chicken

1/4 cup flour
1 tablespoon oregano
4 deboned, skinless chicken breasts
3 tablespoons olive oil
1/3 cup dry white wine
1/3 cup chicken broth
2 tomatoes, diced or 1 can stewed tomatoes
3 tablespoons black olives, sliced of 1 small 2 1/4 ounce can
2 tablespoons capers
2 tablespoons feta cheese, crumbled

Mix flour and oregano. Coat chicken. Brown chicken breasts in oil - five minutes on each side. Add all other ingredients except feta cheese. Simmer 15 minutes or until sauce thicken. Top with feta cheese. Serves 4.

Annette Lear Watson
JACKSON, MS

Chicken a la King

This is one of Mrs. Maud (M.C.) Faulkner's recipes. Mrs. Faulkner had four sons, William, Murry, John, and Dean.

2 tablespoons butter
2 tablespoons flour
1 cup heavy cream
Salt
Pepper
2 cups diced, cooked
 chicken
1/2 cup drained mush-
 rooms, peas or asparagus
2 tablespoons minced
 pimiento
1 egg yolk
2 tablespoons milk

Make white sauce of butter, flour and cream. Season with salt and pepper. Add chicken and drained mushrooms or peas or asparagus which has been heated in a little butter. Add pimiento and egg yolk beaten with milk. Heat thoroughly and serve in pie shells.

Dr. C. M. Murry
OXFORD, MS

Chicken Livers Deluxe

1 onion (chopped)
1/4 cup butter
1-2 pounds chicken livers
1 can sliced mushrooms
Pinch of thyme, salt, and
 pepper
1/3 cup sherry

Sauté onion in butter until soft and clear but not brown. Remove from skillet. Wash chicken livers in cold water and dry. Dust with flour and brown in butter. Brown well, adding more butter if necessary. When brown, return onions to skillet, add mushrooms, thyme, salt, pepper, and sherry. Cover and simmer approximately 15 minutes or until done. Add more sherry if necessary to prevent sticking. Serve over rice or toast points.

Mrs. Cub Amos
DALLAS, TX

Brochette of Chicken Livers

1 pound chicken livers
Bacon
2 eggs
Bread crumbs
1 bell pepper
Shortening

Place the chicken livers on a skewer with alternate pieces of bacon and squares of bell pepper. Salt and pepper well. Dip skewer with contents in well beaten eggs and roll in bread crumbs. Cook for two minutes in very hot shortening. Remove from pan and broil on grill for five minutes, then serve on toast.

Tom Barron
INDIANOLA, MS

Chicken Mary Wilkinson

3 chicken breasts - halved, skinned and boned
1 jar of chipped beef
3 bacon slices, halved
1 can cream of mushroom soup
1 1/2 cartons of sour cream

Rinse very lightly the chipped beef and lay lengthwise in a long pan. Put on top, separately, the chicken breast and, on top of each of these, a piece of bacon. Place the pan in a preheated 350° oven and cook for 35 minutes. Mix mushroom soup and sour cream and spread it over the chicken breasts. Cook for 30 minutes. Put on dinner plates, one for each of six, we hope, hungry guests and garnish with the useless but seemingly indispensable decorative parsley.

Ben Wasson
GREENVILLE, MS

Chicken and Mushrooms in Wine

1 8 ounce bottle Wishbone
  Italian dressing
1/2 bottle dry white wine
  or vermouth
1 pint sour cream
3-4 chickens cut up for 8-
  10 people
1/2 pound mushrooms,
  whole, with stems
  removed
1 small package slivered
  almonds

The day before you plan to serve this, mix to-gether in a shallow baking dish the Wishbone, wine, and sour cream. Taste. Add salt, pepper, more wine, if needed. Put chicken pieces and raw mushrooms in marinade; refrigerate till the next day. About 2 hours before serving set oven at 350°. Remove pan of chicken from refrigera-tor and sprinkle almonds evenly over it. When oven is ready, place pan, uncovered, on a middle rack. Bake 1 to 1 1/2 hours. Taste again and correct the seasoning. Serve with rice and a fresh green vegetable. Serves 8-10 people.

Mary Rinehart Cathcart
ORANO, ME

Oriental Chicken

1/2 cup butter
1/2 cup flour
1 tablespoon salt
1 cup cream
3 cups milk
2 cups chicken stock
2 cups diced chicken, large
  dice
1/2 cup sautéed mush-
  rooms
1/2 cup blanched almonds
1 cup sliced water chest-
  nuts
1/4 cup pimiento, cut into
  strips
1/4 cup sherry

Melt butter in top of double boiler; add flour and salt and cook until bubbly; add cream, milk, and chicken stock, stirring until smooth. Cook over hot water for 30 minutes. Just before serv-ing add remaining ingredients, heating thor-oughly. Serve over cheese soufflé, or in pastry shells, or over rice. You may reserve the mush-rooms, sauté whole and top each service with one. Fresh asparagus served across a grilled to-mato, completes a beautiful plate.

Bess Campbell
INDIANOLA, MS

Pepper Chicken

3 1/2 pounds chicken
1 egg white
2 tablespoons soy sauce
2 tablespoons sherry
3 tablespoons cornstarch
1 cup oil
2 green peppers, chopped
3 chili peppers, chopped
1 (5 ounce) can bamboo
  shoots
1 teaspoon sugar
1 teaspoon salt

Bone and cut raw chicken in 1/2 inch pieces. Use scissors. Beat egg white until foamy and add to chicken. Combine until smooth soy sauce, sherry, and cornstarch. Heat oil and cook chicken about 5 minutes. Drain chicken; leave about 2 tablespoons of oil in pan. Sauté peppers; add shoots, chicken, soy sauce mixture, salt, and sugar. Cook until thick. Serve over rice. Yield: 4 servings.

Susie Calvert
WEST POINT, MS

Chicken Pie

1 3 pound fryer
3 cups cold water
1 tablespoon salt
3 cups milk, heated
Black pepper
Butter

Pastry:
3 cups flour
1 cup shortening
1/3 to 1/2 cup ice water

Cook chicken in tightly covered sauce pan for 1 hour. Cool in stock. Remove and tear into small pieces. Heat stock to boiling. Add 1/2 of pastry which has been cut and torn into 2 inch squares. Add a little black pepper. Cover and boil rapidly a minute or two; turn down fire and boil gently for 5 minutes without peeping. Turn into buttered 9 x 13 inch baking pan. Arrange chicken over sauce. Cover with remaining pastry which has been cut into strips. Dot with butter and black pepper. Pour milk over chicken. Shake pan. Bake at 400° for 15 minutes; turn to 350° and bake another 15 minutes, or until pie is nicely browned. Serves 10-12.

Mrs. Carl Bethea
INDIANOLA, MS

Rolled Chicken Breasts

6 small chicken breasts,
  boned and skinned
6 thin slices ham
6 ounces Swiss cheese cut
  in 6 sticks
6 water chestnuts
1/4 cup all-purpose flour
2 tablespoons butter
1/2 cup water
1 teaspoon chicken flavor
  gravy base (chicken
  bouillon cube)
1 3 ounce can broiled
  sliced mushrooms
1/3 cup sauterne
2 tablespoons all-purpose
  flour
1/2 cup cold water
Toasted sliced almonds

Place chicken pieces, boned side up, on cutting board. Working from center out, pound chicken lightly with wooden mallet to make cutlets about 1/4 inch thick. Sprinkle with salt. Place a ham slice, a cheese stick and sliced water chestnut on each cutlet. Tuck in sides of each, and roll up as for jelly roll, pressing to seal well. Skewer or tie securely. Coat rolls with the 1/4 cup flour; brown in the butter. Remove chicken to baking pan. In the same skillet, combine 1/2 cup water, the gravy base, mushrooms, and wine. Heat, stirring to incorporate any crusty bits from skillet. Pour mixture over chicken in baking pan. Cover and bake in 350° oven 1 to 1 1/4 hours, or until tender. Transfer chicken to warm serving platter. Blend the 2 tablespoons flour with 1/2 cup water. Add to gravy in baking pan. Cook and stir until thickened. Pour over chicken. Garnish with almonds. Serves 6.

Mrs. W. R. Rodgers
ROLLING FORK, MS

Chicken Salad Soufflé

3 pound fryer, cooked and
  cubed
1/4 cup bell pepper
1/4 cup celery
1/2 cup mayonnaise
1/4 teaspoon salt
1/2 cup sharp cheese,
  grated
4 slices bread
2 eggs, beaten
1/2 cup sweet milk
1 can mushroom soup
1 can mushrooms, drained

Spread cubed chicken in 8 x 8 x 2 inch casserole. Spread the mixture of pepper, celery, mayonnaise, and salt on the chicken. Cover with bread. Mix eggs and milk and pour over bread. Let stand in refrigerator over night. Cover with mushroom soup and mushrooms. Bake for 1 hour and 45 minutes at 275°. Remove from oven and sprinkle with cheese. Let stand 20 minutes. Cut into squares and serve.

Mrs. Ben Hilbun
STATE COLLEGE, MS

Chicken Spagetti

4 whole chicken breasts, chopped
4 ribs celery, chopped
1 bell pepper, chopped
2 cans cream of mushrooms soup
1/2 cup chicken broth (can use more)
2 cans sliced mushrooms & juice
1 (9 ounce) package vermicelli - cooked
6 strips of bacon
1 pound sharp cheddar cheese, grated
1 small onion, chopped
Bread crumbs
Butter

Boil chicken in salted water until tender. Fry bacon until crisp and drain. Sauté celery, onion, bell pepper & mushrooms in bacon fat. Add to soup and mushroom juice. Stir in grated cheese. Add spaghetti and chicken that has been cut into pieces. Mix and put into a 3 quart casserole or 2 (1 1/2) quart casseroles. Sprinkle with bread crumbs and crumbled bacon. Dot with butter. Bake at 350° until hot. Serves 12.

Laura Gresham
INDIANOLA, MS

Cold New Orleans Chicken Spaghetti

French Dressing:
1/2 cup vinegar
1/2 cup olive oil
1 teaspoon salt
1 teaspoon sugar
1 teaspoon paprika
1/4 teaspoon garlic powder
2 or 3 drops Tabasco

Can use a Good Seasons bottle for measuring. Add champagne or red vinegar to the water line. Add olive oil to oil line. Add spices and shake well. (Makes an excellent green salad dressing and the spaghetti marinade will not require it all.)

Spaghetti:
1 seven ounce package thin spaghetti or vermicelli
Lawry's seasoned salt
1 small hen or fryer
4 stalks celery, divided
Green pepper
Onion
Salt and pepper
Mayonnaise
1 to 2 tablespoons lemon juice

Cook spaghetti as directed on package. Coat spaghetti in French dressing, season with Lawry's seasoned salt and Tabasco to taste. Mix well and marinate overnight. Cook hen until tender with one stalk celery, green pepper, onion, salt, and pepper. Remove from bone when cool. Cut as for chicken salad. Add 3 stalks chopped celery. Add mayonnaise sparingly and mix. Add lemon juice. Season to taste. Mix with the spaghetti in thin layers. (Garnish with marinated avocado, artichoke hearts, fresh tomatoes, beets or mushrooms.) Serves 6-8.

Augusta C. Barnwell
GREENWOOD, MS

Chicken Tetrazzini

1 bay leaf
1/2 cup onion, chopped
3 pound broiler
1 pint heavy cream
1/4 pound mushrooms or 1
  large can
1/4 pound butter
Salt and pepper to taste
1 tablespoon dry sherry
  (optional)
2 tablespoons dry white
  wine (optional)
2 tablespoons flour
2 tablespoons butter
1/4 pound medium noodles
  or vermicelli
3 tablespoons grated
Parmesan cheese

Simmer chicken until done in just enough water to cover with onion and bay leaves. Remove meat and dice in pieces, medium small. Melt the 1/4 pound butter in skillet and sauté mushrooms 2–3 minutes. Add chicken, cream, wine; season to taste and heat almost to boiling. Knead flour and 2 tablespoons butter together to smooth paste and stir into chicken mixture, continuing to stir until smooth and thickened. Let simmer 5 minutes. Cook spaghetti 7-10 minutes. Drain and spread on bottom of shallow greased casserole. Pour chicken mixture over it and sprinkle with cheese. Bake 375° about 20 minutes. Serves 4.

Mrs. Jean Parkinson
LAUREL, MS

Chicken Stew

6 chicken breasts, cooked
  until tender
1 cup tomatoes
1 can tomato paste
1 cup cream style corn
1 small potato
1/2 package spaghetti,
  cooked
1/2 onion
1 tablespoon butter
Butter
Salt and pepper

Cook chicken until tender and de-bone, saving broth. Add tomatoes, paste, corn, potato, onion, and spaghetti. Season to taste with butter, salt, and pepper. Cook slowly until all vegetables are done. Serves 8.

Good to freeze.

Mrs. Mike Manning
DREW, MS

Mrs. Ada Davidson Neill's Chicken Triangles

1 hen
1 pint cream, scalded
2 tablespoons butter
4 tablespoons flour
2 eggs, well beaten
1/2 teaspoon salt
1/2 teaspoon celery salt
1/2 teaspoon chopped
  parsley
Juice of 1/2 lemon
1 tablespoon white pepper
1/2 teaspoon red pepper

Boil hen, let cool, and cut fine with scissors. Make a roux by mixing melted butter with flour and stirring until smooth. Add cream and seasonings. Before taking from the fire add well beaten eggs. While hot mix with chicken. Spread mixture on shallow dish to cool.

Make 1 recipe of short biscuit dough. Roll flat and thin and cut in squares about 3 1/2 inches wide. Spoon mixture into the square so that you can fold over point to point and mash edges with fork as with pastry. Fry in deep fat until brown or bake if you prefer.

Mrs. A. B. Clark
INDIANOLA, MS

Smoked Turkey

1 turkey 10 to 12 pounds
6 cloves garlic, crushed
1 tablespoon red pepper
1 cup salt
Cooking oil

Use covered pit or oven with fire at one end and smoke vent at other end. Place turkey in large brown sack and tie end tightly (be sure there are no holes). Wet sack thoroughly with cooking oil. Start a good fire, to last 6 - 8 hours. Place on the end away from fire about 10:30 - 11 p.m. and let cook all night. Replenish fire about 6 a. m. and remove turkey from sack. There will be lots of juice; may be used for gravy but salty. Allow 4 hours more for turkey to brown, turning to brown evenly. I use meat thermometer.

Robroy Fisher
GLEN ALLAN, MS

Baked Turkey Soufflé

12 or more slices white bread (crust removed)
4 cups diced cooked turkey (chicken may be substituted)
1/2 pound fresh mushrooms, sliced and sautéed
1/4 cup butter
1 can (8 ounce) water chestnuts (drained and sliced)
1/2 cup mayonnaise
9 slices processed sharp cheese
4 eggs (well beaten)
2 cups milk
1 teaspoon salt
1 can cream of mushroom soup
1 can cream of celery soup
1 jar pimiento (2 ounces)
2 cups buttered bread crumbs

Line a large buttered aluminum baking pan with bread (sides also). Top with turkey, and mushrooms (which were cooked in butter for 5 minutes). Add water chestnuts; dot with mayonnaise; top with cheese slices. Combine eggs, milk, salt, pepper, and pour over all. Mix soups and pimiento and spoon over all. Cover closely with foil and store in refrigerator over night. Bake at 325° for 1 1/2 hours. Uncover and sprinkle bread crumbs on top last 15 minutes. Serves 12.

Sue T. Davidson
INDIANOLA, MS

Dove Breasts

2 dozen dove breasts
1 stick butter
Seasoned flour
1 1/2 cup chopped celery
1/4 cup chopped onion
1/4 cup chopped bell
  pepper
1 (14 1/2 ounce) can
  chicken broth
1/2 carton frozen chives
Mushrooms
4 ounces cooking wine
Salt
Pepper
Curry

Flour dove breasts with seasoned flour; melt stick of butter in electric skillet and brown breasts; remove breast. Put celery, onion and bell pepper into skillet and cook until the onion is transparent. Put doves back in, turn skillet to simmer, add one can chicken broth, put top on skillet and simmer for 3 hours adding more broth if necessary, 1/2 hour before they are done add 1/2 carton frozen chives, mushrooms to taste, 4 ounces cooking wine, salt and pepper to taste and a pinch of curry. Serves 6 - 8.

Alex Gates
SUMNER, MS

Charcoal Dove Breasts

Hunting the native dove of this area, the mourning dove, is great sport in the early fall.

Take the breast of the dove only (as many as are available). Put a dash of Tabasco sauce on the back of each. Sprinkle with Lawry seasoned salt. Wrap each one in a thick piece of bacon. Put several on a skewer. Cook over charcoal - turning occasionally until bacon is crisp.

Variation: Doves may be parboiled in equal parts of sherry, Worcestershire, melted butter and lemon juice before barbecuing as above.

Jimmy Failing
INDIANOLA, MS

Dove Pie

8 doves, whole
1 carrot, diced
1 stick of celery
2 tablespoons of green
  pepper, chopped
2 thin slices of orange peel
1/2 cup cooked mush-
  rooms

Have in a stewpan just enough boiling salted water to cover the birds. Drop the birds, whole into the water; cover, reduce heat, and allow them to simmer until tender. Line a casserole with pie dough, or a good short biscuit dough. Lift the birds from the broth and de-bone. Add remaining ingredients to broth. Allow these to simmer slowly until tender, and thicken with a tablespoon of flour creamed in butter. Place the birds in the casserole, pour over them the thickened broth, and cover with more of the pie or biscuit dough. Place in moderate oven and bake until the crust is a nice brown.

Serve with this green beans cooked with slices of bacon or a piece of ham hock, and a green salad with French dressing.

Mrs. Tom Barron
INDIANOLA, MS

Baked Duck

4 wild ducks
1/2 pound butter (or oleo)
1 cup Wesson Oil
1 large onion, chopped
3 stalks celery, chopped
Salt, pepper
1 teaspoon Lea & Perrins
1 teaspoon liquid garlic
Gravy: sauterne, hot
  sauce, chicken stock,
  wine vinegar

Brown all vegetables in mixture of butter and oil, lift out and put aside for gravy. Add other ingredients. Place duck breasts down in covered dutch oven and cook over low heat five or six hours or until tender. Place ducks on baking pan, pour 1/2 cup wine over them and brown very quickly in hot (450°) oven. Garnish with red crab apples. Remove excess fat before making gravy. Add chicken stock, then the browned vegetables. Sharpen gravy with hot sauce, wine vinegar. Add several tablespoons Sauterne.

Mrs. W. H. Baird
INDIANOLA, MS

Roast Wild Duck

1 duck
Salt
Pepper
1 potato
1 onion
2 teaspoons butter
Garlic clove (optional)
Bacon strips
1/2 cup sherry

Allow 1/2 duck per person. When duck is picked and cleaned, soak in strong salt water for 3 hours. Dry thoroughly inside and out. Rub with salt and pepper. Place a peeled potato and onion inside the duck. Be sure to remove them before serving as they absorb the strong flavor. Have electric roaster preheated; add butter. When butter is hot, place duck in roaster and cook 25 minutes at 500°. Reduce temperature to 250° and cook 2 1/2 hours.

When almost done, add sherry. Lift out duck and strain gravy which may be thickened with a light cream sauce.

Since the secret of cooking wild duck is to get it tender and juicy, an electric roaster is ideal (it steams and basting is unnecessary). Turn duck occasionally. Add a little hot water as the pan gets dry. This recipe may be used with a covered roaster in the oven.

Mrs. Seymour B. Johnson
INDIANOLA, MS

Orange Duckling

2–5 pounds dressed ducks
Lemon juice
Mei Yen seasoning powder
2 bay leaves
1/2 cup honey
1 cup chicken stock
1/2 cup port wine
1 cup red wine vinegar
2 crushed garlic cloves
1/2 teaspoon tarragon
1/8 teaspoon rosemary
1 cup bitter marmalade

Wipe ducklings with damp cloth. Sprinkle all over with lemon juice and Mei Yen powder. Tuck bay leaves inside. Roast at 350° until golden. Pour off fat. Cool and quarter. Return to roaster cut side down.

Over medium heat combine all other ingredients until well blended. Pour over ducklings. Cover roaster and bake 300° for 1 hour. Uncover and bake until golden brown.

Serve garnished with orange halves or kumquats. Serves 8.

Emily Johnson
INDIANOLA, MS

Steamed Frog Legs

Flour
24 frog legs
1 cup finely chopped fresh
  mushrooms
1/4 cup finely chopped
  shallots
1/4 cup finely chopped
  parsley
Salt and pepper to taste
Dry white wine

Flour frog legs and sauté in butter delicately brown on both sides. Season. Sprinkle with parsley and brown thoroughly. In separate skillet, sauté the mushrooms and shallots and sprinkle with wine. When vegetables are tender add legs, cover, and let them steam for a few minutes; serve immediately.

Pete Fisher
INDIANOLA, MS

Smothered Baked Quail (a la Riners)

12 plump quail
6 tablespoons butter
3 tablespoons cooking oil
Salt and pepper to taste
Dash of garlic salt for each
  bird
2 (4 ounce) cans sliced
  mushrooms reserving
  liquid
Mushroom liquid plus 1/2
  cup water
1 (8 ounce) can brown
  gravy (I use 2 packages
  McCormick Brown
  Gravy mix)
1 package cooked wild rice

Wipe quail and rub each bird with butter. Put cooking oil in a large oblong pan; place quail in pan and bake at 350°, uncovered, for about 25 minutes. When quail begin to get tender, remove and add the rest of the butter which has been melted, the salt, pepper and garlic salt. Put pan under broiler, watching carefully until quail are browned. Remove from broiler and add sliced mushrooms, gravy, and liquid. Now that the birds are well smothered, return to 350° oven and cook until tender, basting often. Add more salt and garlic salt if desired. Serve with cooked wild rice. Yield: 12 servings.

Olin K. Boyer (Mrs. C. E. Boyer)
INDIANOLA, MS

Hill Quail

Place each cleaned quail on foil square. Stuff with ground chuck that has been seasoned with freshly ground black pepper and garlic salt. Sprinkle with Lea & Perrin sauce, lemon juice and Tabasco sauce. Wrap quail with strip of bacon secured with toothpicks. Carefully seal foil around quail and bake on cookie sheet in preheated 400° oven 35 to 45 minutes.

Joel Hill, Jr.
GREENVILLE, MS

Crockpot Venison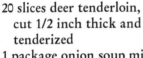

20 slices deer tenderloin, cut 1/2 inch thick and tenderized
1 package onion soup mix
1 can (10 3/4 ounce) cream of mushroom soup
3 tablespoons A-1 Steak Sauce
1 tablespoon Worcestershire sauce
1 small can mushrooms, drained
Salt and pepper, to taste
Sliced onion or minced onion, optional

Place deer in crockpot. Add remaining ingredients and cook on low temperature for 6 hours, stirring occasionally. Serve with white rice.

Seldon Van Cleve
INDIANOLA, MS

Venison Steak

"A slice of venison, a slice of turkey, and a slice of bear meat placed on a stick so that the bear fat seasoned the other meat as it barbecued was considered an Indian luxury."

3/8" slices venison steak,
   all fat removed
Butter
Cracker crumbs
2 beaten eggs
Fresh ground pepper
Salt

Venison must be aged, uncovered on a wire rack under refrigeration for no less than 7 days and preferably 3 or 4 weeks if possible. Broiling or roasting are the better methods for cooking venison and the choice portions are the hind quarters and saddle.

Wash and dry meat thoroughly. These steps are absolutely necessary.

Dip sliced meat into beaten egg, with salt and pepper added. Roll in cracker crumbs and cook in slow (300°) skillet in butter.

Don't turn meat over until red juices appear on top side. Then turn carefully and cook just one or two minutes on other side. Do not overcook, just "struck through" as it were. Season with freshly ground black pepper and serve piping hot with currant jelly or mint sauce. Serve immediately.

W. H. Baird
INDIANOLA, MS

Marinade of Venison or Beef

"Venison and turkey meat stewed with bear oil, served with corn cakes and a beverage of acidulated honey and water was a favored Indian meal."

Tenderloin of venison or
  beef
1/2 cup beef consommé
1/2 cup red wine
1/3 cup soy sauce
1 1/2 teaspoon Lawry's
  seasoned salt
1/4 cup chopped onion
1 tablespoon lime juice
2 tablespoons honey or
  brown sugar

Mix all ingredients and marinate meat overnight. Do not cook meat in marinade. Marinade may be heated separately and used as a sauce over meat. Add a little flour to thicken marinade, if you like, to be used as thick gravy.

Mary Ann Allen
INDIANOLA, MS

Vegetables

Boiled Artichokes - Hollandaise

6 or more artichokes
2 stalks celery
1 onion (sliced)
1 1/2 tablespoons lemon
    juice
2 quarts water
1 tablespoon salt

Remove artichoke stems and tough outer leaves. Soak 30 minutes in cold water. Add artichokes to boiling water with seasonings and be sure water covers vegetables. Put lid on and boil for 30 to 35 minutes (until tender). Drain and serve with Hollandaise sauce.

Mrs. Billups Allen
STARKVILLE, MS

Asparagus Casserole

1 can (10 1/2 ounce) green
    asparagus and juice
Cracker crumbs
4 hard boiled eggs
1 can of cream of mush-
    room soup
3 tablespoons sauterne or
    wine
Garlic powder - dash
2 tablespoons butter
3 or 4 dashes Tabasco
1 teaspoon Worcestershire
    sauce
Salt, pepper and about 1
    teaspoon sugar
Grated cheese (sharp)
Toasted slivered almonds

Into buttered casserole alternate layers of asparagus, eggs, cracker crumbs and mushroom soup which has been mixed with asparagus juice, wine, butter and seasonings. Top with grated cheese and slivered almonds. Bake at 350° for about 25 or 30 minutes. Serves 6 to 8.

Mrs. Frank Pigford, Jr.
CHAMPAIGN, IL

French Cut Beans with Water Chestnuts

5 packages frozen French cut beans
1 or 2 medium onions chopped
1 (8 ounce) can mushrooms
1 stick butter
1/4 cup flour
2 cups warm milk. (May substitute Cream of Mushroom soup for flour and milk)
1 cup light cream
3/4 pound sharp Cheddar cheese
1/8 teaspoon Tabasco
2 teaspoons soy sauce
1 teaspoon salt
1 tablespoon Accent (optional)
1 (5 ounce) can water chestnuts, sliced and drained
3/4 cup almonds, sliced
1 clove garlic
1 teaspoon paprika
1/2 teaspoon chili powder

Sauté mushrooms and onions in butter. Add all ingredients except beans and nuts. Add pre-cooked beans. Layer this mixture with a layer of chestnuts and more beans topped with almonds. Fills 2 casseroles. Bake at 375° for 20 minutes. Serves 12-15.

Mrs. James Robertson
INDIANOLA, MS

Pearl's Harvard Beets

3 cups beets, sliced or diced
1/2 cup sugar
1 tablespoon cornstarch
1/2 teaspoon salt
1/2 cup mild cider vinegar
2 tablespoons butter

Cook sugar, cornstarch, salt and vinegar and stir until clear in double boiler. Add beets and butter. Serve warm. Serves 6.

Mrs. Dewitt S. Lovelace, Jr.
INDIANOLA, MS

Green Beans in Sour Cream

2 cans green beans
1 onion
1 tablespoon vinegar
1 tablespoon salad oil
Salt and pepper

Drain the beans and toss together with sliced onion rings. Marinate with vinegar and salad oil. Sprinkle with salt and ground pepper. Marinate at least one hour; over night is better.

Dressing:
1 cup sour cream
1/2 cup mayonnaise
  (homemade)
1 teaspoon lemon juice
1/4 teaspoon dry mustard
1 teaspoon prepared
  horseradish
1 teaspoon onion juice
2 teaspoons chives, frozen
  and chopped

Mix all ingredients, add to green beans and serve cold.

Bess S. Campbell
INDIANOLA, MS

Green Beans with Topping

2 cans green beans,
  drained
2 tablespoons bacon
  drippings
2 medium onions, chopped
1 large clove garlic
1 cup water

Topping:
1/2 stick butter
1/2 cup bread crumbs
1/2 cup pecans
Pinch of salt

Sauté onions and garlic in bacon drippings. Add drained beans and 1 cup water. Simmer one hour. Combine ingredients and cook over low heat until golden brown, stirring constantly.

Serve the topping over beans. Serves 8.

This topping is good over other vegetables and the topping does not need to be hot when served.

Mrs. Opie Little, Jr.
INDIANOLA, MS

String Bean Casserole

2 onions, chopped
1 tablespoon caraway seed
1 tablespoon Accent
Salt and pepper to taste
3 No. 2 cans string beans
1 can mushroom soup
1 cup sharp cheese, grated
4 slices cooked bacon
Ritz crackers
1/4 pound butter
Tabasco
Paprika

Brown onion in small amount of butter. Add seed, Accent, salt and pepper. Add beans and liquor from 3 cans. Cook 1 hour. Drain and save 4 tablespoons of liquor. Add soup, cheese, crumbled bacon, cracker crumbs, butter and paprika on top. Cook 30 minutes at 375°. Serves 8.

Mrs. W. B. Fletcher, Jr.
INDIANOLA, MS

Confetti Lima Beans

3 packages (10 ounces each) frozen baby lima beans
3 tablespoons butter
1 cup onions, chopped
1 can whole button mushrooms, drained with liquid reserved
1/4 can pimiento, chopped
1 tablespoon all purpose flour
2 cups sour cream
1/2 teaspoon salt

Cook lima beans according to directions on package. Drain. Melt butter in a large skillet. Add onions and sauté until transparent. Add mushrooms and cook five minutes. Add pimento and flour. Stir until flour is smooth. Add sour cream, liquid drained from mushrooms, salt and cooked lima beans. Heat gently.

Mrs. Andrea Polasini
LELAND, MS

Broccoli in Wine

1 bunch broccoli
1/2 cup olive oil
1/2 cup white wine
1 large garlic clove, crushed
Pinch cayenne pepper

Wash and trim broccoli and cut stalk lengthwise if thick. In a large skillet, combine 1/2 cup of oil and wine, garlic clove, and the pepper. Add broccoli and bring the liquid to a boil over high heat. Cover the pan, reduce the heat, and steam slowly for 5-10 minutes or just until tender.

Mrs. James Thompson
JACKSON, MS

Broccoli Casserole

2 packages (10 ounces each)
  frozen broccoli
1/4 cup minced onion
6 tablespoons butter
5 tablespoon flour
1 teaspoon dry mustard
3/4 teaspoon salt
1/8 teaspoon marjoram
1/8 teaspoon accent
3 dashes hot pepper sauce
2 1/2 cups milk
2 chicken bouillon cubes
5 egg yolks, beaten
1 1/2 cups grated sharp
  cheese
1 (4 ounce) can sliced
  mushrooms
3 tablespoons slivered
  almonds
Dash of paprika

Arrange cooked broccoli on serving platter. Sauté onions in butter. Blend in flour and seasonings. Add milk and bouillon cubes. Cook over medium heat, stirring constantly until mixture thickens and comes to a boil. Add a little of the hot sauce to eggs. Stir into remaining hot sauce. Add cheese. Stir until blended. Add mushrooms. Pour three cups of the sauce over broccoli. Store remainder for future use. Sprinkle with almonds and paprika. Bake 350° 20 minutes or until brown. Yield: 6 portions.

Mrs. C. W. Denton
INDIANOLA, MS

Broccoli Casserole Elegante

1 large onion, chopped fine
1/2 stick butter or oleo
3 packages chopped
  broccoli
2 cans mushroom soup
1 1/4 packages garlic cheese
1 teaspoon monosodium
  glutamate
1 small can mushrooms
1/2 cup chopped almonds,
  divided
1/2 cup bread crumbs

Sauté onion in butter. Add broccoli and cook until tender. Add mushroom soup, cheese, monosodium glutamate, mushrooms, and 1/4 cup almonds. Sprinkle rest of almonds and bread crumbs on top. Bake at 300° until bubbly. Will serve 10 generously.

Mrs. Anne Aden
MADISON, MS

Stuffed Cabbage

1 large cabbage
3/4 pound pure ground
  beef
1/2 cup rice, uncooked
1/2 teaspoon salt
1/4 teaspoon black pepper
1 large onion, chopped fine
1/8 teaspoon cinnamon
1/4 teaspoon basil
1 (14 ounce) canned
  tomatoes with juice
1 clove garlic
1 lemon, sliced

Separate cabbage leaves and blanch in boiling water until limp. Remove and drain. Cut into large leaves, removing tough vein. Mix other ingredients and for each roll use an amount about the size of your finger; squeeze together an place on leaf; fold in tips of leaf and roll. Put in heavy pot and arrange rolls in layers. Add 1 can tomatoes, water to cover, 1 chopped clove garlic and slice one lemon, arranging slices on top of rolls. Add salt and pepper to taste. Put a plate on top of rolls to anchor them. Cook slowly for about 1 hour.

Sonya R. Fox
SUNFLOWER, MS

Carrot Ring

2 bunches carrots
2 tablespoons sugar
4 crackers
3 tablespoons butter
3 tablespoons onion,
  chopped
1 green pepper, chopped
1/2 cup celery, minced
1 egg
1 can petit peas
2 tablespoons butter

Cook carrots until tender. Season with salt and pepper. Mash; add sugar and crumbled crackers. In butter, cook onions, celery, pepper slowly. When tender add to carrot mixture. Add beaten egg.

Have ring mold greased and heated. Put carrot mixture in mold; place in a pan of hot water. Cook 30 minutes in oven 350°.

Invert on plate; fill center with buttered petit peas. Marvelous and colorful!

Mrs. Glenn Rutledge
STATE COLLEGE, MS

Corn Pudding

2 cup creamed corn
1 1/4 tablespoon sugar
1 tablespoon flour
2 eggs
1/4 teaspoon salt
1/2 cup milk
1/3 cup butter

Mix all ingredients together in baking dish and bake at 300° for approximately 45 minutes. Serves 6.

Mrs. W. W. Gresham
INDIANOLA, MS

Mexican Corn

3 tablespoons shortening
1/2 cup chopped onion
1/2 cup chopped celery
2 cups drained tomatoes
3 cups corn, fresh or whole
  canned kernel
2 teaspoons salt
2 small chili peppers
1/4 teaspoon chili powder

Sauté celery and onion in oil. Add remaining ingredients and simmer 30 minutes. Excellent for barbecues! Serves 6 to 8.

Eleanor N. Failing
INDIANOLA, MS

Stewed Corn

1 dozen ears corn
1 cup cream
2 tablespoons butter
Salt and Pepper
Cayenne

Take one dozen ears of green, tender, sweet corn. Cut off the kernels (using a sharp knife); then scrape the cob. Put the corn into a saucepan with just enough water to keep it from burning. Boil about 20 minutes. Add 1 cup of heavy cream, 2 tablespoons butter and season to taste with salt and pepper and cayenne. Boil ten minutes longer and serve piping hot.

Mrs. C. J. VanArsdall
INDIANOLA, MS

Corn Tamale Casserole

2 cans cream corn
1 cup milk
2 tablespoons flour
2 tablespoons sugar
1/2 stick butter or oleo
1 medium onion, grated
1/2 teaspoon salt
Red pepper to taste
1 can tamales
1 small pimiento chopped
1 cup American cheese,
  grated

Combine first 8 ingredients; cook on top of stove until semi-thick. Remove from heat and add pimientos. Place half the corn mixture in baking dish, then add a layer of tamales, 1 can and its liquid. Pour remaining corn over tamales. Cook in 350° oven until bubbly. Add grated cheese. Leave in oven only long enough to toast cheese lightly.

Mrs. C. C. Swayze
YAZOO CITY, MS

Eggplant Antipasto

Good hot as vegetable or dip; also, good cold.

1/3 cup olive oil
3 cups peeled and cubed
  eggplant
1/3 cup chopped green
  pepper
1 cup chopped onion
1 (4 ounce) can sliced
  mushrooms
2 cloves or more crushed
  garlic
1 small can tomato paste
2 tablespoons wine vinegar
3/4 cup chopped green
  olives, big pieces
1 1/2 teaspoons sugar
1 teaspoon oregano
1 teaspoon salt
1/4 to 1/2 teaspoon pepper

Heat oil, add eggplant and other ingredients in Dutch oven, cover, cook 10 minutes stirring occasionally. Then add, tomato paste, vinegar, green olives, sugar, oregano, salt, and pepper. Stir, simmer until eggplant is done, approximately 30 to 40 minutes.

Susan Noble
NEW ORLEANS, LA

Baked Eggplant Radosta

2 large eggplants
2 eggs, beaten
1 1/2 pounds peeled
  shrimp, sautéed,
  chopped
Salt and pepper
1/2 cup minced parsley
1 cup bread, moistened
1/2 cup minced onion
1/2 cup Italian cheese
1 cup minced green pepper

Cut eggplants in half and boil until soft. Scrape insides into bowl and mix with minced onion, green pepper, parsley, bread, cheese, salt, and pepper. Sauté cooked shrimp, and eggs. Fill shells. Sprinkle bread crumbs over top and bake at 350 until done. Serves 8.

Mrs. Ike Nunnery, Jr.
ARCOLA, MS

Eggplant au Gratin

4 small eggplants
2 large onions, sliced
12 crackers, crumbed
2 tablespoons butter
1 pound sharp cheese,
  grated
2 eggs, beaten
Salt and pepper, to taste

Peel and boil eggplants in salted water until soft. Strain off water and mash. Fry onions in butter. Combine eggplant, onions, eggs and cheese. Salt and pepper to taste. Place in greased casserole, cover with cracker crumbs, dot with butter. Bake in moderate oven for 45 minutes. Serves 8 to 10.

Mrs. H. A. Pehl
INDIANOLA, MS

Escalloped Eggplant

2 medium eggplants
2 tablespoons butter
1 medium onion
1 medium green pepper,
  chopped
2 or 3 pieces celery,
  chopped
2 eggs, beaten
2 tablespoons flour
1 cup milk
1 pound sharp cheese,
  grated
Cracker crumbs

Peel eggplant; cut in cubes and soak 1 or 2 hours in salted water. Drain, cover with fresh water and cook until tender. Sauté onion, celery and pepper in butter. Add flour and milk and cook until thick. Add the eggs and eggplant, which has been drained and mashed. Place in buttered casserole; top with cheese and Ritz cracker crumbs that have melted butter added to them. Bake in 325° - 350° oven until bubbly.

Katie Gooch
INDIANOLA, MS

Kathleen Claiborne's Eggplant and Oysters

"The late Mrs. Claiborne, an artist in cookery, challenged a criticism of Southern cooking printed in a national magazine. The editor and staff accepted her invitation to "come to dinner" and traveled many miles to lose an argument. They, like James Street, were forced to agree that, in the main, down south, delectable cuisine is found only in the home."

1 medium egg plant
4 tablespoons chopped
  onion
1/4 cup butter
1/2 cup dry bread crumbs
Salt to taste
1 pint oysters
1/2 cup light cream

Peel, cube and cook eggplant, drain. Sauté onion and add crumbs and salt. Heat oysters until they curl. Mix all ingredients. Add cream. Put in casserole. Cover with crumbs. Bake at 350°, until heated through. Serves 6.

Augusta C. Barnwell
GREENWOOD, MS

Garden Casserole

"This is at its best in late summer when there's an excess of garden squash, eggplant and tomatoes."

1 medium - large eggplant, peeled
4 small crookneck summer squash or (2 medium zucchini squash)
1 onion
4 large tomatoes, peeled
Salt and pepper
Olive oil
Fresh chopped oregano, basil and parsley. (If fresh is unavailable, used dried sparingly).
6 - 8 ounces mozzarella cheese, shredded or sliced thinly
Crushed crackers
Parmesan or Romano cheese, grated

Preheat oven to 350°. Cut peeled eggplant in half lengthwise and then crosswise into thin "half-moon" slices. Place them in a colander and toss them with a few teaspoons of salt. Leave to drain 30 minutes. Meanwhile, slice squash, onions, and peeled tomatoes thinly. Lightly oil two 1 1/2 quart casseroles. Rinse eggplant and drain well.

Divide half of the tomato slices between the two casseroles; salt and pepper lightly. Divide half of the onions between the casseroles, layering on top of tomatoes. Divide half of the eggplant between casseroles. Drizzle lightly with olive oil and salt and pepper lightly. Divide half of squash between casseroles. Sprinkle with a generous tablespoon of chopped fresh herbs (or 1 teaspoon dried). Repeat preceding 4 steps using rest of vegetables.

Cover casseroles with mozzarella. Bake 45 minutes, well-covered with a tight fitting lid, or foil. Remove covers; sprinkle with crushed crackers and grated Parmesan or Romano. Bake 15 more minutes uncovered.

Kate Failing
INDIANOLA, MS

Grits Casserole

1 cup grits
1 teaspoon salt
4 cups water
1 stick butter
1 roll garlic cheese
3 eggs, slightly beaten
1/3 cup milk

Cook grits in salted water until done. Then add butter, cheese, eggs, milk; stir until melted and smooth. Place in 1 1/2 quart casserole and bake for 1 hour at 325° - 350°. Serves 6-8 people.

Can be made ahead and frozen until ready for use.

Mrs. R. L. Bambauer
CHARLOTTE, NC

Tom-ful-la Casserole (Hominy)

1 cup white sauce (medium)
1 medium size onion
1 cup grated cheese
3 small Jalapéno peppers, chopped & deseeded
1 large can hominy (drained)
1/4 stick butter or oleo

Sauté onion in butter. Mix all ingredients and pour white sauce over same. Bake in casserole at 350° until hot and bubbly. Serves 8.

Mrs. Anne Aden
MADISON, MS

Indian Okra

2 pounds young okra
1 onion
1 garlic bud
4 pieces bacon
1 can tomato paste
Salt
Cayenne Pepper
1 bay leaf
Parsley
Roux
2 tablespoons flour
2 tablespoons butter

Soften okra, onion, garlic in bacon drippings; add tomato pulp. Make very thick roux and add tomato juice and a little water if needed. Add seasonings. This should be very thick with no juice. Add parsley five minutes before serving.

Mrs. Burton Moore
INDIANOLA, MS

Baked Onion Casserole

8 large white onions,
  quartered
1 cup brown sugar
1 1/2 sticks oleo
1/2 cup dry sherry
  sliced almonds

Completely fill a 9" x 13" casserole with onions. Sprinkle sugar over onions. Mix melted oleo and sherry and pour over onions. Top with sliced almonds. Bake 45 minutes, 350°.

Mrs. Ernie Baker
INDIANOLA, MS

Onion Pie

1 cup fine cracker crumbs
1/2 stick (1/4 cup) melted
  butter
2 cups thinly sliced onions
2 tablespoons butter
2 eggs, lightly beaten
3/4 cup milk
3/4 teaspoon salt
Dash pepper
1/4 cup grated Cheddar
  cheese
Paprika
Parsley

Mix together thoroughly cracker crumbs and butter. Press the mixture into the bottom and around sides of an 8-inch pie plate. In skillet sauté onions in butter until they are transparent. Spoon them into the crumb-lined pie plate and pour over them a mixture of eggs, milk, salt and pepper. Sprinkle top with grated cheese and a little paprika. Bake in 350° oven for 30 minutes or until knife comes out dry. Garnish with parsley and serve hot. Serves 4. Delicious with roast beef or steaks.

Mrs. Duke Goza
RULEVILLE, MS

Sweet and Sour Onions

4 large onions
1/4 cup cider vinegar
1/4 cup butter
1/4 cup boiling water
1/4 cup sugar

Slice onions and arrange in a 1 quart baking dish. Mix the rest of the ingredients and pour over onions. Bake in 300° oven for one hour.

Mrs. C. W. Denton
MARKS, MS

French Fried Onion Rings

2 large onions (white)
1 cup flour
1 teaspoon baking powder
1 cup prepared cracker
  meal from grocery *
1/2 cup milk
Fat for deep frying

Cut onions into 1/3 inch slices, separate and drop into cold water. Sift flour and baking powder together. Dip each slice onion into flour, then into milk and last into meal. Let dry a little. May be done a day ahead and kept in cool place. Fry lightly in deep hot fat, turning once; drain on brown paper. Serves 6.

*Rolled crackers cause onion rings to wilt. Prepared cracker meal from grocery is the secret of crisp rings.

Mrs. Carl Bethea
INDIANOLA, MS

English Pea Casserole

1 cup diced celery
1 cup diced green pepper
2 cans of tiny English
  peas, save about 1/2 of
  juice
1 small jar chopped
  pimiento
6 hard boiled eggs
1 cup chili sauce
1 tablespoon
  Worcestershire sauce
1 can of mushroom soup
1 cup grated cheese
  (Wisconsin)

Sauté celery and pepper in butter. Put in bowl with peas, pimiento, 5 boiled eggs, chili sauce and Worcestershire. Put in layers. Top with some soup to which the pea juice has been added. Also save a few egg slices for top. Top all this with grated cheese. Bake 30 minutes at 350°. Serves 8 easily.

Mrs. Frank Pigford, Jr.
CHAMPAIGN, IL

Stuffed Bell Pepper, Creole

16 large peppers
2 cloves garlic, chopped
4 onions, chopped
1/2 cup butter
1 cup chopped ham
1 cup water
1 cup tomato juice
1 No. 2 can tomatoes
2 eggs, well beaten
4 cups cracker crumbs
Salt and pepper to taste
1 teaspoon sugar
Bread crumbs
Melted margarine
Dash of paprika

Chop 4 of the peppers leaving in seeds. Sauté in butter with garlic and onions until tender. Add ham, water, tomato juice and tomatoes. Cook until liquid is absorbed. Stir in eggs and cracker crumbs. Season to taste. Cut off tops and remove seeds from remaining 12 peppers. Parboil with sugar until slightly tender. Stuff with tomato mixture. Cover lightly with bread crumbs, margarine and paprika. Bake at 350° for about 20 minutes or until peppers are piping hot. Serves 12.

Mrs. Eustace Conway
BUENA VISTA PLANTATION, VICKSBURG, MS

Browned Paprika Potatoes

6 medium sized potatoes
3 tablespoons melted bacon
  drippings
1/2 cup corn flake crumbs
2 teaspoons paprika
1 teaspoon salt

Pare potatoes; brush with melted fat. Roll potatoes in mixture of corn flake crumbs, paprika and salt. Place in greased pan and bake at 425° for about 45 minutes.

Katie B Gooch
INDIANOLA, MS

Roasted Parmesan Potatoes

1/4 cup soft butter or oleo
1/2 cup mayonnaise or
  salad dressing
1/2 cup grated parmesan
  cheese
2 tablespoons finely
  chopped green onion
1/4 teaspoon
  Worcestershire Sauce

Prick potatoes with fork. Wrap each in foil. Place in hot coals for 1 hour turning every 10 minutes. Combine above ingredients - criss-cross slash in top of potato-squeeze open. Put heaping tablespoon of mixture into each potato and serve.

Mrs. S. Leonard Young
GREENWOOD, MS

Potato Casserole

6 large potatoes
2 cups sour cream
1 cup milk
2 cups sharp cheese, grated
1 stick butter
2/3 cup onions, tops and all

Boil potatoes in jackets. Chill until cold. Shred on grater. Melt butter in double boiler. Add cheese gradually, saving a small amount to set aside. Mix together sour cream and milk. Add to cheese mixture. Add onions. Stir all together. Add to shredded potatoes. Put in casserole and bake at 350° for 45 minutes. Sprinkle remaining cheese on top the last 5 minutes of baking. Serves 8 to 10.

Mrs. Jimmy Lee
GREENVILLE, MS

Stuffed Potatoes

3 pounds potatoes, cooked, drained and mashed
1/2 cup butter
1 (8 ounce) cream cheese
1 jar pimientos, chopped & drained
1 green bell pepper, chopped
1 bunch green onions, chopped
1 cup parmesan cheese, grated
1/4 cup milk
1 cup cheddar cheese
Salt and pepper to taste

Mix all ingredients. Use mixer until desired consistency as with mashed potatoes. Add a little more milk if necessary. Bake at 350° in 9 x 13" baking dish until heated through. Serves 8.

Linda Lee
HORSESHOE BAY, TX

Plantation Sweet Potato Pone

This grand old dish, similar to Sweet Potato Puddin', makes one smack the lips and say: "That's what I like about the South!".

4 large sweet potatoes
Grated peel of 1 lemon
Grated peel of 1/2 orange
2 eggs, beaten
1/2 cup brown sugar
1/2 teaspoon cinnamon
1/2 cup butter
1/2 teaspoon nutmeg
1/2 teaspoon ground cloves
1/2 cup molasses
2/3 cup milk
1/3 cup bourbon

Grate raw sweet potatoes, then the lemon and orange peel. Beat eggs and sugar and stir into potato mixture. Then add the spices, molasses, milk, bourbon and butter. Mix thoroughly, then bake slowly for 1 hour in buttered casserole. Serve hot. About 8 servings.

Mrs. George Fondren
INDIANOLA, MS

Ratatouille

2 cups pared and sliced
  eggplant
2 cups yellow or zucchini
  squash, sliced
3 tomatoes, peeled and
  sliced
3 medium onions sliced
2 bell peppers sliced into
  rings
1/3 cup oil (1/2 olive oil
  and 1/2 cooking oil)
2 cloves garlic
1/3 teaspoon cumin
1/2 teaspoon dill
1/3 teaspoon oregano
1 teaspoon salt

Arrange vegetables in a shallow baking dish or pan. Crush garlic with salt and add to oil. Add cumin, dill, and oregano to oil. Pour oil mixture over vegetables. Cover dish or pan with top or foil. Bake for 1 hour at 350° or until vegetables are done. Serves 8-10.

Mrs. George P. Hopkins, Jr.
GULFPORT, MS

Armenian Rice

1 cup rice
2 cups chicken broth
1 stick butter
4 buttons garlic, chopped
1 cup broken nested
  vermicelli
1 large bell pepper, cut in
  large pieces
1 can mushrooms
1 small can ripe olives
  halved
1 can water chestnuts

Wash rice until water is clear. Place washed rice in casserole and cover with chicken broth. Melt butter in skillet and cook garlic until golden brown. Remove garlic and add vermicelli to butter. Cook the macaroni until a dark brown. Add remaining ingredients to casserole and mix well. Place lid on casserole and cook in 350° oven for about 40 minutes. The rice will be done when all the broth has cooked away. Serves 8.

Burton Moore
INDIANOLA, MS

Brown Rice

1/2 stick butter
1 cup white rice
1 can (10 1/2 ounce) french
  onion soup
1 can (10 1/2 ounce) beef
  broth
1 small can mushrooms,
  drained

Melt butter in casserole placed in pre-heated 350° oven. Add other ingredients and mix well. Cover uncovered for 40 minutes or until firm.

Michelle Van Cleve
INDIANOLA, MS

Cumin Rice

1 stick butter
1 cup rice
1 cup total chopped green
  onion, bell pepper and
  fresh mushrooms
2 cans consommé
1 teaspoon cumin powder
Salt and pepper
1 tablespoon
  Worcestershire sauce

Melt butter. Brown rice, onion, bell pepper and mushrooms. Then add consommé, cumin, salt, pepper, and Worcestershire. Let come to a boil and then put lid on and turn very low. Cook 30 minutes.

Mrs. Bingby Jackson, Jr.
HOLLY GROVE, AR

Emerald Rice

4 cups cooked rice
1 package chopped spinach
1/2 cup chopped green
  pepper
1/4 cup chopped onion
1 cup cream, whipped
4 eggs, separated
1/3 cup Parmesan cheese
1/2 teaspoon paprika
3/4 teaspoon salt

Sauce:
1 cup sour cream
3 tablespoons chives
3/4 teaspoon salt

Cook spinach according to directions on package. Whip cream. Beat yolks and whites separately. Beat whites until soft peaks form. Combine all ingredients. Fold in egg whites last. Bake in 2-quart mold in pan of hot water 45 minutes at 350°. Serves 6-8.

Mix sauce and serve over rice.

Mrs. J. M. Heathman, Jr.
INDIANOLA, MS

Hopping John

Black eyed peas
Rice

Cook equal portions of blackeyed peas and rice. Cook the peas with a piece of salt pork, hog jowl or ham hock. Cook rice in usual manner. About 30 minutes before serving, mix them and let simmer. In the south, blackeyed peas cooked with hog jowl are served on New Year's Day to bring prosperity throughout the year. Some prefer stewed tomatoes added to peas instead of rice.

Mrs. Bill Buchanan
INDIANOLA, MS

Rice and Red Beans

"This is cajun eating. I got the recipe from a Negro woman who stayed with me when Ike Stone was a baby; her home was originally South Louisiana." Have a tossed salad, French bread, coffee, and enjoy yourself!

Red beans or kidney beans
1 cup rice
Salt meat
Chopped onions
Garlic to taste

About noon, put 1/2 package of red beans (I have to buy kidney beans) on the stove in a large boiler. Cover with water. Cover and cook at a slow boil all afternoon, adding water to make a real thick juice. About an hour before you plan to eat, put on your rice, and make by your usual method. Use 1 or 2 cups (one cup will be enough for 5 or 6 people.) Then fry quickly in a hot skillet 10 to 12 slices of fat meat or salt meat. Put in with beans. Then sauté in the grease 1 onion chopped, 1 garlic section chopped (or more or less according to taste). Add the onions, garlic and grease drippings to the beans and salt to taste. Allow to continue cooking until the rice is done. At the table serve with a mound of rice covered by the beans and all its meats and juices.

Mrs. W. C. Trotter, Jr.
GREENVILLE, MS

Variation: Add 2 tablespoons green pepper and 1 tablespoon pimento.

Mrs. Joe S. Green
INDIANOLA, MS

Soubise

2/3 cup rice
1 1/2 teaspoon salt
4 quarts rapidly boiling
  water
4 tablespoons butter
2 pounds (6 to 7 cups)
  thinly sliced yellow
  onions
1/4 cup whipping cream
1/4 cup grated Swiss cheese
2 tablespoons softened
  butter
1 tablespoon minced
  parsley
Salt and pepper

Drop rice into rapidly boiling water with salt, and boil for exactly 6 minutes. Drain immediately. Put 4 tablespoons butter in heavy 3 quart fireproof casserole. When butter is foaming over medium heat, stir in onions. As soon as they are well coated with butter, stir in rice. Cover. Cook in 300° oven for 1 hour stirring occasionally. The rice and onions should become very tender and usually a very light golden yellow. Add seasonings. May be cooked several hours in advance and reheated. Just before serving, stir in cream and cheese and then butter (2 tablespoons). Taste for seasoning. Turn into hot vegetable dish and sprinkle with parsley. Serves 4.

Jane Watkins
WASHINGTON, D.C.

Justine's Creme D'epinard (Creamed Spinach)

2 cups cooked, chopped
  fresh spinach
2 heaping tablespoons
  cream sauce
Dash of Worcestershire
  sauce
Dash Tabasco
Salt and pepper to taste
4 tablespoons Hollandaise
  sauce

Mix together spinach, cream sauce, and the seasonings and heat. Divide the hot spinach among the four individual casserole dishes or one large casserole and top with Hollandaise. Lightly brown in a very hot oven.

Justine's Restaurant
MEMPHIS, TN

Spinach Madeleine

2 packages frozen chopped
  spinach
4 tablespoons butter
2 tablespoons flour
2 tablespoons chopped
  onion
1/2 cup evaporated milk
1/2 cup vegetable liquor
3/4 teaspoon celery salt
1/2 teaspoon salt
1 teaspoon Worcestershire
  sauce
1/2 teaspoon black pepper
3/4 teaspoon garlic
1 (6 ounce) roll Jalapeno
  cheese
Red pepper to taste

Cook spinach by directions and save liquor. Melt butter in pan, add flour and blend until smooth but not brown. Add onion and cook until soft but not brown. Add liquids slowly stirring constantly until smooth and thick. Add seasonings and cheese which has been cut into small pieces. Stir until melted. Combine with cooked spinach. Better if saved 24 hours. Cover with bread crumbs. Cook at 350° for 30 minutes. Serves 6 to 8.

Sue P. Wiggins
INDIANOLA, MS

Spinach with Sour Cream

1 package frozen chopped
  spinach
1 tablespoon grated onion
2 eggs, beaten
1/2 cup sour cream
1 cup grated Parmesan
  cheese
1 tablespoon flour
2 tablespoons butter
Salt and pepper to taste

Cook frozen spinach in small amount of water with onion until thawed. Add eggs and rest of ingredients with spinach and onions and bake in greased casserole for 25 to 30 minutes in 350° oven, or until center is set. Do not over cook as it will separate. Serves 4 and is extremely rich.

Wister Henry of Wister Henry Gardens
BELZONI, MS

Shugah Casserole

4 or 5 shugahs, or zucchi-
  nis, strung and sliced
3 small eggplant, cut in
  cubes
12 large onions, chopped
2 stalks celery, chopped
1 bell pepper, chopped
1 1/2 pounds ground meat
1 dozen cooked shrimp
1 can mushroom soup
2 small medium ripe
  tomatoes
1/2 cup grated cheese
Soy sauce
Worcestershire sauce
Salt
Pepper
Cooking oil

Stir ground meat and 1 onion in oil until done. Season with soy, Worcestershire, salt and pepper. Set aside. Heat skillet and add 3 tablespoons oil. Sauté onion, pepper and celery until clear. Add eggplant and shugah. Stir 2 or 3 minutes until coated with oil. Add 1/2 cup of water, cover and cook 5 to 7 minutes. Stir occasionally. Season same as meat. Layer vegetables, meat and shrimp and soup in casserole. Top with tomatoes cut in wedges. Cover and bake in 350° oven 1 hour. Uncover; top with cheese and cook 30 minutes.

Note: Shugah seeds available from us in Merigold, MS.

Lee and Pup McCarty
MERIGOLD, MS

Squash Casserole

3 medium squash, cut into
  small pieces
1/4 cup sour cream
1 tablespoon butter
1/2 cup grated cheese
1/2 teaspoon salt
1/8 teaspoon paprika
1 beaten egg yolk
1 tablespoon chopped
  chives
3 strips bacon, fried dry
  and crumbled
Bread crumbs
Butter to dot top

Simmer squash until tender. Drain well. Combine next five ingredients, stirring over low heat until cheese melts. Remove from fire. Stir in beaten egg yolk, chives, and bacon. Add squash. Cover with bread crumbs. Dot with butter. Brown in oven 350°.

Mrs. Gene Stansel, Jr.
RULEVILLE, MS

Squash Casserole Superb

1 pound (10 small) yellow
  squash
1 teaspoon salt
1 stick butter
1 cup chopped onion
1/2 cup chopped celery
1/4 cup finely cut mush-
  rooms
1/4 cup chopped pimiento
1/4 cup chopped green
  pepper
1 cup raw oatmeal
3/4 cup and 2 tablespoons
  milk
1 whole egg, slightly
  beaten
2 hard boiled eggs,
  chopped
Pepper to taste
Ritz crackers, crushed

Wash and cut squash into 1 inch rounds. Put into boiler and cover with water. Add salt and cook until just tender. Drain, mash and place in large mixing bowl. Sauté the following in the butter: onion, celery, mushrooms, pimiento, and green pepper. Add this to well mashed squash. Add raw oat meal (quick kind if desired), milk, whole egg, boiled egg and pepper. Mix well and refrigerate over night. When ready to cook be sure squash mixture is room temperature. Place in buttered casserole, cover with crushed Ritz crackers. Bake 30 minutes at 400°. Serves 8 to 12.

Mrs. W. E. Van Cleve
JACKSON, MS

Squash Croquettes

4 or 5 fresh squash (cut up)
1 small onion (cut up)
Salt and pepper to taste
1 egg (beaten)
1/4 cup grated cheese
1 cup cracker crumbs (fine)
1/4 stick butter

Cook squash and onion in small amount of water, with salt added and drain well, then mash. Add egg, butter, cheese and 1/2 cup cracker crumbs. Mix well. Shape into balls and roll in remaining crumbs. Fry in deep fat.

Mrs. J. C. Totten
HOLLY SPRINGS, MS

Summer Squash Casserole

6 medium yellow crooked-
    neck squash, cut in
    cubes
1/2 stick butter
1 teaspoon black pepper
1/2 teaspoon salt
1 egg
1 tablespoon grated onion
1/2 cup cracker crumbs
3/4 cup grated cheese,
    divided
1/2 teaspoon paprika

Cook squash, drain and process in food processor (or mash with potato masher). Add melted
butter, salt, pepper, onion and cracker crumbs.
Taste and adjust seasoning. Add slightly beaten
egg and 1/2 cup grated cheese and mix. Place in
1 quart casserole. Top with remaining 1/4 cup
cheese and sprinkle with paprika. Bake at 350°
for 20 to 25 minutes. Serves 4 to 6.

Mrs. W. C. Speer, Jr.
INDIANOLA, MS

Baked Green Tomatoes

2 1/2 pound green toma-
    toes, sliced 1/4 inch
1/2 teaspoon sugar
Salt and pepper to taste
3/4 cup bread crumbs
3 tablespoons butter
1/2 teaspoon oregano
1/4 teaspoon basil
1/4 teaspoon thyme
1/3 cup parmesan cheese

Slice tomatoes and arrange overlapping in oil
coated rectangular baking dish. Sprinkle layers
with 1/2 teaspoon sugar and salt. Add freshly
ground pepper to taste. Lightly brown 3/4 cup
bread crumbs in 3 tablespoons butter. Combine oregano, basil and thyme and add to bread
crumbs. Sprinkle crumbs over tomatoes and top
with parmesan cheese. Dot generously with butter. Bake at 350° for 45 minutes.

Lynn Eastland
INDIANOLA, MS

Creole Tomatoes

4 large tomatoes
2 green peppers
1 small onion
Salt
Cayenne Pepper
4 tablespoons butter
1 cup milk or cream
4 tablespoons flour

Cut tomatoes in half crosswise; lay cut side up in a baking pan and sprinkle with the peppers and onion which have been finely chopped. Season well with salt and cayenne. Put a small piece of butter on each tomato. Pour 1/2 cup water in pan and bake in moderate oven. When tomatoes are almost tender, pour over them a brown sauce made by browning flour in butter and stirring in milk or cream. Bake a few minutes longer.

Mrs. S. G. Mounger
GREENWOOD, MS

Tomato Stuffed with Mushrooms

8 firm but ripe tomatoes
4 tablespoons butter
1 1/4 pounds fresh mushrooms
1 cup sour cream
1 tablespoon and 1 teaspoon flour
3 ounces soft Roquefort cheese
1/4 teaspoon fine herbs
1 teaspoon chopped parsley
2 tablespoons dry sherry
Salt
Pepper
Blanched almonds or sesame seeds

Scoop out soft part of tomatoes and drain upside down. In large skillet melt butter and sauté the mushrooms until all liquid is gone. Mix sour cream with flour and blend into the mushrooms over low heat until thick and bubbly. Stir in the sherry, fine herbs, parsley, salt, and pepper. Cool. Stuff tomatoes loosely. Sprinkle with seed or almonds. Bake at 350° for 15 minutes.

Mrs. Vivion (Emily S.) Johnson
INDIANOLA, MS

Fresh Tomatoes with Pesto

Pesto
2 cups fresh basil leaves,
  washed and dried
4 large garlic cloves, peel
  and chop
1 cup shelled pecans
1 cup olive oil
1 cup freshly grated
Parmesan cheese
1/4 cup Romano cheese
Salt, to taste
Fresh ground pepper, to
  taste

Combine basil, garlic and pecans in food processor and chop. Add olive oil in a slow stream. Stop motor, and all other ingredients, process briefly.

Serve over fresh tomatoes in summer. May also serve over pasta.

Susan Robertson Allen
INDIANOLA, MS

Fried Green Tomatoes

4 large green tomatoes
1/2 cup meal
1 teaspoon salt
1/4 teaspoon pepper

Mix meal with salt and pepper. Slice tomatoes 1/4 inch thick. Dip each slice into seasoned meal mixture. Place seasoned vegetable in heavy skillet containing melted bacon fat. Fry slowly until brown, turning once. Yield: 6 servings.

Mrs. Will French
INDIANOLA, MS

Sunflower Tomatoes

1 sweet onion, chopped
2 - 3 cloves garlic, minced
  or pressed
1 bell pepper, chopped
1 small skillet regular
  cornbread (6-8" skillet)
1 large can whole tomatoes
  & juice, squeezed
Cajun seasoning to taste
Shredded cheddar cheese

Sauté onion, bell pepper, and garlic in bacon drippings or olive oil until soft. Add cornbread, tomatoes, and seasonings to taste. Do not overmix, mixture should be lumpy. Pour into oiled casserole and top with a little shredded cheddar, stirring a little into mixture if you like. Bake at 350° until mixture is bubbly and cheese is melted.

Trish Berry
INDIANOLA, MS

Stuffed Baked Tomatoes

6 to 8 firm ripe tomatoes
Lump of butter
Dash salt and cayenne
  pepper
1 tablespoon grated onion
1 tablespoon
  Worcestershire sauce
Small chopped garlic
1 medium size can deviled
  ham
1/2 cup chopped green
  pepper
1 cup chopped celery
1 medium can mushrooms

Cut off stem end and scoop out tomatoes; place in baking pan; add a little salt in each.

Mix remaining ingredients except mushrooms. Cook until tender, adding mushrooms last 10 minutes of cooking time.

Add enough cooked white rice to give body; filling tomatoes with this mixture, covering with bread crumbs, dotting with butter, and sprinkling with paprika, bake in 375° oven until tomatoes wrinkle. If stuffing used for green bell peppers, parboil peppers after cleaning inside.

This was one of the favorite recipes of Mrs. Ruth Stephenson, mother of the Rev. George Stephenson, rector of St. Stephens 1938-1941.

"Streak of Lean 'N Streak of Fat"

Turnip Greens
Cornfield peas
Turnips
Fried Okra

Boil piece of salt pork in a pot of water for half hour, then add turnip greens; boil one hour or more, until tender. Dip out with perforated spoon. Serve with hot pepper sauce. Season to taste.

Boil piece of salt pork in a pot of water for 1 hour. Add cornfield peas, adding salt just before they are done. Drain and serve.

Wash, peel, cut in thin slices across the grain, put in pot with piece of fresh pork or salt meat, add enough cold water to cover. When the water has stewed down low, mash the turnips and season with salt and pepper. Set back on the range and stir frequently until the water is dried out. Do not boil too long. They are sweeter when cooked quickly. A little sugar may be added to the taste. Cooking time - forty minutes to an hour.

Chip fresh okra in 1/4" cubes. Salt and pepper it and roll in cornmeal. Drop chips into iron skillet of bacon grease or salt pork grease, until lightly browned.

Mrs. Joe Green
INDIANOLA, MS

Creole Zucchini

2 onions, chopped
3 ribs celery, chopped
1 small green pepper
1 clove garlic, minced
1 bay leaf
1 large can tomatoes
3 or 4 medium zucchini
1/4 cup oil

Brown onions, celery, garlic and pepper in oil. Add tomatoes and bay leaf; simmer covered 1 hour. Slice squash thin and add. Remove bay leaf. Simmer 1 hour, remove cover and cook longer if it is too juicy. Serves 6 to 8.

Eleanor N. Failing
INDIANOLA, MS

Zucchini and Eggs

Oil
2 - 3 small zucchini, thinly sliced, (do not peel)
1 large onion
1 clove garlic
1/4 teaspoon basil
1/2 cup Parmesan cheese
Salt and pepper to taste
6 eggs

Heat large frying pan with a little oil and add zucchini, onions, garlic, and basil. Cook slowly. In a separate bowl mix eggs, Parmesan cheese, salt, and pepper. When zucchini mixture is tender, add egg mixture. Cook until eggs are scrambled.

Karen K. Carpenter
INDIANOLA, MS

Breads
and
Sandwiches

Banana Fritters

1 cup sifted flour
1 teaspoon baking powder
1/2 teaspoon salt
2/3 cup milk
Bananas, cut into one-
  inch pieces
1 tablespoon lemon juice
  (optional)
1 egg separated
1 tablespoon sugar
  (optional)
1 tablespoon melted oleo

Mix flour, baking powder, salt, and milk. Add egg yolk, lemon juice, and butter. Fold in stiffly beaten egg whites. Add sugar and bananas. Fry in deep fat. Drain on paper towel.

Augusta C. Barnwell
GREENWOOD, MS

Banana Muffins

2 1/4 cup sugar
3 sticks margarine (soft-
  ened)
3 cups cake flour
1 1/2 teaspoon soda
3 eggs, beaten
6 ripe bananas
Pinch of salt
2 cups pecan pieces
1 1/2 teaspoons vanilla

Cream together eggs, butter, and sugar. Mash bananas and add to creamed mixture. Then add sifted dry ingredients, pecans, and vanilla. Spoon into greased muffin tins, filling about 3/4 full. Bake at 375° for 15 - 20 minutes.

These are delicious for breakfast or a snack! They freeze well, and extra batter can be stored in refrigerator about a week.

Ellen Clayton
INDIANOLA, MS

Herb Batter Bread

1 1/4 cup milk
1 teaspoon caraway seeds,
  poppy seeds, instant
  minced onion, dried
  chervil
1/2 teaspoon dried oregano
2 tablespoons sugar
2 tablespoons salt
4 tablespoons butter
2 packages yeast
1/2 cup water
2 eggs beaten well
1/2 teaspoon nutmeg
4 1/2 cups flour

Heat milk, herbs, sugar and salt to scalding point, add butter and cool to lukewarm. Add yeast that has been softened in the 1/2 cup water. Stir in eggs, nutmeg and flour and beat vigorously for 2 minutes. Cover and let rise until more than double. Stir down with fist or wooden spoon. Beat hard 1/2 minute or more. Turn into a 2 quart casserole dish or small 8" tube pan. Sprinkle top with poppy seeds, coarse salt, and teaspoon minced onion softened in water. Let rise 20 minutes. Bake at 375° for 45 minutes to 1 hour.

Don't let the length of this scare you. It's so easy to make and so good, especially hot!

Searcy Lawler
ROSEDALE, MS

Toasted Herb Bread Rolls

1 loaf thinly sliced bread,
  decrusted
1/2 cup butter, softened
1/2 teaspoon savory
1 teaspoon sweet basil
2 tablespoons chopped
  chives

Add herbs to butter and spread mixture on the bread slices. roll the slices starting at the corner, pinning with tooth pick. Bake in 350° oven for approximately 35 minutes. Remove pick before serving. Can be served with meal or as an appetizer.

Jean Kent E. Barron
BOCA RATON, FL

Angel Biscuits

5 cups flour
1/4 cup sugar
3 teaspoons baking powder
1 teaspoon soda
1 teaspoon salt
2 cups buttermilk
1 cup shortening
2 tablespoons water
1 package yeast

Mix first 5 ingredients in a large bowl. Make a well in flour; add shortening and remaining ingredients. Mix well. Roll as for any type biscuits. Dip small biscuits in melted butter before placing in pan. Cook 400° 15 minutes.

Mrs. Jack E. Harper, Jr.
INDIANOLA, MS

Old-Fashioned Biscuits

7 cups flour (plain)
1 teaspoon soda
2 teaspoons baking powder
1 teaspoon salt
1 1/2 cups crisco
1 cup butter (oleo)
2 cups buttermilk

Mix well, then add buttermilk. Roll dough thin - place one biscuit on top of another. (This enables one to butter each biscuit after baking). Bake at 375° until brown.

Penda Johnson
INDIANOLA, MS

Bran Muffins

2 cups boiling water
2 cups 100% bran cereal
1 heaping cup shortening
3 cups sugar
4 eggs, beaten
1 quart buttermilk
5 cups flour
5 teaspoons baking soda
1 teaspoon salt
4 cups all bran cereal
Nuts and raisins, if
  desired

Cream shortening and sugar, add eggs. Add 100% bran that has been soaked in buttermilk. Sift flour, soda, and salt. Add to above mixture. Add all bran alternately with water. Store, covered, in refrigerator. Makes one gallon. Stores in refrigerator 4 - 6 weeks. Bake 15 minutes at 400°.

Mrs. J. P. Fisher
INDIANOLA, MS

Brown Bread

1 cup flour
3 tablespoons sugar
2 teaspoons baking powder
2 cups whole wheat flour
1 cup all bran cereal (not
   raisin bran)
1 cup molasses and 1 cup
   raisins
1/2 teaspoon soda in 2
   cups buttermilk

Sift together flour, sugar, and baking powder. Add but do not sift whole wheat flour and cereal. Add remaining ingredients.

Mix well, put in greased bread pan (long narrow one is best); bake in 350° oven about 45 minutes until tested done in middle with a tester or clean broom straw. This keeps well in refrigerator in summer; freezes well. Good for cream cheese sandwiches or just with butter. Especially good with baked beans, the traditional New England Saturday night supper.

Mrs. Phil (Louise B.) Mayhall
GREENVILLE, MS

Hot Cakes

3 eggs, beaten
4 cups flour
4 heaping teaspoons
   baking powder
2 teaspoons salt
1/2 cup water
Sweet milk, enough for
   pouring consistency
1/2 cup cooking oil or
   melted butter

Beat eggs in large bowl or mixer; add milk, oil. Sift in dry ingredients. Be sure griddle is moderately hot, about 400°. No grease needed.

Mrs. J. T. Lancaster
SUNFLOWER, MS

Holland Carrot Bread

2 cups sifted flour
2 teaspoons baking soda
2 teaspoons cinnamon
1/2 teaspoon salt
1 1/2 cups sugar
1 1/2 cups cooking oil
3 eggs
2 teaspoons vanilla extract

In a large bowl sift together first 4 ingredients. Make a well in the center and put in remaining ingredients.

With electric mixer beat well on medium speed until well blended. Fold in 2 cups carrots, grated. Turn the mixture into 2 well greased and floured loaf pans and bake in a slow oven (300°) for 1 hour or until bread test done. If desired, add 1 cup nuts or raisins after folding in the carrots.

Wister Henry
BELZONI, MS

Cheese Bread

2 packages yeast
2 tablespoons sugar
1 teaspoon garlic salt
1/2 teaspoon regular salt
1/2 cup Parmesan cheese
1 1/2 cups warm milk
2 beaten eggs
4 tablespoons melted oleo
5 1/2 cups sifted flour

Dissolve yeast in 1/2 cup warm water. Scald 1 1/2 cups milk and let cool to just warm. Add to milk - sugar, garlic salt, salt, dissolved yeast, beaten eggs, melted oleo, and cheese. Add 3 cups flour and beat until smooth, scraping sides of bowl. Work the remaining flour (2 1/2 cups) with spoon and finally with hands. Cover and let rise 1 hour. Punch down and divide in two parts. Place in 2 greased loaf pans. Let rise until almost at top of pan. Bake at 350° forty-five to fifty minutes or until brown.

Louise Boyd Hendon
INDIANOLA, MS

Chocolate Muffins

2 sticks oleo
1 1/2 cup sugar
4 eggs
1 cup flour
4 squares semi-sweet
  chocolate
1 teaspoon vanilla
  flavoring
3 cups pecans

Cream oleo and sugar. Melt chocolate in a double boiler. Add chocolate, eggs, flour, vanilla, and pecans to mixture. Pour into tiny muffin tins. Bake 350° for about 35 minutes. Yields approximately 18 muffins.

Mrs. Jack Carter
ROSEDALE, MS

Corn Fritters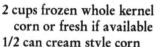

2 cups frozen whole kernel
  corn or fresh if available
1/2 can cream style corn
  (omit if using fresh corn)
2 eggs
1/2 to 1 cup flour
1 tablespoon or more
  sugar
2 or 3 green onions,
  chopped (optional)
3 - 4 slices bacon, fried
  crisp (optional), save
  drippings
Salt and fresh cracked
  pepper to taste
Oil for frying

Combine all ingredients. Make a "Test Fritter". Taste and adjust for consistency and seasoning. Good fried in oil or margarine with just a little bacon grease.

Trish Berry
INDIANOLA, MS

Corn Light Bread

2 cups plain meal
1/2 cup plain flour
3/4 cup sugar
1/2 teaspoon soda
1 teaspoon salt
1 teaspoon dry yeast
2 cups buttermilk
3 tablespoons melted
    shortening

Sift together meal, flour, sugar, soda and salt. Add yeast and mix well. Then, add buttermilk and melted shortening, and stir until just mixed. Bake in greased loaf pan 55 - 60 minutes. Let stand in pan 15 minutes before removing.

Kathy Allen
INDIANOLA, MS

Cornbread-Delta Style

1 1/2 cups white or stone
    ground meal
3 tablespoons all-purpose
    flour
1 1/2 teaspoons baking
    powder
1 teaspoon salt
2 to 3 tablespoons shorten-
    ing (melted and hot)
1 1/2 cups milk (if you
    prefer buttermilk then
    add 1/2 teaspoon soda
    and delete the baking
    powder)
1 egg beaten

Beat egg until light; add a little of the liquid; mix this with the flour and meal which has been sifted with soda and salt. Add the melted shortening and sufficient liquid to make a smooth batter and beat well. Have the pan in which the bread is to be baked sizzling hot when the batter is put in. Bake in preheated oven 450°. An 8" black iron skillet is best for baking cornbread.

Alberta Green
INDIANOLA, MS

Cornbread Dressing

"A must for Thanksgiving and Christmas dinners. Good for all year round."

Egg Bread, crumbled
3/4 cup celery, chopped
1/3 cup butter
1/8 teaspoon pepper
1 teaspoon Poultry
　Seasoning
2/3 cup onion, chopped
1 teaspoon salt
3 eggs, beaten
2 cups (or more) broth

Sauté onions and celery in butter over low heat. Combine with egg bread and seasonings. Add eggs and mix well. Add broth, mix until smooth. Pour into buttered dish. Bake at 350° until set and brown (about 45 minutes).

Mrs. Larry Hudson
MOORHEAD, MS

Egg Bread (for dressing)

"Good by itself also. But a must for good 'southern' dressing."

1 1/2 cups corn meal
2 teaspoons baking powder
1 teaspoon sugar
1/2 teaspoon soda
1 1/2 cups buttermilk
1/2 cup flour
3/4 teaspoon salt
4 tablespoons oil
2 eggs, beaten

Sift dry ingredients. Combine milk, eggs, and oil. Mix with dry ingredients. Pour into well greased VERY HOT pan (I use cast iron skillet). Bake in hot oven (425°) 25 minutes or until golden brown.

Mrs. Larry Hudson
MOORHEAD, MS

Mexican Cornbread

1 cup corn meal
1 teaspoon baking powder
1 teaspoon salt
1/2 teaspoon soda
1/2 pound grated cheese
2 tablespoons flour
1 medium onion, grated
3 hot peppers, chopped
1/4 cup Wesson oil
1 cup sweet milk
2 eggs
1 small can creamed corn

Mix together and bake at 450° for 30 minutes. Use a medium sized skillet or 1 quart casserole.

Mrs. Harold Tapley
SHAW, MS

Jettie's Hot Water Cornbread

2 cups corn meal
1 teaspoon salt
1 tablespoon vegetable oil
Pinch sugar
Boiling water

Mix dry ingredients. Add enough boiling water to make mix of corn bread consistency. Add vegetable oil, mix and fry in hot grease until golden brown - turning once. Each hoecake should contain 2 tablespoons batter. These are delicious with fresh vegetables.

Mrs. Burton Moore
INDIANOLA, MS

Kentucky Oyster Dressing

3 cups buttermilk made
  into cornbread (without
  sugar)
3 cups celery, diced
2 cups white onions, diced
1/2 cup salad oil
8 slices of bread, stale
1/2 cup fresh parsley,
  chopped
1/2 teaspoon black pepper
3 cups congealed chicken
  stock
1/2 cup oyster liquid
2 to 3 pints oysters,
  drained
1 teaspoon sage if desired
3 eggs, beaten

Sauté onions and celery in salad oil over low heat until clear. Remove grease from congealed chicken stock and heat until liquid. Put stale bread in slow oven until golden. Combine crumbled cornbread with liquids and mix. Add onions, celery, oil from skillet, sage, pepper, and parsley. Make fine bread crumbs of white bread with rolling pin or blender and add to mixture. Add oysters and eggs and mix. Turkey may be stuffed or dressing may be baked in large greased baking dish at 375° for about one hour or until brown. Serve with giblet gravy.

If you have no chicken stock you may boil five pounds of chicken necks in water until very tender, drain and refrigerate until congealed.

Mary Steele Nabors
INDIANOLA, MS

Wild Turkey Dressing

3 cups cooked wild rice
2 cups bread crumbs (corn
  bread)
1 cup minced onion
1 cup diced celery
1 garlic clove, minced
1 tablespoon chopped
  parsley
1/2 cup butter
2 teaspoons salt
1 teaspoon black pepper
1 teaspoon sweet basil
1/2 cup chopped bell
  pepper
1/2 teaspoon sage
1/2 teaspoon rosemary
1 cup sliced mushrooms
2 cups stock from turkey

Fry onions until transparent in the butter and then add the bell pepper, celery, garlic, and parsley mixing constantly over low heat. When cooked down slightly add the remaining ingredients and mix in a good size bowl moistening the ingredients with turkey stock to soft consistency. Stuff the turkey with the dressing or cook in a separate pan.

Tom Barron
INDIANOLA, MS

Crackling Bread

2 cups cracklings
1/2 teaspoon baking soda
1 cup buttermilk (more if
  thick)
2 cups corn meal
2 tablespoons fat
Salt pork

Render salt pork to make cracklings. Mix baking soda with buttermilk and add to corn meal a little at a time, stirring until smooth. Stir in cracklings and fat. Form pones, molding between palms. Bake at 350° for 12 to 20 minutes. Yield: 6 portions.

Serve at dinner with vegetables or dunk in buttermilk to enjoy as a noontime snack, or serve with turnip greens and garden relish. Cook greens with pod hot pepper to flavor.

Mrs. John Neill
GREENWOOD, MS

Dill Casserole Bread

1 packet dry yeast
1/4 cup warm water
1 cup warm creamed
  cottage cheese
2 tablespoons sugar
1 tablespoon instant
  minced onion
1 tablespoon melted butter
2 teaspoons dill seed
1 teaspoon salt
1/4 teaspoon soda
1 unbeaten egg
2 1/4 to 2 1/2 cups flour

Soften yeast in water. Combine in mixing bowl: cottage cheese, sugar, onion, butter, dill seed, salt, soda, egg and softened yeast. Add gradually flour to form soft dough, beating well after each addition. Cover and let rise in warm place, 80 - 90° until doubled, about 50 - 60 minutes.

Stir down dough, turn into well greased 8 inch round casserole. Let rise 30 - 40 minutes. Bake at 350° for 30 - 40 minutes. Brush with butter and salt.

Kay Johnson
INDIANOLA, MS

Hush Puppies

1 cup self-rising meal
1/2 cup self-rising flour
1 teaspoon sugar
1 teaspoon baking powder
2 large eggs
2 medium onions chopped
  fine
1/2 cup milk

Combine meal, flour, baking powder, sugar, chopped onions and eggs; to this add the milk and stir thoroughly. This batter should be the consistency of thick cake batter. If the batter is too thick add 1 or 2 tablespoon of milk or if too thin thicken with a small amount of flour. Drop by spoonfuls in hot fat. If they do not form a ball immediately in the hot fat, the batter is not thick enough and it must be thickened as above.

Mrs. Bob Rutherford
ROLLING FORK, MS

Nut Date Bread

1/2 cup brown sugar
2 tablespoons shortening
1 egg
1/2 cup nuts
1 cup dates
1 teaspoon soda
1 1/2 cups flour

Pour 1 cup of boiling water over the dates; add 1 teaspoon soda. Add to sugar, shortening and egg that have been mixed together. Then add flour and nuts. Put in loaf pan, greased and floured. Bake about one hour at 350°.

Kate W. Patterson
INDIANOLA, MS

Tiny Orange Muffins

2 orange rinds grated
1/2 cup butter or oleo
1 cup sugar
1 cup buttermilk
1 teaspoon soda
2 cups flour
2 eggs

Sauce:

1 cup brown sugar
1 cup orange juice

Mix all together. Bake 15 minutes in 400° oven in small greased muffin tins.

To make sauce boil brown sugar and orange juice. Dunk muffins in sauce while hot.

Makes about 45-48 small muffins.

Rebecca Barrett
INDIANOLA, MS

Orange Nut Bread

2 eggs
1 cup sugar creamed with
   2 tablespoons melted
   butter
3 1/2 cups flour sifted
3 teaspoons baking powder
1/2 teaspoon salt
1 cup milk
1 cup chopped nuts
Peel of 4 oranges

Cream eggs, sugar and melted butter. Add all other ingredients except orange peel, mix well and set aside. Shred finely the orange peel and boil 5 minutes in 1 cup water and 1 teaspoon soda. Rinse and drain. Add 1 cup sugar and 3/4 cup water. Cook until thick, very little juice. Add this mixture to the batter and bake in 2 loaf pans about 1 hour.

Mrs. Bob Barron
INDIANOLA, MS

Pumpkin Bread

3 cups sugar
3 1/2 cups flour
1 cup Wesson oil
3/4 cup orange juice
2 cups mashed pumpkin
4 eggs, slightly beaten
1 1/2 teaspoon salt
2 teaspoons soda
1 teaspoon nutmeg
1 teaspoon cinnamon
1 cup raisins
1 cup pecans

Mix ingredients together in large mixing bowl. Beat with electric mixer. Grease and flour 4 small coffee cans. Fill half full with mixture (this will rise to the top of can). Bake at 350° for one hour; remove from oven and let cool for 10 minutes. Remove from can and wrap in plastic wrap.

"The Big Orange Colored Pumpkin was highly developed by the Indians before America was settled by the Europeans."

Mrs. W. M. Pitts
INDIANOLA, MS

Sixty Minute Rolls

5 cups flour
2 teaspoons salt
1 heaping tablespoon sugar
3 level tablespoons shortening
1/2 cup sweet milk, scalded and cooled
1 cup warm water
2 packages yeast

Dissolve the yeast in warm water; add the cool, scalded milk, and 1/2 teaspoon of the sugar. Sift 2 1/2 cups flour in bowl: add salt and sugar. Cut in shortening. Add yeast mixture and beat vigorously until smooth and bubbling. Add remaining flour, making a firm dough easily handled without sticking. Mold as desired. Let stand in a warm place until double in bulk (30 or 40 minutes). Bake in medium oven 20 minutes.

Mrs. Ben S. Jones
WOODVILLE, MS

Ice Box Rolls

1 quart milk
1 cup shortening
1 cup sugar
2 packages yeast
1/4 cup water
Flour
1 teaspoon soda
2 teaspoons baking powder
1 teaspoon salt

Three generations at Eureka plantation have called for Willie to pass the rolls, please. They are worth calling for.

Place milk, shortening and sugar on stove, heating thoroughly but don't boil. Cool until milk is warm. Dissolve yeast in water and add to milk mixture. Stir in enough flour to make a batter. Let rise 2 hours or double bulk. Add soda, baking powder and mix thoroughly; add enough flour to make stiff dough. Make rolls, brushing with butter on fold and on top. Place in greased pan to rise for 2 hours. Bake at 350° until brown. Makes 6 to 7 dozen and will keep in refrigerator for several days.

Willie Tillis
INDIANOLA, MS

Sally Lunn

1 yeast cake
4 1/4 cups flour
2 cups sugar
1 cup milk
2 eggs, separated
1 cup butter, melted

Dissolve yeast cake in 2 tablespoons water. Add 1 cup flour and milk to make a soft batter. Beat. Set aside for about an hour until it becomes bubbly and begins to rise.

Beat yolks and sugar until light and creamy. Add butter, remaining flour and well beaten whites. Knead dough well in bowl and cover. Let rise until double in bulk. Pour out on well-floured board. Work down. Roll out to 1/2" thick, cut with biscuit cutter. Put in greased muffin rings. Let rise until doubled. Bake in rather quick oven. The softer the consistency of the dough the better and lighter the Sally Lunn.

This has been handed down five or six generations.

Mrs. S. G. Beaman
GREENWOOD, MS

Scotch Shortbread

2 sticks butter (no substitute)
1/2 cup confectioners
sugar
1/4 teaspoon baking
powder
2 cups plain flour
1/8 teaspoon salt
2 teaspoons almond
flavoring (optional)

Cream butter and sugar until light. Add almond flavoring if desired. Sift flour, salt, and baking powder together into a soft dough. Press out into 2 ungreased 8" round cake pans. Prick with a fork and cut into twelve wedges. Bake at 325° for from 45 minutes to 1 hour until golden brown.

Mrs. Mavis Porter
COLUMBIA, SC

Irish Soda Bread

2 cups flour
1 teaspoon baking powder
1/2 teaspoon baking soda
1/2 cup sugar
1/4 teaspoon salt
1/2 cup currants or raisins
1 tablespoon caraway seeds
3/4 cup buttermilk

Preheat oven to 350°. Sift dry ingredients together. Stir currants and caraway seeds into dry ingredients. Add buttermilk. Don't over beat dough. Slowly shape into a round loaf - it will be sticky so use floured hands. Do not knead.

Bake on a lightly greased and floured pan for 45 minutes. (I like to use a tin pie pan.) *Optional - the top of the dough can be slashed with a sharp knife in a criss-cross pattern before baking.

Yield 1 free - form loaf.

Kate Failing
INDIANOLA, MS

Easy Spoonbread

1 egg beaten
1 1/2 cups buttermilk
1 1/2 cups corn meal
1 teaspoon salt
1 teaspoon sugar
1 teaspoon baking soda
1 teaspoon baking powder
1 1/2 cup boiling water
2 tablespoons shortening

Scald corn meal, and boiling water. Stir well. Add salt, baking soda, baking powder, buttermilk and egg. Mix well. Place shortening in baking dish and melt in 350° oven. Add melted shortening to cornmeal batter. Pour into baking dish and cook 45 minutes to 1 hour.

Delightful eaten as is or with butter, but best of all with smothered chicken gravy.

Mrs. Harlan Swango
GULFPORT, MS

Spoonbread

1 1/2 cups water
1 teaspoon salt
1 cup white corn meal
2 tablespoons butter
1 cup sweet milk
2 eggs, separated

Bring water and salt to boiling point. Gradually stir in corn meal. When smooth, add butter, milk, well beaten yolks of eggs. When mixed well fold in 2 egg whites beaten stiff. Pour into greased baking dish; bake in moderate oven about 30 minutes, or until firm.

Congressman G. V. "Sonny" Montgomery
RECIPE FROM MONTGOMERY FAMILY

Spiced Muffins

1 cup sugar
1/2 cup butter
2 cups flour
2 cups raisins
2 cups water
1 egg
1 teaspoon cloves
1 teaspoon soda
1 pinch salt

Put raisins and water on to boil for 15 minutes. Take off when boiled down to one cup water. Cream butter, sugar, and egg. Sift soda, spices, and salt with flour. Combine and bake 400° about 20 minutes in greased muffin tins.

Mrs. Tom Pitts
INDIANOLA, MS

Buttermilk Waffles

2 cups sifted flour
1/2 cup shortening
2 cups buttermilk
2 large eggs
1 teaspoon salt
1 teaspoon soda
1 teaspoon baking powder

Sift all dry ingredients together, cut in shortening with pastry blender or fork. (DO NOT MELT). Best eggs until fluffy and add to buttermilk. Pour this mixture into flour and shortening mixture and stir just until mixed. Batter should be lumpy with particles of shortening. This makes 12 (4x4) very crisp waffles.

Mrs. Thomas G. Abernethy
OKOLONA, MS

Hot Cheese Planet Puffs

2 jars Old English cheese
1 egg
Red pepper to taste
1 1/4 sticks oleo
Loaf of thin sliced sand-
  wich bread

Have all ingredients room temperature. Process cheese, egg, red pepper, and oleo until well blended. Cut crust from bread. Make sandwiches spreading cheese mixture thin. Cut each sandwich in 3 strips and ice with cheese mixture. Refrigerate overnight. Bake in 350° oven 10 to 12 minutes. These freeze nicely.

Mrs. H. W. Ray
INDIANOLA, MS

Baked Chicken Salad Sandwiches

20 ounces boned chicken
6 chopped hard boiled eggs
1 cup sliced stuffed olives
4 tablespoons grated onion
1 1/2 cup mayonnaise
24 white sandwich bread
  slices, crust removed
  and cut in half
1 cup soft butter
1 (10 ounce) old English
  sharp cheese spread at
  room temperature

Day before: Mix chicken, eggs, olives, onion, mayonnaise. Trim crusts; butter half of bread; spread generously with chicken mixture. Top with remaining slices of bread. Blend remainder of butter with cheese to form smooth paste. Spread over tops of sandwiches; cover well with foil or Saran after placing on baking sheet.

Twenty minutes before serving heat thoroughly in 400° oven uncovered until hot and cheese begins to brown.

Katie Gooch
INDIANOLA, MS

Layered Hawaiian Loaf

1 loaf Hawaiian Bread
1 recipe favorite pimiento
  cheese
1 recipe Knorr spinach dip
1/2 pound shaved ham
  (baked ham)
1 carton cream cheese &
  pineapple

Slice round loaf of bread horizontally four times. Put shaved ham on bottom slice, pimiento cheese on the next, spinach dip on the next layer, and cream cheese and pineapple on the final layer. Top with final slice of bread. Refrigerate until ready to serve. Cut as you would a layer cake.

Linda Lee
HORSESHOE BAY, TX

Broiled Seafood Sandwich

6 ounces cream cheese
2 teaspoons lemon juice
1/4 teaspoon salt
4 ounces fresh crabmeat or
  1 can crabmeat
2 boiled eggs, chopped
1/2 teaspoon celery salt or
2 tablespoons finely
  chopped celery
3 whole buttered buns
6 tomato slices
Olives for garnish

Mix cream cheese, juice, salt, crabmeat, eggs, and celery. Lightly toast bun halves, top each with tomato slice and crab mixture and broil. Garnish with olives.

Mrs. John Hughes
GREENWOOD, MS

Two Different And Delicious Sandwiches

Bacon Sandwich:

1 pound bacon, cooked
  and chopped
1 bunch green onions and
  tops, chopped
3 cups mayonnaise

Mix and spread. Makes 20 sandwiches.

Olive Pepper Pecan Sandwich:

1 cup green pepper,
  chopped
1 cup ripe olives, chopped
1 cup pecans, chopped
1 cup mayonnaise, or less

Mix first three ingredients. Add enough mayonnaise to moisten and spread. Makes 16 sandwiches.

Adelaide Hunt
RUSTON, LA

Beverages

———□———

Café Brulot

1 (4-inch) cinnamon stick
12 whole cloves
Peel of 2 oranges, cut in
thin slices
Peel of 2 lemons, cut in
thin slivers
6 lumps sugar
8 ounces brandy
2 ounces curacao
1 quart strong black coffee

"Wine measurably drank, and in season, bringeth gladness to the heart, and cheerfulness to the mind." Ecclesiasticus 31:28

In a Brulot Bowl or chafing dish, mash cinnamon, cloves, orange and lemon peel, and sugar lumps with a ladle. Add brandy and curacao and stir together. Carefully ignite brandy and mix until sugar is dissolved. Gradually add black coffee and continue mixing until flame dies out. Serve in demitasse or brulot cups.

Herman De Cell
YAZOO CITY, MS

Kathleen Claiborne's Iced Coffee

2 quarts milk
2 quarts half and half
cream
2 ounce jar instant coffee
1 cup boiling water
1 tablespoon sugar
1/2 gallon coffee ice cream
Pinch of salt

Dissolve coffee in boiling water. Combine all ingredients, stir well and serve in mugs or punch cups.

Augusta C. Barnwell
GREENWOOD, MS

Buena Vista's Irish Coffee

Black coffee
3 sugar cubes
Jigger of Irish whiskey
Whipping cream

This recipe originated at Shannon Airport, Ireland and was brought back to Buena Vista, San Franciso.

Like the French Market in New Orleans, this is the place to go in San Francisco for all, whether enroute to the opera or out to sea as a fisherman.

Preheat glass with very hot water. Fill, let stand and empty. Fill glass 3/4 full of hot, black coffee before glass has cooled. Drop 3 cocktail cubes of sugar into coffee. Stir until dissolved completely. Add full jigger of Irish whiskey for correct taste and body. By pouring over a spoon, top with a head of lightly whipped whipping cream. Your Irish coffee is ready to enjoy. Serve to your guests while piping hot. (If you do not have coffee glasses, any stemmed glass may be substituted)

Arthur Clark, Jr.
INDIANOLA, MS

Champagne Punch

6 bottles sauterne wine
2 large bottles soda
Sweeten with simple syrup
  (2 cups sugar to 1 cup
  water)
2 jiggers brandy or bour-
  bon
2 bottles champagne
2 cans peach halves (for
  decorating)

"If you drink anything containing alcohol, you can drink nothing better, as Thomas Jefferson told you long ago, and every intelligent doctor will tell you today, than a good light wine, red wine especially diluted with water, through-out the meal, with perhaps a small wine glass pure at the end. The French take that because 'it keeps the blood in the stomach where it is needed for digestion for at least half an hour after the end of a meal." Arthur Brisbane.

Makes 2 1/2 gallons.

Lucy Fisher
INDIANOLA, MS

Frostee Fruit Punch

6 packages lemon-lime
  Kool-aid
6 quarts water
3 cups sugar
2 large cans frozen lemon-
  ade
4 cans water
5 large cans pineapple juice
2 large cans orange juice
5 bottles of ginger ale

Combine all ingredients except ginger ale. Freeze in 5 (1 gallon) jars. Thaw about 3 hours before serving. Add one bottle of gingerale to each gallon. 140 (4 ounce) servings.

Mrs. Leslie Fletcher
INDIANOLA, MS

Milk Punch

1 1/4 ounce bourbon or
  brandy
3 ounces breakfast (light)
  cream or milk if you
  prefer
1 teaspoon super-fine
  powdered sugar
1 dash vanilla
Nutmeg

A great football weekend reviver!

Shake thoroughly ingredients which have been place in a shaker. Strain into an 8 ounce highball glass, and top with nutmeg.

Jimmy Lear
INDIANOLA, MS

Shaw Punch

2 ounces citric acid
2 quarts boiling water
4 quarts cold water
7 cups sugar
1 can frozen orange juice
  (small)
1 big can pineapple juice

This has been used over and over during the stage of life when quantity was important for school children.

Pour boiling water over acid to dissolve. Add sugar, cold water and juices. Freeze to a mush or frappe stage. Serves 50.

Mrs. Jimmy Simpson
SHAW, MS

Virginia Punch (150 Years Old)

6 lemons
1 pint Jamaican rum
1 pint good bourbon
1 1/2 pounds granulated
  sugar
3 cups strong green tea

Squeeze juice from lemons over sugar. Add cold tea. Remove seeds but leave the rinds of the lemons. Let stand two (2) hours. Strain through cheese cloth. Add spirits. Makes 5 pints. Bottle and put on ice.

Member of Church of Nativity
GREENWOOD, MS

Mrs. Johnson's Recipe for Spiced Tea

6 teaspoons tea
2 cups boiling water
1 small can frozen lemon
  juice
1 small can frozen orange
  juice
1 1/2 cups sugar
2 quarts water
1 stick of cinnamon

Pour water over tea and let cool. Strain and add lemon juice, orange juice, sugar and cinnamon. Simmer mixture for 20 minutes. If too strong, add water. Add extra sugar to taste. This recipe makes 16 to 20 cups.

L. B. J. RANCH, STONEWALL, TX

Laura Richards, 1860 Eggnog

8 large eggs
8 rounding tablespoons
  granulated sugar
1/2 cup thick cream,
  whipped
1 cup good whiskey

To each egg allow a rounding tablespoon of granulated sugar, 2 tablespoons of good whiskey, 1 tablespoon of thick sweet cream. Separate the eggs; beat the yolks until thick and lemon colored. Add the sugar gradually and beat until the grains of the sugar are dissolved. Pour the whiskey very slowly over the well beaten yolks and sugar, beating well. Then stir in the thick whipped sweet cream and, last, fold in the stiffly beaten whites. Do not stir them but fold in gently. The whites must be beaten until the dish can be inverted without their slipping. When ready to serve (the nog should not stand many minutes), fill the glasses and top them with whipped cream and a slight sprinkling of grated nutmeg. Be sure to mix the egg whites thoroughly but gently with eggnog. The cream must be whipped to stiff froth.

This recipe makes eight glasses 1/2 pint, cooking school size. If you prefer the "Nog" weaker, add more cream, whipped or unwhipped, but be sure it is thick and sweet.

Josephine Early Pickens
INDIANOLA, MS

Overnight Eggnog

16 egg yolks
12 tablespoons sugar
1 quart whiskey
1 quart cream

Beat egg yolks until stiff; add sugar and beat well (no whites). Add whiskey, slowly. Fold in stiffly beaten cream and refrigerate overnight. (To be eaten with a spoon.)

Mrs. J. P. Fisher
JONESTOWN, MS

Syllabub

5 cups whipping cream
1 cup of sherry
1 cup sugar (scant cup), sifted
3 lemons (juice and grated rind of lemons)

To 5 cups whipping cream add 1 cup sherry, cup of sugar and the juice of 3 lemons. Grate the yellow rind of lemons before squeezing. Whip the cream with above ingredients until stiff. Put into syllabub cups and serve. You may add a large teaspoon of vanilla, if desired. Garnish with nutmeg.

Variation: 1 cup sweet wine or 1 cup madeira wine instead of sherry.

"This was my grandmother's recipe brought to Altorf Plantation when she came as a bride in 1840."

Chancellor and Mrs. Jim Thames
ALTORF PLANTATION, VICKSBURG, MS

Bayou Bouillon

2 parts Vodka
3 parts beef bouillon
Dash lemon juice
Dash Tabasco
Dash Worcestershire sauce
Salt and pepper to taste

Mix and serve over ice.

Ed Gooch
INDIANOLA, MS

Black Russian

1 jigger Vodka
1 jigger Kahlua

Stir and serve over ice.

Morris Lewis, Jr.
INDIANOLA, MS

Bloody Mary

1 1/2 cans V-8 juice
  (1 quart, 14 ounce size)
Fifth of vodka
4 ounces Worcestershire
  sauce
3/4 cup lemon juice
6 shakes of Tabasco
Celery salt

Mix all ingredients except celery salt. Shake celery salt over drink; celery salt on top of drink is secret of its success.

W. C. Speer, Jr.
INDIANOLA, MS

Colonial Wars Cocktail

2 quarts whiskey
Peel of 3 lemons
Peel of 3 oranges
2 tablespoons Angostura
  bitters
8 or 9 ounce grenadine
  (about 2/3 of 12 ounce
  bottle)

This is an old recipe from Charleston, S. C. and is delicious.

Chop the outer yellow peel fine. Bruise as much as possible and let soak in whiskey for 6 to 8 hours (no longer). Be sure not to include any of the inner skin of the lemon or oranges. Filter. Combine with grenadine and bitters. Shake in cocktail mixer with ice and serve, or if served in a punch bowl, add 1 quart of dry ginger ale and ice.

Mrs. Vassar Hemphill
PALOMA PLANTATION, GREENWOOD, MS

Julep Time in the Mississippi Delta

Anywhere in the Delta—
Anytime between noon and midnight,—
from May to September

Take 1 rounded teaspoon
   granulated sugar
2 teaspoons water
Add 1 1/2 to 2 jiggers aged
   quality bourbon
3-4 sprigs freshly cut mint
   at least 4 - 5" long (use
   extreme care not to
   bruise sprigs).

Stir vigorously until sugar dissolves. Place mint sprigs into mixture in refrigerator and allow to bleed for thirty minutes. Discard mint. Pour in prepared mixture, stirring vigorously with silver spoon to frost goblet. Add ice to goblet brim and garnish with mint sprig.

Sip your julep slowly. Let its aroma permeate your soul and be at peace with the world... yes, those were the days!

Colonel Rebel

Mississippi Gambler

12 lemons (juice of)
4 cups quality bourbon
   whiskey
4 cups water
1 cup sugar

Extract juice. Reserve 8 lemon rinds. Combine lemon juice, whiskey, water, and sugar, stirring well. Add 8 rinds and pour mixture into an old fashioned churn or crock (caution: do not use a metal container). After 24 hours, squeeze rinds and remove. Strain. Mixture improves with passage of time. Two days before serving place in deep freeze. When ready to serve, scoop out iced slush (it will not freeze) into silver julep cups; garnish with mint leaves and use cocktail straw. Yield: Enough for 4 drinking Southern gentlemen or 16 nice ladies!

Arthur Clark, Jr.
INDIANOLA, MS

Old-Fashioned

1 1/2 ounces bourbon
1 to 1 1/2 teaspoons sugar
  water
1/2 inch thick orange slice
  (six pieces to orange)
Dash bitters
1/2 teaspoon cherry juice
Crushed ice
Top with one stemmed
  cherry

Sugar Water: All the sugar that can be dissolved in 2 pints of water with gentle heat–cool.

Secret of drink: Muddle orange slice well into the liquid mixture.

Bill Ross
INDIANOLA, MS

Plantation Stirrup Cup

1 jigger quality bourbon
1/4 jigger Grand Marnier
1/2 jigger brandy

Stir. Pour over crushed ice in old fashioned glasses. Sip...do not worry...it will all work out!

Waldemar Prichard
INVERNESS, MS

Sazerac Cocktail

1 lump sugar
1 dash Angostura bitters
2 dashes Peychaud bitters
1 1/4 ounces straight rye
  whiskey (90 proof)
3 dashes absinthe
Twist of lemon peel

To mix a Sazerac requires 2 Old Fashioned glasses. One is filled with ice and allowed to chill. In the other put sugar with just enough water to moisten. Then crush with bar spoon or muddler. Add Angostura and Peychaud bitters, rye and ice cubes and stir to mix and chill. Empty the ice from the first glass, dash in the absinthe, twirl to thoroughly coat inside of glass, and discard excess. Strain whiskey-bitters mixture into absinthe-coated glass, and add twist of lemon peel. Serve without ice.

Janie Dale
GREENWOOD, MS

Whiskey Sours

1 quart water
5 lemon rinds
1 cup sugar
1 pint lemon juice
1 1/2 quarts whiskey

"The Yawin' and Pitchin' Variety"

Boil rinds in sugar and water 5 minutes. Cool. Remove rinds. Add remaining ingredients. Put in freezer overnight. This will not freeze solid. Serve as slush in champagne glasses. It is very potent. Serves 10 to 20.

Jimmy Failing
INDIANOLA, MS

Jellies, Pickles and Relishes

—□—

Blackberry or Strawberry Jam

Wash berries and then cap. To 1 measure of berries put 2 measures of sugar. (For example: 10 cups berries to 20 cups sugar). If berries are not very acid use less sugar. Mix together and let stand until syrup forms. Place on stove and stir often. When it comes to a rolling boil, let boil 10 minutes. Take off and cool. Stir occasionally. Pack in one-pint sterilized jars.

Mrs. W. H. Harper
GREENWOOD, MS

Fig Preserves

Select firm, ripe figs. Peel. Place figs in large boiler over low heat. Add 1 pint of sugar for each pint of figs with 1 tablespoon water per pint. When sugar has dissolved, increase heat and cook until figs are transparent (about 10 minutes). For each pint of figs 2 slices of lemon may be added if desired. Pack in clean, hot jars, cover with syrup, and seal.

Corine Sellers
INDIANOLA, MS

Pear Honey

1 quart shredded or grated
  pears
1 to 2 (no. 2) cans crushed
  pineapple
1 1/2 pounds sugar or
1 pound sugar and
1 bottle Karo

Drain thoroughly the juice from shredded pears and add other ingredients. Cook until transparent and pack in jars. Seal.

Mrs. Allen Puckett
COLUMBUS, MS

Pepper Jelly

1 cup ground sweet pepper,
  green and red
2 pods hot pepper, ground,
  green or red
1 1/2 cups cider vinegar
6 cups sugar
1 or 2 drops green food
  color in vinegar
1 bottle Certo

Mix all ingredients; bring to a rolling boil. Remove from heat and let stand for 30 minutes. Put back on heat and let come to a full boil for 2 minutes. Pour in bottle of Certo. Stir for 5 minutes. Pour up and let set; then seal with paraffin.

Mrs. H. G. Fisher
INDIANOLA, MS

Sunkist Strawberry Preserves
(Brought from Tennessee many years ago).

4 cups strawberries
4 cups sugar

Wash and cap berries. Place sugar and berries in heavy boiler and leave until juice has formed. Boil vigorously for ten minutes. Pour into very shallow pans and place in the sun (plastic may be placed over the berries to protect them). Leave for days directly in the sun until the sauce is thick and they retain their bright red color. Place in jars and seal.

Mrs. Millicent L. Prichard
INVERNESS, MS

Chow-chow Pickle

1 gallon chopped green
   tomatoes
1 cup salt
1 gallon cabbage, shredded
1/2 cup hot pepper (red
   and green)
1 quart onions, finely
   chopped
1 pint celery
3 pounds sugar
5 tablespoons dry mustard
2 tablespoons ginger
1 tablespoon cloves
2 tablespoons tumeric
1 tablespoon cinnamon
1 cup white mustard seed
White vinegar

Chop green tomatoes fine. Cover tomatoes with salt. Let set for one hour. Squeeze all salt out of tomatoes. Add other ingredients; cover with vinegar and cook for forty-five minutes. Seal in hot sterilized jars.

Mrs. A. B. Clark
YAZOO CITY, MS

Kosher Dill Pickles

Cucumbers
1 tablespoon salt
3 tablespoons vinegar
1 teaspoon pickling spice
1 tablespoon mustard seed
1/2 hot green or 1/2
   teaspoon crushed red
   pepper
1 or 2 cloves garlic, cut in
   half
Fresh green dill (some top
   and some stem)

Sterilize quart jars. Into each jar put all ingredients. Wash cucumbers thoroughly, using a vegetable brush. Pack freshly picked cucumbers into jars. Pack tightly (preferably small ones). Cover with boiling water to the neck of jar–never any further as the brine begins to work and will sometimes seep. Seal tightly at once. Always use new lid inserts. Turn jars upside down for a few hours to see if they are not leaking and are thoroughly sealed. These pickles can be kept for months, but are usually ready to be eaten in 10 days.

Mrs. Raymond Goff
ROME, GA

Garlic Pickles

1 gallon sour pickle
1 whole crown of garlic
  pods
5 pounds sugar
1 box pickling spice

Drain vinegar from pickle. Slice pickle in 1/2 inch slices in jar. Put layer of sugar, layer of pickle. Spice and garlic pods between each layer. Let pickles set for two weeks.

Mrs. Leroy Deavenport
GREENVILLE, MS

Mama's Peach Pickle

1 bushel peaches
1 gallon and 1 quart
  brown cider vinegar
2 cups water
1 1/2 to 2 tablespoons salt
  (according to sweetness
  or acidity of peaches)
1 teaspoon powdered
  cinnamon
1/2 teaspoon allspice
10 to 12 pounds white
  sugar (2 pounds save)
6 sticks cinnamon
3 whole cloves to each
  peach

Peel peaches. Be sure they are firm, either free-stone or cling peaches. Cling make firmer pickles but freestone are easier to eat. Stick 3 whole cloves in each peach.

Place all ingredients in large kettle except peaches and reserve 2 pounds sugar, 1/2 tablespoon salt to add if necessary according to taste. cook sugar, water, spices (tied in cheesecloth, reserve 1/2 tablespoon), salt until syrup begins to thicken a little. Add as many peaches (with cloves stuck in) as practical to handle. Cook until peaches soften (but still firm) and slightly clear—not dark.

Fill sterilized jars with peaches, removed from kettle with a slotted spoon to drain.

Cook juice down a little, then thin liquid and add rest of peaches. Cook as before. When jars are filled then pour over peaches to fill all jars. Seal and store. (The extra 2 pounds of sugar and 1/2 tablespoon salt are to be added if needed, according to taste). Yield: 16-18 quarts.

Florence Sillers Ogden
ROSEDALE, MS

Oil Pickles

50 cucumbers
1 quart small white onions
1 ounce white mustard
  seed
2 cups salt
White cider vinegar
1 ounce celery seed
1/2 ounce ground pepper
1 pint olive oil

Slice unpeeled cucumbers and peeled onions thinly into large bowl, putting salt over each layer. Let stand 3 hours and drain. If too salty, rinse in cold water. Place in layers in stone jar sprinkling spice mixture over each layer and part of oil. When all is used, cover with vinegar. After 2 weeks, seal in jars.

Mrs. James O. Eastland
DODDSVILLE, MS

Ripe Tomato Pickle

1 gallon chopped ripe
  tomatoes
1 gallon chopped cabbage
1 quart chopped onions
6 chopped bell peppers
6 chopped hot peppers
1 cup salt
3 pounds sugar
1/2 gallon vinegar
2 tablespoons ground
  mustard
2 tablespoons ginger
1 tablespoon tumeric
1 tablespoon celery seed
1 tablespoon cloves
  (ground)
1 tablespoon cinnamon

Pour salt over vegetables and drain in bag for two hours.

Combine remaining ingredients and boil 20 minutes in open kettle. Seal in jars.

Mrs. John C. Lake
INDIANOLA, MS

Watermelon Rind Pickles

7 pounds watermelon rind
7 cups sugar
2 cups vinegar
1/2 teaspoon oil of cloves
1/2 teaspoon oil of cinnamon

Cover rind with water and cook until tender. Make a syrup of vinegar, sugar, oil of cloves and oil of cinnamon. Cook for five minutes.

Drain water off the watermelon rind and pour hot syrup over rind and cover. Drain syrup off the rind and heat syrup for 2 days. The third day, heat rind and syrup together. Put in jars and seal.

Mrs. Robinet W. Tredway
RICHMOND, VA

Florida Beans

3/4 cup salad oil
1/2 cup (scant) sugar
3 cans vertical pack green
  beans
3/4 cup vinegar
5 cloves garlic

Drain beans. Pack in jars or dish. Simmer other ingredients 5 minutes. Pour boiling liquid over beans. Cover tightly. Next day drain, boil liquid again - pour over beans. Cool. Refrigerate. Keeps well.

Mrs. Bill McKamy
GLEN ALLAN, MS

Cucumber Catsup

Cucumbers
Onion
Salt
Black and red pepper
White mustard seed
Horseradish
Vinegar
Sugar
Tumeric

Grate the cucumbers and sprinkle with salt. To every 3 dozen cucumbers grate 1/2 dozen large onions and a little horseradish. Press the cucumbers after they are grated until all the water is out. Save the water and measure. Add to pulp as much vinegar as there is water. Add sugar and a little tumeric, season with black and red pepper and white mustard seed. Mix thoroughly. Put in bottles and cork tight.

This recipe comes from a cookbook dated May, 1905, belonging to Sue Garrard Kennan.

Charlotte Garrard Paty
GREENWOOD, MS

Chutney

This recipe is excellent poured over a bar of softened cream cheese and served with crackers. It is also a fine relish for any number of meat or vegetable dishes.

10 pears, diced fine
3/4 pound seedless raisins
2 1/2 cups dark brown
  sugar
3 tablespoons ground
  ginger
1 1/2 teaspoons salt
1 clove of garlic, minced
2 cups cider vinegar
1 small piece of ginger root

Combine all ingredients and simmer slowly about forty minutes until fruits are tender and syrup is thick. Pour into hot pint jars, leaving 1/4 inch of head space. Adjust caps. Process 10 minutes in a boiling water bath. Recipe may be halved if less is desired. Makes 8 pints.

Tom Barron
INDIANOLA, MS

Cranberry Chutney

1 cup sugar
1 onion, chopped
1 clove garlic, chopped
6 whole cloves
1 teaspoon cinnamon
2 cardamom seeds, peeled
  and crushed
Generous dash cayenne
  pepper
1/4 teaspoon ground
  ginger
1/2 teaspoon salt
1/4 cup vinegar
2 cups fresh cranberries
1 cup seedless raisins
1/3 cup brown sugar

Combine first 9 ingredients with 1 cup water; simmer 5 minutes. Add rest of ingredients and simmer gently 10 to 12 minutes. Serve chilled. Makes 2 pints.

Mrs. R. E. Davisson
VAN NUYS, CA

Jellied Cranberry Relish

2 oranges, quartered and
  seeded
1 quart cranberries
1 1/2 cup sugar
2 envelopes unflavored
  gelatin
1 1/2 cups bottled cran-
  berry cocktail juice

Put orange quarters and cranberries through food chopper, using medium blade. Add sugar and mix well. In sauce pan, sprinkle gelatin on the cranberry juice to soften. Place over low heat, stirring constantly, until gelatin is dissolved. Remove from heat, stir into orange-cranberry relish. Turn into mold. Chill until firm.

Mrs. Jamie Whitten
CHARLESTON, MS

Ginger Mint Relish

1 cup washed, fresh mint
  leaves, packed
1/4 inch slice peeled fresh
  ginger root or
2 tablespoons chopped
  preserved ginger
1 1/2 cups dark raisins,
  rinsed and drained
1/4 cup Indian pickle relish
1 teaspoon shredded
  orange peel
Few drops lemon or
  orange juice

Grind mint leaves, raisins, and ginger together. Stir in pickle relish, orange peel, and lemon or orange juice. Chill for several hours. Marvelous relish with lamb! Yield: 1 pint.

Mrs. Charles O. Dean
LELAND, MS

Pear Relish

2 quarts coarsely ground
  pears
6 large onions
6 large bell peppers
1 hot pepper
6 dill pickles
1/2 cup salt
1 quart vinegar
2 tablespoons dry mustard
1 tablespoon tumeric
1 tablespoon flour
1 tablespoon celery seed
Cayenne pepper

Grind pears, onions, peppers and dill pickles and cover with 1/2 cup salt. Let stand overnight. Squeeze dry and add to the hot mixture made of the vinegar and other ingredients. Mix well: bring to a boil and boil 5 minutes. Put into clean jars and seal. Makes 7 pints.

Mrs. W. R. Gwin
INDIANOLA, MS

Sauerkraut Relish

1 can sauerkraut
1 cup onion, chopped
1 cup celery, chopped
1 green pepper, chopped
1 small jar pimientos
  (optional)
1 cup sugar
1/3 cup oil
1/4 - 1/3 cup vinegar

Drain sauerkraut. Combine sugar, oil, vinegar. Pour over vegetables and marinate overnight or longer. Keeps several weeks in refrigerator.

Joan Griffin
RICHMOND, VA

Cakes and Toppings

Angel Food Cake Dessert

1 tablespoon or envelope
  Knox gelatin
2 tablespoons water
3/4 cup Hershey chocolate
  syrup
8 English toffee, or 8
Heath bars, crushed
1 pint whipping cream
1 Angel Food cake

Dissolve gelatin in hot water. Add to syrup. Cool and fold in crushed Heath bars and whipped cream (not too stiff). Tear cake into small pieces. Place in 9" x 13" pyrex dish and pour mixture over cake pieces. Let refrigerate at least 2 hours or over night. Cut in squares and serve.

Mrs. C. K. Holland
COLUMBUS, MS

Ambrosia or Wedding Cake

Mrs. McClatchey is well known for her wedding cakes.

1/2 cup shortening
1 cup sugar
3 1/2 cups cake flour
3 teaspoons baking powder
1/2 teaspoon salt
1 1/2 cups ice water
1 teaspoon coconut
flavoring
1/2 teaspoon lemon
flavoring
1/2 teaspoon orange
flavoring
4 egg whites (room temp.)
and 1 cup sugar

Cream shortening and 1 cup sugar. Sift, measure, and resift dry ingredients. Alternate with ice water and mix into creamed mixture. Add flavoring. Beat whites stiffly adding 1 cup sugar; fold this into cake mixture. Bake in two 9" pans 30 minutes at 350°.

For frosting and decorating:

1 cup shortening
3 pounds confectioners'
sugar
6 unbeaten egg whites
1 teaspoon coconut
1 teaspoon orange
1 teaspoon lemon flavoring

For AMBROSIA CAKE fill with favorite ambrosia and ice with boiled icing. Sprinkle with coconut.

For WEDDING CAKE the above recipe will fill two 9" or two 8" or one 14" or 1-6" plus 1-10" pans. Cover tops of layers with pineapple preserves, stewed apples or some fruit that will not spoil quickly. This icing can be adjusted for desired consistency with water or sugar. Dip knife in hot water to smooth after icing. The same mixture may be tinted and used for decorating and used in pastry tube. Also keeps well in the refrigerator.

Mrs. Bill McClatchey
SUNFLOWER, MS

Green Apple Cake with Cream Cheese Icing

2 cups sugar
1/2 cup strong black coffee
1 1/2 cup oil
4 eggs well beaten
2 teaspoons cinnamon
1/2 teaspoon all spice
1/2 teaspoon ground cloves
1/2 teaspoon nutmeg
1 teaspoon salt
2 teaspoons baking powder
1 teaspoon baking soda
3 cups flour
1 cup raisins (dredged in 2
    tablespoons flour)
3 cups raw apples (sour
    and firm) chopped fine

Mix together sugar, coffee, eggs, oil, and dry ingredients, add raisins and apples. Bake in 1 1/2 to 2 inch cake pans at 350° about 30 minutes.

Cream cheese icing:

1 (8 ounce) package cream
    cheese
3/4 stick butter
1 pound box powdered
    sugar
1 tablespoon vanilla

Beat cheese and butter together. Add vanilla, then beat in sugar until light. Ice cake and put in cool place to set up.

This cake freezes well. It can be baked in a tube pan as a pound cake.

Mrs. Honey Morris
INDIANOLA, MS

Applesauce Cake Elaine

1 cup butter
2 cups sugar
2 cups applesauce
2 teaspoons soda (dissolved
  in small amount of
  water)
1/2 teaspoon lemon and
  vanilla flavoring
4 cups sifted cake flour
2 cups nut meats
2 cups raisins
1 cup bourbon
2 teaspoons each: cloves,
  cinnamon, nutmeg

Flour the nut meats and raisins. Mix all ingredients thoroughly in a very large mixing bowl. Grease and flour pans. This will make either one cake in a large tube pan or two loaf pans. Bake at 325°.

Mrs. Robert M. Randall
INDIANOLA, MS

Apricot Lemon Cake

1 box yellow cake mix
4 eggs
3/4 cup apricot nectar or 1
  large jar apricot baby
  food
3/4 cup oil
1 tablespoon lemon extract

Icing:
1 1/2 cups confectioners
  sugar
2 lemons grated, rind and
  juice

Combine ingredients. Pour in greased and floured bundt pan. Bake at 325° for 45 minutes. Cool 5 minutes. Turn out on plate. Poke holes with a fork and spoon icing over hot cake.

Mimi Alexander
INDIANOLA, MS

$100 Chocolate Cake

2 cups sugar
1/2 cup butter or oleo
2 eggs
2 cups all-purpose flour
2 teaspoons baking powder
1/2 teaspoon salt
1 teaspoon vanilla
4 ounces square chocolate
  (melted and cooled)
1 1/2 cups sweet milk
3/4 cup nut meats

Cream sugar and butter, add beaten eggs and chocolate. Sift together flour, baking powder, and salt. Add alternately with milk. Add chopped nuts and vanilla. Bake in two 9" layer pans at 350° about 20 to 25 minutes, or bake in tube cake pan for 45 minutes.

Icing:

1 1/2 ounces square
  chocolate, melted
1/4 cup butter or marga-
  rine
1 teaspoon salt
Confectioners' sugar
  (almost a 1 pound box)
1 tablespoon vanilla
1 tablespoon lemon juice
1 egg

Combine butter with melted chocolate then add egg, beat until smooth; add vanilla, lemon juice, and sugar.

I usually put cake in refrigerator over night. It seems to be much better.

Joan Hughes
INVERNESS, MS

Chocolate Sheet Cake

2 cups sugar
2 cups flour
1/2 teaspoon salt
1 stick oleo
1/2 cup Crisco
3 tablespoons cocoa
1 cup water
2 eggs
1/2 cup buttermilk
1 teaspoon vanilla
1 teaspoon baking soda

Bring to a boil and pour over dry ingredients. Mix well and add 2 eggs and 1/2 cup buttermilk to which 1 teaspoon soda has been added and 1 teaspoon vanilla. Mix well and pour into greased and floured pan about 11 inches by 15 inches. Bake 20 minutes in 350° oven. When cake has been baking 15 minutes start to prepare icing.

Icing:

1 box powdered sugar
3 tablespoons cocoa
1 stick oleo
6 tablespoons sweet milk
1 teaspoon vanilla
1 cup chopped nuts

In saucepan put 1 box powdered sugar, 3 tablespoons cocoa, 1 stick oleo, 6 tablespoons milk, 1 teaspoon vanilla and 1 cup chopped nuts. Melt over heat but do not boil. Pour over cake while hot. Do not take cake from pan until it has been cut in squares.

Mrs. Dozier Lester
INVERNESS, MS

Lemon Fruit Cake

1 pound butter (no substitute)
2 cups sugar
1 quart broken pecan meats
1 pound white raisins
3 cups flour
6 eggs (separated)
1 teaspoon soda (level measure)
1 tablespoon warm water
1 (2 ounce) bottle lemon extract

Cream butter and sugar. Add beaten egg yolks. Add raisins and nuts to 1/2 cup flour. Add flour to butter, sugar and egg mixture. Then add raisins and nuts. Add soda, water, and extract. After all has been folded in then fold in the beaten egg whites (beaten to soft peaks). Bake in tube pans or 3 loaf pans. Use waxed paper or oiled brown paper on pan bottoms. Bake in 250° oven until light brown. I prefer loaf pans.

Mrs. Milton Barnett
INDIANOLA, MS

White Fruit Cake

1/2 pound citron, candied
1/4 pound lemon peel, candied
1/4 pound orange peel, candied
1 (6 ounce) glass apple brandy
1 pound crystallized cherries
1 pound crystallized pineapple
1/2 pound black walnuts
1/4 pound English walnuts
2 pounds white seedless raisins
1 pound almonds
1 1/2 dozen eggs
1 1/2 pounds sugar
1 1/2 pounds flour
1 1/2 pounds butter

Flour all fruits and nuts with extra flour. Cream butter and sugar. Add eggs one at a time (beaten well); then add flour and brandy alternately. Add floured fruits. Bake in a very slow oven about 4 hours at 200° or 250°.

Pour a cup of sherry wine over each cake and let set over night after the cakes are cold. This recipe makes 3 good size cakes.

Mrs. Robinet W. Tredway
RICHMOND, VA

Coffee Cake

Quick and easy for weekend guests.

1 cup sugar
1/2 cup butter, creamed
2 eggs, separated
1 1/4 cup cake flour
1 teaspoon baking powder
1/4 teaspoon salt
1/3 cup milk
1 teaspoon vanilla (optional)

Mix egg yolks with all ingredients. Add well beaten egg whites and mix. Spread into 9 x 13 inch greased pan.

Topping:
1 1/2 tablespoon flour
1/3 cup sugar
3 teaspoons cinnamon
1 cup chopped nuts
Butter

Mix flour, sugar, and cinnamon and sprinkle over cake. Cover with chopped nuts and dot with butter. Bake in 350° oven for 20–30 minutes.

Mrs. Alex Heathman
INDIANOLA, MS

Fudge Cakes

4 squares bitter chocolate,
   melted
4 eggs
2 cups sugar
2 sticks butter
1 cup flour
2 cups pecans, chopped
1 teaspoon vanilla
Pinch salt

Grease and flour 2 square cake pans. Cream butter and sugar and add eggs one at a time. Add chocolate. Mix flour with nuts and add to chocolate mixture. Add vanilla. Bake in 350° oven for 15 to 20 minutes. Let cool then cut into squares.

Mrs. Morris Lewis, Jr.
INDIANOLA, MS

Mother's Gingerbread

1 cup butter
1 cup sugar
3 eggs
1 cup thick molasses
3 cups cake flour, sifted
2 teaspoons soda
3/4 teaspoon cream of
   tartar
1 teaspoon ginger
1 teaspoon cinnamon
1 cup buttermilk

Cream butter and sugar. Add eggs and molasses. Sift dry ingredients together and alternating with butter, add to mixture. Pour in greased pan (size 14" x 10" x 2") and bake about 1 hour in 350° oven.

Gingerbread Topping

Bananas
Lemon juice
Whipped cream, divided

Make two layers of gingerbread. Slice bananas thinly, dip into lemon juice. Add to whipped cream and spread between layers. Top with plain whipped cream.

Mrs. Jack Montgomery, Jr.
INVERNESS, MS

Icebox Cake

1 pound butter
1 pound sugar
1 dozen eggs, separated
4 (1 ounce) squares chocolate, melted
1 pound nuts, chopped,
  lightly toasted
2 dozen macaroons
1/2 cup whiskey
1 1/2 dozen lady fingers

Cream butter and sugar for 20 minutes. Beat egg yolks for 6 minutes and add to sugar mixture. Pour in melted chocolate. Fold in stiffly beaten egg whites. Add nuts. Soak macaroons in whiskey. Lightly spray spring form pan with Pam. Place lady fingers around side of pan. Put layer of macaroons on bottom of pan. Add cake mixture and macaroons in alternate layers until pan is filled. Refrigerate.

Sylvia Patterson (Mrs. H. C.)
CLARKSDALE, MS

Jam Cake (Mrs. George Wilson's)

1 cup butter
2 cups sugar
4 egg yolks (beaten)
4 egg whites (beaten)
1/2 teaspoon nutmeg
1 cup sweet milk
3 cups sifted flour
2 teaspoons baking powder
3 teaspoons cinnamon
3 teaspoons allspice
1 cup jam

Cream butter and sugar and beat until fluffy. Alternate the flour (to which the dry ingredients have been added) with milk. Add the jam. Fold in stiffly beaten egg whites, and thick, lemony-beaten yolks. Grease and flour cake pans (2 large or 3 small) and bake 40 minutes in a 400° oven. Frost with caramel icing.

Mrs. Charles R. Harris
GREENWOOD, MS

Lady Baltimore Cake

1 cup butter
3 cups sugar
4 eggs
1 cup milk
3 1/2 cups cake flour
4 teaspoons baking powder
2 teaspoons vanilla
2 teaspoons almond
 extract
1/2 cup water

Frosting:

3 cups sugar
1 cup water
3 egg whites (stiffly
 beaten)
3 teaspoons corn syrup
2 cups seeded raisins
2 cups toasted pecans or
 walnuts
12 dried figs or chopped
Maraschino cherries
Almond and vanilla
 extract

In electric mixer, cream butter, and 2 cups of sugar added gradually and beat until the consistency of whipped cream. Add eggs, one at time, and beat thoroughly. Sift baking powder and flour 3 times and add alternately with milk, using a wooden spoon for blending. Bake in two 11" greased cake pans in 350° oven 30 minutes. Make a thick syrup of 1 cup sugar and 1/2 cup water. Flavor with almond and vanilla. Spread this over your layers as soon as you remove them from the pans.

Mix sugar, water and syrup. Cook until it forms a firm ball in cold water (250°). Pour gradually into the stiff egg whites, beating constantly. Now add raisins, pecans and figs and cherries, all cut finely. Raisins and figs may be soaked overnight in sherry or brandy, if desired. Add almond and vanilla extracts to taste. Spread between layers, on top and sides of cake.

This is a very flavorful and rich cake. Maraschino cherry juice may be added to the icing to make the cake a light pink.

Mrs. R. L. Morrison
HATTIESBURG, MS

Lemon Cup Cakes

6 eggs, beaten separately
2 cups sugar
1/2 lemon (rind and juice)
1/2 cup water, boiling
2 cups flour, sifted

Topping:
3 cups sugar
1 1/2 lemons (juice and rind)
2 oranges (juice and rind)

Beat egg yolks; add 2 cups sugar and beat together thoroughly. Add lemon juice and rind, water and flour. Fold in stiffly beaten egg whites. Use well-greased small muffin pans, filled 1/2 full. Bake in 450° oven about 5 or 6 minutes. Prepare topping night before baking if possible. Mix sugar, fruit juices, and rind together. Stir occasionally. While still hot, dip cakes in topping. After dipping, place cakes on wax paper.

Mrs. Sam Fowlkes
GULFPORT, MS

Lemon Dessert Cake

2 envelopes gelatin
1/2 cup cold water
8 egg yolks
1 cup lemon juice
2 cups granulated sugar
1 teaspoon salt
2 teaspoons finely grated lemon rind
8 egg whites
1 cup whipping cream
20 lady fingers

Soften gelatin in water. In double boiler combine 8 egg yolks, lemon juice, salt and 1 cup sugar. Cook over boiling water, stirring constantly, until mixture coats back of spoon. Into custard, stir softened gelatin and 2 teaspoons finely grated lemon rind. Cool.

In large bowl beat 8 egg whites until they hold shape. Gradually beat in the other cup of sugar until mixture holds peaks. Whip cream, and gently fold mixtures together. Line sides of 9 inch spring form pan with about 20 split lady fingers. Spoon in mixture and smooth on top. Refrigerate 8-12 hours. Remove side of pan and slide on plate. Pretty to serve at table. Serves 12.

Jean Kent E. Barron
BIRMINGHAM, MI

Milky Way Cake

4 Milky Way candy bars
2 sticks margarine
2 cups sugar
4 eggs
1 cup buttermilk
2 1/2 cups flour, sifted
1/4 teaspoon soda
2 teaspoons vanilla
1 cup pecans, lightly
　　toasted, chopped fine

Melt candy bars and 1 stick margarine over hot water. Let cool. Cream 1 stick margarine with sugar. Add eggs 1 at a time. Add buttermilk alternately with flour and soda. Fold in vanilla and nuts. Bake in greased, lightly floured Bundt pan, 1 1/2 hours at 300°.

Mrs. Norman Henke
INDIANOLA, MS

Miss Laura's Nut Cake

1 pound seedless white
　　raisins
2 quarts shelled whole
　　pecans
4 cups flour, divided
2 cups sugar
1/2 pound butter, not oleo
6 eggs
2 full teaspoons baking
　　powder
1 cup bourbon

Put raisins to soak in warm water 1 hour until they are soft. Drain. Mix the pecans well with the raisins and dredge with 1 cup of flour. Cream sugar and butter well. Add eggs, one at the time. Sift three cups flour with the baking powder and add slowly. Add the bourbon all at once, beating constantly to keep from cooking the mixture with it.

Add pecans and raisins last, mixing with hands. Press batter into a tube pan with two layers of waxed paper in bottom, top one of which has been greased along with rest of pan. Press especially well at side and around spout. Cover with another pan just fitting the cake pan. Place in 250° oven with skillet of water underneath to keep from burning and to steam. Cook 3 and 3/4 hours.

Shelby Grantham
JACKSON, MS

Aunt Elise's Orange Cake

1 cup shortening
2 cups sugar
3 cups flour
4 eggs
4 teaspoons baking powder
1 teaspoon salt
1 teaspoon vanilla
1/2 cup milk
1/2 cup orange juice
1/2 orange rind, grated

Cream shortening and sugar. Add eggs. Add sifted dry ingredients alternately with liquids. May add 2 to 4 tablespoons more liquid. Bake in 2 (9 inch) pans for 35 minutes at 375°. Fill with orange filling. Top with more filling or divinity icing. Seven minute frosting may be substituted.

Orange cake filling:

1 cup orange juice
1/2 orange rind, grated
1 cup sugar
1/2 cup flour
Pinch salt
2 egg yolks, beaten
2 tablespoons butter

Cook all ingredients except butter until thick and clear. Add butter. Cool. This is better with fresh orange juice. Will fill 2 layers.

Mrs. R. J. Allen, Jr.
INDIANOLA, MS

Plum Cake

2 jars of strained plum or
  prune baby food
2 cups self-rising flour
2 cups sugar
1 cup oil
3 eggs
1 teaspoon cinnamon
1 teaspoon cloves
1 cup chopped nuts,
  lightly toasted

Combine thoroughly all ingredients. Bake in tube pan 1 hour at 325°.

Mrs. W. B. Fletcher, Jr.
INDIANOLA, MS

Pineapple Cake

2 sticks butter
2 cups sugar
3 cups sifted cake flour
4 eggs
1 cup milk
3 teaspoons baking powder
1 tablespoon vanilla

Filling:
2 1/2 cups crushed pine-
    apple
3/4 cup sugar
1 egg
1 tablespoon flour or
    cornstarch
1 teaspoon butter
1/2 teaspoon vanilla

Topping:
7 Minute boiled white
    icing

Cream butter and sugar. Add eggs unbeaten - one at a time, and cream until well blended. Sift flour, baking powder and add alternately with milk; add flavoring. Bake in 3 - (9 inch) pans on 350° for about 20 minutes.

Mix sugar and flour; beat egg and pineapple. Cook until thick, stirring often (about 10 minutes). Remove from heat and add butter and vanilla, then put between layers (but not on the top layer). Use 7 minute boiled white icing for topping cake.

Mrs. Armeen Weber, Jr.
YAZOO CITY, MS

Strawberry Meringue Cake

2 cups sifted cake flour
4 teaspoons baking powder
1/2 cup butter or marga-
  rine
1 1/4 cups sugar
5 egg yolks, well beaten
3/4 cup milk
1 teaspoon vanilla extract
1/3 cup confectioners'
  sugar
1/4 cup sugar
5 egg whites, stiffly beaten
1 quart fresh strawberries
1/2 cup sugar

Sift flour once, measure, add baking powder, and sift together 3 times. Cream butter; add 1 1/4 cups sugar gradually and cream together until light and fluffy. Add egg yolks and mix well. Add flour alternately with milk. Beat after each addition. Add vanilla extract. Bake in two greased 9-inch cake pans at 375° about 25 minutes. Remove from pans and cool.

Fold confectioners' sugar and 1/4 cup sugar slowly into beaten egg whites. Beat until stiff, but not dry. Place the two layers on a baking sheet. Pile meringue lightly on top of each layer and bake at 350° to brown (about 15 minutes).

Wash and hull the berries. Reserve a few choice ones for garnishing. Crush remaining berries with 1/2 cup sugar. Spoon between the layers. Garnish top with whole berries. Serve at once.

Moody Hall
BELZONI, MS

Perfect Pound Cake

2 sticks butter
1 stick oleo
1 pound sifted powdered
  sugar
1 sugar box sifted flour
1 tablespoon vanilla
6 large eggs

Cream shortening; add sifted powdered sugar and beat well. Add 2 eggs, flavoring and flour that has been sifted three times. Add remaining eggs, beating after each addition. Bake at 300°, one hour, or until done.

Mrs. Pattie M. Norris
INDIANOLA, MS

Mattie Belle's Sour Cream Pound Cake

1 cup soft butter (2 sticks)
2 2/3 cups sugar
6 eggs
3 cups sifted flour
1/2 teaspoon salt
1/4 teaspoon soda
1 cup sour cream
1 teaspoon vanilla

Cream butter and sugar until light. Add eggs one at a time, beating thoroughly after each. Sift dry ingredients 3 times and add alternately with sour cream to first mixture, beating until smooth. Add flavoring. Pour into 9" tube pan that has been greased. Bake in moderate oven (350°) 1 hour and 20 minutes. Let stand in pan on rack about 5 minutes.

This is delicious.

Mrs. B. W. Sory
INDIANOLA, MS

Beth's Chocolate Pound Cake

2 sticks butter
2 cups sugar
4 eggs
2 small cans Hershey
  syrup
1/2 teaspoon soda
1 cup buttermilk
2 1/2 cups cake flour
1/4 teaspoon salt
1 teaspoon vanilla
7 small Hershey bars,
  melted

Cream butter and sugar. Add eggs one at a time. Add 2 cans chocolate syrup. Add soda to buttermilk. Add flour, salt, and buttermilk, alternately. Last add melted Hershey bars and vanilla.

Bake in 325° oven for one hour in a tube or Bundt pan.

Mrs. Frank Crosthwait, Jr.
INDIANOLA, MS

Mrs. Wilson's Chocolate Pound Cake

4 sticks butter
3 cups sugar
5 eggs
3 cups cake flour
1/2 teaspoon salt
1/2 teaspoon baking
  powder
4 rounding tablespoons
  cocoa
1 cup milk
1 tablespoon vanilla

Sift together dry ingredients. Cream butter and sugar on high speed of mixer. Drop in whole eggs one at a time. Cut mixer down to low speed. Add dry ingredients alternating with milk. Add vanilla and pour into large greased tube pan. Bake 1 hour and 35 minutes in 325° oven.

Mrs. Jack Montgomery, Jr.
INVERNESS, MS

Queen Elizabeth Cake

1 cup dates
1 cup hot water
1 1/2 cups cake flour, sifted
1 teaspoon baking powder
1/4 teaspoon salt
1/4 cup butter
3/4 cup sugar
1 egg
3/4 teaspoon baking soda

Topping:
5 tablespoons butter
3 tablespoons cream
1/2 cup brown sugar,
  firmly packed
1 cup chopped nut meats

Cook dates and water until paste like. Start oven at 325°. Grease an 8" square cake pan and line with brown paper. Sift flour, baking powder, and salt together. Work butter until creamy, gradually work in sugar. Add unbeaten egg and beat in very well. Mix soda into cooled, cooked dates and stir into batter with dry ingredients. Pour into pan, bake 45 minutes or until done. While cake bakes, mix topping ingredients in saucepan and boil 3 minutes. When still warm, spread evenly on top of baked cake. Slide under broiler 4 inches from tip of flame or unit and broil 2 minutes. Cool in pan on rack. Freezes beautifully. Allow 2 1/2 to 3 hours to thaw.

Mrs. Charles Dean
LELAND, MS

Shortcakes

2 cups self-rising flour
8 tablespoons sugar
1/2 cup butter or butter
flavored shortening
2 beaten eggs
2/3 cup evaporated milk

Mix flour and sugar; cut in butter until mix is like coarse crumbs. Add eggs and milk; stir only to moisten. Bake in greased tart pans or 8-inch cake pan at 350° for 15 - 20 minutes. Makes 12 tarts. Great for strawberry shortcake. Freezes well.

Vickie Hester
INDIANOLA, MS

Slippery Sam Cake

1 1/2 stick butter
1 1/2 cups sugar
4 eggs
2/3 cups milk
1 teaspoon vanilla
2 1/2 cups flour
2 1/2 teaspoons baking
powder
1/4 teaspoon salt

Caramel icing:

2 3/4 cups sugar
1 cup flour
2 egg yolks
1 cup milk
1 teaspoon vanilla
1 stick butter

Cream butter and sugar; add whole eggs one at a time while beating; add combined milk and vanilla alternately with combined dry ingredients. Bake at 300° for 25 minutes in 2 layer pans. Ice with caramel icing.

Mix sugar (except for 3 tablespoons) with flour. Beat egg yolks well; add milk and flour, sugar mixture. Bring to a boil while browning the 3 tablespoons sugar. Add browned sugar to boiling mixture and cook to soft ball state (360°). Take from stove; add butter and vanilla. Cool, beat and spread.

Mrs. Hilliard Lawler
ROSEDALE, MS

Yellow Cake And Coconut Icing

1 cup shortening (butter)
2 cups sugar
3 cups sifted flour (do not pack or shake down)
3 teaspoons baking powder
1 teaspoon salt
4 eggs, separated
1 cup milk
2 teaspoons vanilla (or little less)

Icing:
1 1/2 cups sugar
1/2 cup water
1 teaspoon vinegar
1/4 teaspoon salt
3 egg whites
2 cups fresh coconut

Beat shortening until soft, gradually add sugar and beat until very light. Beat egg yolks until light and slightly thick. Add to sugar mixture. Blend well. Add vanilla.

When measuring flour, do not pack dry ingredients together. Add flour and milk alternately to first mixture. Mix well. Beat egg whites until they stand in peaks. Add to batter (fold in well).

Grease and flour (put oil paper in pan bottom) of 3 nine-inch cake pans. Bake at 350° for about 25 minutes.

I usually just use 2 layers for the cake because 3 makes the cake too tall. Give the third layer to children while hot.

Icing:
Cook the first four ingredients over medium heat until they spin a good thread. Egg whites must be at room temperature and must be beaten until stiff. Add salt. Turn mixture on highest speed and gradually pour sugar mixture over whites. Do not pour sugar mixture too fast or pause in beating. Spread between layers of cake and spread 1 cup of coconut over it. Put on top layer and sprinkle with remaining coconut. Keep in cool place.

Mrs. Louis Graeber
MARKS, MS

Easy Caramel Frosting

1 1/3 cups brown sugar
1/4 teaspoon salt
1/2 cup milk
3 tablespoons butter
1 teaspoon vanilla
3 cups powdered sugar,
  sifted

In heavy saucepan, combine brown sugar, salt, and milk; bring to a boil. Cook slowly for 5 minutes or until slightly thickened. Remove from heat and add butter and vanilla. Cool slightly. Add powdered sugar; beat until smooth or good consistency for spreading.

Mrs. J. P. Fisher, Jr.
INDIANOLA, MS

Quick Chocolate Icing

7 tablespoons milk
2 squares chocolate
1 1/2 cup sugar
1 tablespoon Karo
1 stick butter
1 teaspoon vanilla

In heavy saucepan, melt on low heat. Turn heat to high and when mixture begins to boil, cook 1 minute not stirring. Add 1 teaspoon vanilla and chill. Beat until thick.

Mrs. Francis Stevens
JACKSON, MS

Divinity Icing or Puffs

2 1/2 cups sugar
1/2 cup light corn syrup
1/2 cup water
2 stiffly beaten egg whites
1/2 teaspoon vanilla

Cook sugar, syrup and water to thin syrup stage. Slowly pour 1/3 of mixture over egg whites beating constantly. Using a candy thermometer, cook remaining syrup to 234°; add 1/2 of this to eggs, beating. Cook remaining syrup to 248° on the candy thermometer and add to egg mixture; add vanilla; beat until mixture holds shape and will drop from a spoon.

Mrs. Bill McClatchey
SUNFLOWER, MS

Lemon Icing

1 cup sugar
1/4 cup water
1 tablespoon butter
1/4 cup cornstarch
6 tablespoons lemon juice
1 teaspoon lemon peel
3 egg yolks
2 tablespoons milk
3 tablespoons cold water

Mix sugar, 1/4 cup water and butter in pan. Add cornstarch, and 3 tablespoons cold water. Cook slowly until clear, about 8 minutes. Add lemon juice, and lemon peel. Cook slowly, then add egg yolks, which have been beaten with milk. Stir constantly, and cook until spreading consistency.

Mrs. J. M. Gilbert
INDIANOLA, MS

Candies and Cookies

---□---

Chow Mein Candy Clusters

2 (6 ounce) packages
  butterscotch morsels
1 (3 ounce) can chow mein
  noodles
1 small can cocktail
  peanuts, optional

Melt butterscotch bits in double boiler until thoroughly dissolved, stirring constantly. Remove from heat and stir in chow mein noodles coating all carefully.

Add the peanuts and mix quickly.

Drop on wax paper with teaspoon.

Mrs. Anne Aden
MADISON, MS

Never-Fail Divinity

3 cups sugar
1 cup Karo
2/3 cup water
1 cup sugar
1/2 cup water
3 egg whites, beaten until
  stiff
1 teaspoon vanilla
1 cup chopped pecans

Cook sugar, Karo and water until it spins a thread. While this is cooking, beat egg whites in mixer until stiff.

Pour this first cooking in egg whites slowly. While you are pouring first cooking into egg whites start your second cooking of sugar and water until it forms a hard ball. Add to first mixture until almost stiff. Add vanilla and pecans. Drop on wax paper or foil, using two teaspoons.

Mrs. W. I. Hollowell
INDIANOLA, MS

Chocolate Fudge

4 cups sugar
3 squares unsweetened
  chocolate
4 tablespoons (heaping)
  white Karo
1 large can evaporated
  milk
3/4 cup boiling water
1/2 stick butter
1 teaspoon vanilla
3 cups chopped nuts

Combine first 5 ingredients and over "medium-hot" heat stir constantly, while rapidly boiling. Near end of cooking time lower heat while continuing to stir. When a "medium firm" ball forms in cold water, remove from heat. With a damp sponge, wipe away all sugar particles from the sides of the container. Pour into electric mixer bowl. Put in 1/2 stick butter and let stand (1 to 1 1/2 hours) until just warm. Beat mixture until it loses its glow and will not run. Add 1 teaspoon vanilla and 1 quart chopped nuts. Pour onto butter platter and cut before candy hardens.

Mary Steele Nabors
INDIANOLA, MS

Light Opera Fudge

2 cups sugar
2/3 cups sweet milk
2 tablespoons brown Karo
  syrup
1/2 stick butter
2 teaspoons vanilla flavoring
Pinch of salt
1 cup chopped nuts

Mix all above ingredients, except pecans, in a heavy boiler. Stir until mixture begins to boil. Boil slowly until candy thermometer registers soft ball stage. Set aside to cool. When luke warm beat by hand until creamy and begins to hold shape. Add nuts. Drop by teaspoon on waxed paper. Makes about 30 pieces.

Mrs. E. S. Van Cleve
INDIANOLA, MS

Glass Candy

"Fun for children to break apart."

2 heaping cups sugar
2/3 cup white karo
  syrup
1/2 cup water
1 teaspoon oil of
  cinnamon or pepper-
  mint (from a drug
  store)

Dissolve sugar and bring all ingredients to a boil. Cook until 300° on a candy thermometer. Add 1 teaspoon oil of cinnamon or peppermint (from a drug store) and a few drops of food coloring. Pour in a pie pan to cool. Crack with a knife handle.

Mimi Alexander

Crystallized Grapefruit Peel

2 grapefruit
1 teaspoon salt
3 cups sugar
1 teaspoon ginger and red
  food color or 1 teaspoon
  mint and green food
  color

Use the peel from two grapefruit. Cut into quarters and grate all of the hard yellow surface off. Wash and soak in salt water over night. (About 1 teaspoon of salt to 1 quart of water). Next morning, wash and soak again in clear, cold water about 2 hours. Wash again and then boil the quarters about 45 minutes, until tender. Press the water out gently and cut into small strips. Set aside. Boil 3 cups sugar and 1 cup of water. Add 1 teaspoon ginger and red food color or 1 teaspoon mint and green food color. When this has formed a syrup, add the strips of grapefruit peel. Boil until most syrup is absorbed. Remove strips and carefully roll in sugar. Dry on waxed paper.

Mrs. H. P. Sherrod
INDIANOLA, MS

Candied Orange Peel

1 1/2 cups sugar
3/4 cup water
3 large navel oranges
Powdered sugar or granu-
  lated sugar

Take off orange peeling in quarters. Cover with cold water and bring to a boil slowly. Boil several minutes then drain. Again cover with cold water and boil until tender. Drain and cut in strips.

Make sugar syrup and add orange strips. Cook until practically all liquid is absorbed. Lift out peel a few at a time and roll in powdered or granulated sugar.

Mary Steele Nabors
INDIANOLA, MS

Martha Washington Candy
Wonderful Christmas candy!

2 boxes powdered sugar
1 stick oleo
1 can sweetened condensed
  milk
1 can Baker's coconut
4 cups pecans, chopped
1 (12 ounce) Baker's semi-
  sweet chocolate chips
1 2" x 4" block paraffin

Mix sugar, butter, milk, coconut and pecans. Roll in small balls. Heat paraffin and chocolate chips in pan. Dip balls and place on wax paper to cool. The first mixture may be stored in the refrigerator and later dipped in chocolate.

Julia Alford
INDIANOLA, MS

Peanut Brittle

3 cups raw peanuts
2 cups sugar
2/3 cup white Karo
1/3 cup water
Small piece of paraffin
  (1/2" square)
2 teaspoons baking soda

Place all ingredients except soda in heavy sauce pan. Cook to 300° on candy thermometer. Remove from heat. Stir in soda. Pour onto buttered cookie sheet.

Mrs. Opie Little, Jr.
INDIANOLA, MS

Pecan Brittle

2 cups sugar
1/2 cup white Karo
1/4 cup water
3 cups pecans
1 teaspoon soda
1 teaspoon vanilla
2 tablespoons butter

Combine sugar, Karo, and water. Bring to a boil, then add pecans (broken or halved). Cook slowly until the syrup is brown. Remove from heat and add the other three ingredients. Pour as thinly as possible on to a well-greased cookie sheet. Allow to cool and then break into small pieces.

Mrs. H. P. Sherrod
LELAND, MS

Pralines

1 cup light brown sugar
1 cup sugar
5 tablespoons water
1 tablespoon butter
1/2 pound chopped pecans

Combine sugar, water, and butter. When mixture begins to boil rapidly, add pecans. Boil, stirring constantly, until mixture forms large bubbles on top and looks sugary. Remove from fire, drop by teaspoon on well buttered platter.

Mrs. Guy Price
LYON, MS

South Carolina Candy

1 stick butter
1 1/2 cups vanilla wafer
  crumbs
1 package chocolate chips
1 cup chopped pecans
1 cup shredded coconut
1 can condensed milk

Melt butter in oven in 6" x 9" or 8" x 8" baking pan. Add crumbs to make crust on the bottom. Add remaining ingredients in order, spreading evenly. Bake 350° for 30 - 35 minutes. Cool completely. Cut in squares. This is very rich.

Mrs. H. J. Munnerlyn
BENNETTSVILLE, SC

Almond Keifling (Cocoons)

2 sticks butter
8 tablespoons powdered
 sugar (1 or 2 more if
 necessary)
2 tablespoons water
2 tablespoons almond
 extract
2–3 cups cake flour
1–2 cups almonds (or
 pecans)

Cream butter, and sugar and water with extract. Work in flour to a crumbly state. Add finely chopped almonds or pecans. Roll into small cocoons. Bake at 200° until a little dry (not brown). Then turn into tray of powdered sugar and coat each cocoon well. Chill them and store in airtight container. Keeps well if hidden!

Mrs. Honey Morris
INDIANOLA, MS

Almond Crispies "Megthalota"

(Old Greek recipe)

2 pounds almonds
1 1/2 cups sugar
4 egg whites
2 tablespoons rose water

Mix finely chopped almonds and sugar. Beat egg whites until stiff and fold in the almonds and sugar. Blend together and add rose water.

Drop by teaspoon on a greased cookie sheet and bake in an oven 300° for 15 minutes. Makes approximately 25 - 30.

Mrs. R. M. Randall
INDIANOLA, MS

Bourbon Balls

2 1/2 cups crushed vanilla
  wafers
1 cup pecans
1 cup powdered sugar
2 tablespoons cocoa
3 tablespoons white Karo
1/4 cup bourbon

Grind vanilla wafers and pecans in food chopper and mix with cocoa and sugar. Stir Karo into bourbon and pour over dry ingredients. Mix until all is moistened and then shape into small balls and roll in powdered sugar.

Mrs. James O. Eastland
DODDVILLE, MS

Bourbon 'N Butter Cookies

1 cup butter
1 cup sugar
1 egg
3 cups sifted flour
1 tablespoon whiskey

Cream real butter and sugar. Add egg, flour, and whiskey. This will be stiff. Form small balls; place on cookie sheet. Press down with fork. Bake 12 to 15 minutes at 350°. Remove immediately. Yield 6 dozen.

Mrs. Don Shultz
METAIRIE, LA

Brown Sugar Brownies

1 1/2 sticks butter or
  margarine
1 box brown sugar
3 eggs
1 1/2 cups flour (self-rising)
1 package (6 ounce) chocolate chips
1 cup nuts, chopped,
  lightly toasted

Melt butter. Add brown sugar. Mix well and let cool. Add beaten eggs and mix well. Add flour, chocolate chips, and nuts. Bake in greased and floured pan in 350° oven for 25 or 30 minutes.

Mary Louise McGregor
INDIANOLA, MS

Brown Sugar Cookies

1 pound brown sugar
1 pound chopped pecans
1 pound butter
2 whole eggs
4 cups flour
1 tablespoon baking
   powder
1 tablespoon cinnamon

Mix thoroughly; roll in small roll and wrap in wax paper. Place in refrigerator until thoroughly chilled. Slice and bake on baking sheet until brown in 350° oven.

Mrs. Walter Sillers
ROSEDALE, MS

Mrs. Water's Chocolate Goodies

12 ounce sack of semi-
   sweet chocolate chips
4 tablespoons sugar
1 can condensed milk
1 stick butter (cut in
   pieces)
1 cup flour
1 cup chopped pecans
1 teaspoon vanilla

Melt in double boiler chocolate chips and sugar. Add milk and butter. Remove from heat and add flour, pecans, and vanilla. Stir and then let sit for 10 minutes. Drop by teaspoon on an ungreased cookie sheet. Bake at 350° for 10 minutes *exactly*. Remove promptly with a spatula and place on wax paper to cool. (The secret to these cookies is not to over bake.)

Louise Gresham
INDIANOLA, MS

Cream Puffs

1/2 cup butter
1 cup of boiling water
4 eggs
1 cup flour

Put butter in a saucepan and add the boiling water gradually, while stirring constantly. Place over heat and boil until butter is melted. Then add the flour at once and stir vigorously. Cook until mass is smooth and thick and does not stick to sides. Remove paste and allow to cool slightly. Then add unbeaten eggs one at a time, beating in each egg thoroughly. With a spoon or a pastry bag drop the mixture on a greased baking sheet 1 1/2 inches apart. Bake at 400° for 35 minutes. When cool split and fill with sweetened whipped cream.

Kathe Berge
INDIANOLA, MS

Danish Tart

1/2 pound butter
3 tablespoons sugar
2 1/2 cups plain flour
1/2 cup chopped ground
   pecans
1 teaspoon vanilla
Strawberry preserves

Blend butter and sugar, then flour. Then add other ingredients. Pinch off small pieces and roll into small balls. Put on a floured board and press indention in middle with thimble. Fill hole with strawberry preserves. Bake at 350° until brown.

Ann Gresham
INDIANOLA, MS

Date Bars

3 eggs, well beaten
1 cup sugar
1 teaspoon baking powder
1/2 teaspoon salt
1 cup flour
1/2 pound dates, cut fine
2 cups pecans, cut fine
1/2 teaspoon vanilla
Powdered sugar

Grease and flour a 9 inch pan and line with brown paper. Sift flour, baking powder and salt together and sift a little over nuts and dates.

Cream sugar and eggs well and gradually add the flour mixture. When well mixed add the nuts and dates with the vanilla and pour into the prepared pan. Bake at 325° until set in the middle. Remove from oven and turn out of the pan and cut into finger size strips and roll very lightly in powdered sugar.

Mrs. John C. Beard
INDIANOLA, MS

French Swiss Cookies

1/2 pound butter
1 cup sugar
1 egg separated
2 cups sifted flour
2 1/2 teaspoons cinnamon
Colored candies or ground
    nuts

Cream butter and sugar thoroughly. Beat in egg yolk and add flour and cinnamon and blend well. Roll pieces of the dough between buttered palms into 1 inch balls. Place balls on ungreased baking sheet about 2 inches apart. Press paper thin with floured spatula. Paint with egg white and sprinkle with colored candies or ground nuts. Bake 350° for 10 or 12 minutes. Yield: 6 dozen 2 1/2 inch cookies. 100 year Old Mississippi recipe.

Mrs. W. C. "Chuck" Trotter
INDIANOLA, MS

Fruit Cake Cookies

1 cup sugar
3 eggs
3/4 cup margarine
2 cups unsifted flour
1 teaspoon cinnamon
1/4 teaspoon nutmeg
1 scant teaspoon allspice
   (optional)
1 teaspoon soda
1 teaspoon baking powder
1 pound raisins
Pecans (1 pound or more)
Candied cherries (optional)

Mix all ingredients. Place by teaspoonful on cookie sheet and bake at 325° until edges look slightly brown.

Mrs. Wallace Carter, Jr.
ROLLING FORK, MS

Ginger Cakes 1872

1 quart molasses-warm
3 level tablespoons soda
1/2 cup lard
Powdered sugar
Flour for soft dough

Mix and roll out thin and bake at 350° for 10-12 minutes.

Mrs. Sallie M. Falkner
OXFORD, MS
(SUBMITTED BY: MRS. C. M. MURRY, OXFORD, MS)

Ginger Cookies

3/4 cup shortening
1 cup sugar
1 beaten egg
4 tablespoons molasses
2 cups flour
2 tablespoons baking soda
1 teaspoon ground cloves
2 teaspoons cinnamon
1/4 teaspoon ginger

Cream together shortening, sugar, egg, and molasses. In a separate bowl mix and sift together flour, soda, cloves, cinnamon, and ginger. Combine mixtures together in electric mixer. Pinch off a small amount and roll into balls. Press onto an ungreased cookie sheet with a sugared glass. Bake at 350° for 10 - 12 minutes. Makes about 3 dozen.

Louise Gresham
INDIANOLA, MS

Sue's Icebox Cookies

1 cup dark brown sugar
1 cup melted Crisco
2 cups nuts, cut up
1 teaspoon soda
1 teaspoon vanilla
1 cup white sugar
3 whole eggs (beaten
   together)
4 1/2 cups flour
1 teaspoon salt

Cream sugar and Crisco. Add beaten eggs, then rest of ingredients. Make rolls of the dough about 8 inches in length. Chill or freeze the dough. When ready to bake - slice and place on cookie sheet in moderate oven.

Mrs. W. C. Trotter
GREENVILLE, MS

Willie's Icebox Cookies

2 cups brown sugar
1 cup shortening
2 eggs
2 1/2 cups flour
1/4 teaspoon salt
1 teaspoon soda
1 teaspoon vanilla
2 cups chopped nuts

Cream sugar, shortening, and eggs together. Add other ingredients and make into rolls. Wrap in wax paper and keep in freezer. Slice and bake at 350°.

Mrs. Rodgers Brashier
INDIANOLA, MS

Lemon Crumb Squares

They taste like tiny lemon ice box pies.

2 cups condensed milk
1/2 cup lemon juice
1 teaspoon grated lemon rind
1 1/2 cups sifted flour
1 cup uncooked oatmeal
1 teaspoon baking powder
2/3 cup butter
1/2 teaspoon salt
1 cup dark brown sugar, packed

Blend together milk, juice and rind of lemon and set aside. Sift together flour, baking powder and salt. Cream butter, blend in sugar. Add oatmeal and flour mixture and mix until crumbly. Spread half the mixture in an 8x12x2" buttered baking pan and pat down; spread condensed milk mixture over top and cover with remaining crumb mixture. Bake at 350° for about 25 minutes, until brown around edges. Cool in pan at room temperature for 15 minutes; cut into small squares and chill in pan until firm.

These are best served at least slightly chilled.

Mrs. R. L. Morrison
HATTIESBURG, MS

Lemon Glazed Cookies

1 cup unsalted butter
1/3 cup powdered sugar
1 cup all purpose flour
2/3 cup cornstarch

Icing:
2 1/2 cups powdered sugar, sifted
1/2 cup butter, melted
2 tablespoons lemon juice

Preheat oven to 350°. Beat butter and 1/3 cup powdered sugar on medium speed until creamed. Sift flour and cornstarch. Add to butter. Blend until smooth. Drop by small teaspoons full on ungreased cookie sheet. (Will not rise, so press to desired shape and thickness.) Bake until lightly browned, about 15 minutes.

Combine 2 1/2 cups powdered sugar, melted butter and lemon juice. Let cookies cool a bit and then while still warm, mound 1/2 teaspoon of icing on each. Icing will melt. Let cool until hard.

Kathy Allen
INDIANOLA, MS

Meringue Puffs

2 egg whites
3 drops vinegar
1/2 teaspoon water
1/8 teaspoon salt
1/2 cup granulated sugar
1/4 teaspoon vanilla

Beat whites stiff but not dry; add vinegar, water and salt. After adding these beat a little more adding sugar gradually - then vanilla.

Grease cookie sheet well and drop by tablespoonsful, making dent in the middle and bake an hour at 250°.

Mrs. B. J. Spear
TAMPA, FL

Peanut Butter Cookies

1 cup sugar
1 cup brown sugar
3/4 cup melted shortening
3/4 cup peanut butter
2 well beaten eggs
2 teaspoons vanilla
3 cups flour
3/4 teaspoon salt
1 teaspoon soda

Mix sugar with shortening and peanut butter. Add eggs and vanilla and beat until smooth. Sift flour, salt and soda and add to first mixture. Roll small amount of dough in hand and flatten with tines of fork or form dough into rolls; wrap in wax paper; chill and slice. Bake on greased cookie sheet at 400° for 8-10 minutes.

Mrs. Tom Pitts
INDIANOLA, MS

Pecan Bites

1 cup brown sugar, packed
1 egg white, slightly
   beaten
Pinch salt
1 1/2 or 2 cups pecans cut
   in halves
1 teaspoon vanilla

Combine all ingredients. Line pan with foil and grease well with margarine. Heat oven 450° for 10 minutes. Turn heat off before putting cookies into oven. Bake 8 minutes.

Kathy Allen (from my Mother, Katherine Keach)
INDIANOLA, MS

Travis House Pecan Kisses

1 egg white
1 cup brown sugar, firmly
    packed
1 tablespoon flour
1/2 teaspoon salt
1 cup pecans, chopped in
    large pieces

Beat egg white until stiff, gradually add combined sugar, flour, salt, beating constantly. Add nuts. Bake on buttered cookie sheet. Place two inches apart and drop by teaspoon. Bake in slow oven, 325° about 20 minutes until slightly brown. Do not let them get too done. Makes two dozen.

Mrs. Alex Armour
RICHMOND, VA

Potato Chip Cookies

1 pound butter
2 teaspoons vanilla
1 cup crushed potato chips
1 cup sugar
3 1/2 cups flour
6 ounces butterscotch
    morsels (optional)

Soften butter. Add other ingredients and bake on greased cookie sheet at 350° until brown. Cook 12 - 15 minutes. This makes 7 - 8 dozen.

Ellen Clayton
INDIANOLA, MS

Raspberry Filled Cookies

"The elderly lady who gave me this recipe made me promise I'd never make these cookies in the State of Kentucky as they were her livelihood. She was booked solid making them for elegant receptions and the like. Although you won't whip them up in 20 minutes, you'll never forget them, or regret your expenditure of time."

2 sticks (1 cup) butter or margarine, at room temperature
1 cup sugar
2 extra large eggs, at room temperature
1 teaspoon vanilla extract, or 1 teaspoon almond extract
3 cups flour
1 teaspoon baking powder

For the filling:
Raspberry jam, warmed if needed to spread easily

For the glaze:
1 cup powdered sugar
1 tablespoon warm water
Brandy (optional)

Leave eggs and butter out of refrigerator overnight to come to room temperature. Cream butter and sugar together until light and fluffy. Add eggs one at a time, beating well to fully incorporate. Add extract; then sift in flour and baking powder. Beat well. Don't be tempted to add extra flour. Refrigerate dough overnight, or a minimum of 6 hours.

Roll in batches to the thinness of pie crust. Cut with a 2 - inch lightly floured cookie cutter, (a little flour on rolling pin and board helps). Bake 5 minutes in a preheated 350° oven.

Allow cookies to cool on pans for 10 minutes before removing. Spread raspberry jam thinly between cookies and sandwich together. Glaze with mixture of powdered sugar, water, and enough brandy or extra water to allow the glaze to be brushed across the tops with a pastry brush.

They freeze beautifully when layered with wax paper.

Kate Failing
INDIANOLA, MS

Grandma's Tea Cakes

1 cup sugar
1 stick oleo
2 teaspoons baking powder
1 egg
2 cups flour
1 teaspoon nutmeg
2 teaspoons vanilla

Cream sugar and oleo until light and fluffy. Then add egg, flour (a little at a time), baking powder, nutmeg and vanilla. (More flour may be needed to make a stiff batter) Very Important Note: Wrap in waxed paper and refrigerate overnight or at least 3 hours. Roll out on floured board and cut in desired shape. Bake at 350° until lightly browned. Makes 3 or 4 dozen cookies.

Mrs. James Corder
INDIANOLA, MS

Lemon Tea Cakes

4 hard boiled eggs (use
  yolks only)
2 sticks butter
1 lemon (rind and juice)
1 cup sugar
1 1/2 raw eggs (use raw
  yolk in mixture: save
  white for topping)
4 cups flour
1 tablespoon vanilla
Pecan halves

Cream butter and sugar, add the grated yolks of 4 hard boiled eggs, and 1 1/2 raw egg yolks. Save the white of egg to rub over the tops of the cookies. Add vanilla and grated rind and lemon juice. Add flour. Roll thin. Cut with cookie cutter and brush with slightly beaten egg white. Sprinkle sugar and put 1 pecan on each cookie. Bake in hot 400° oven.

Hoke Stone
LAMBERT, MS

Fruit and Frozen Dessert

Brandied Fruit

This start or magic potion must be handled with respect. Pour brandy into a stone jar that has a tight-fitting lid. Suggested fruits to use: cherries, pineapple, strawberries, peaches, apricots or any fruit without a large seed. Use the same amount of sugar as fruit, and a fifth of brandy.

When you share this potion, remember the one to whom you give this fruit must be worthy. You must never let the content of the stone jar get below three cups or the fermentation will stop. Most jars hold 8 cups. Every two weeks you may add one cup of sugar and one cup of canned fruit in this order: pineapple chunks, sliced peaches, and maraschino cherries cut in halves. You must not add later than three weeks but a day or two delay will not be disastrous. Keep a calendar for adding water and fruit.

Keep the jar in view, for it is a wonderful conversation piece. Never refrigerate. Keep the fruit in a slightly warm spot. The apothecary jars are just right because there is room for expansion and the lid rises with pressure when necessary. This may be used as a sauce for desserts and meats. Ready for testing in about a week.

Mrs. Frank Baker
INDIANOLA, MS

Cherries Jubilee

1 tablespoon cornstarch
1 tablespoon sugar
1 pound can pitted black
   cherries
3 or 4 strips orange peel
Dash lemon juice
1/2 cup warm brandy

Mix sugar and cornstarch. Add liquid from cherries and the orange peel. Cook until thick. Discard peel. Add cherries and lemon juice. At table add warm brandy and ignite, averting face to avoid flames. Serve over vanilla ice cream.

Mrs. Joel Hill, Jr.
GREENVILLE, MS

Coupe Sicelienne

1 pineapple, shredded
3 oranges (pulp)
3 bananas, sliced
Powdered sugar
2 tablespoons maraschino
   juice
1 tablespoon lemon juice
Few grains salt

Ice:
1 quart strawberries
1 cup sugar
1 cup water
Lemon juice

Mix ingredients; sweeten to taste, and chill. Serve in champagne glasses having glasses two-thirds full. Cover fruit to fill glasses with strawberry ice and garnish with strawberries.

Strawberry ice: strawberries, sugar, lemon juice – let berries, sugar, stand two hours; then mash; squeeze through cheese cloth; add water and lemon juice; taste; then freeze.

Helen Neill Henry
INDIANOLA, MS

Peach Melba

Serve with light pound cake or sponge cake, sliced for individual servings.

3 big peaches, real yummy ones in appearance and flavor
1 vanilla bean or a tablespoon of vanilla extract
3 cups of water
2 cups of sugar
1 package frozen raspberries, thawed

Make simple syrup — you remember the kind grandpaw used to keep on a shelf to make his toddies — Lordy, don't I wish people still drank toddies! — with sugar and water by boiling and vanilla added.

Poach peaches in this until just tender (naturally, you peel and remove pits first).

Strain raspberries through a fine sieve. Put your peaches, after chilling them, in dessert dishes, and pour raspberry sauce over them. One per person gives you six splendid servings and it's just too bad if your guests want more, because there ain't none left.

Ben Wasson
GREENVILLE, MS

Sherried Strawberries

4 egg yolks
1 cup sugar
2 to 4 tablespoons sherry
2 boxes strawberries (sliced in half)
1 cup whipping cream

Combine yolks and sugar in double boiler, stirring constantly for about 15 minutes. Remove from flame and add sherry. Chill. When cold, add 1 cup whipped cream. Chill. Just before serving combine sherried mix with strawberries. Serves 8.

Mrs. Marshall Nesbitt
PACIFIC PALISADES, CA

Strawberry Charlotte

2 envelopes unflavored
  gelatin
3/4 cup sugar (divided)
1/4 teaspoon salt
4 eggs (separated)
1/2 cup water
2 (10 ounce) packages
  frozen strawberries
  (divided)
2 tablespoons lemon juice
2 teaspoons grated lemon
  rind
8 whole lady fingers, split
  in half
1 cup cream, whipped

Mix gelatin, 1/4 cup sugar and salt in top of double boiler. Beat egg yolks and water together. Add to gelatin mixture. Add 1 package frozen sliced strawberries. Cook over boiling water stirring constantly until strawberries are thawed and gelatin dissolved (about 8 minutes). Remove from heat and add other package strawberries, lemon juice and rind. Stir until berries are thawed. Chill until mixture mounds when dropped from spoon. Stand split lady fingers around edge of an 8 inch spring pan. Beat egg whites until stiff. Beat in remaining 1/2 cup sugar. Fold in gelatin mixture. Fold in whipped cream. Turn into pan and chill until firm. Remove from pan and garnish with more cream and berries if desired. Serves 12.

Mrs. William Dulaney
TUNICA, MS

Sherry Delight

3/4 cup sugar
1 cup cold water
6 oranges
1 1/2 stick cinnamon
  broken in small pieces
Rind of 2 lemons and
  reserve juice
Rind of 2 oranges and
  reserve juice
3 tablespoons gelatin
1/4 cup cold water
1/2 cup sherry wine

Boil all ingredients except gelatin, 1/4 cup cold water, and juices until the sugar is well dissolved. Soak 3 packages of gelatin in cold water. When sugar and water mixture are very hot pour in gelatin and stir. Add juices from the squeezed oranges and lemons. This should be about a pint or more. If it is not, then add more juice from the oranges. Strain this mixture. When cool add 1/2 cup sherry wine. Serves 6 to 8 people. Make and serve the same day. Mold until firm in cups.

Mrs. Leonard Patterson
ROME, MS

Wine Jelly

2 packages Knox gelatin
1/4 cup cold water
3/4 cup boiling water
1/4 cup sugar (or more to taste)
1 1/2 cup orange juice (fresh if possible)
7 teaspoons lemon juice (fresh if possible)
1 1/4 cups cream sherry (Harvey's Bristol Cream or Meier's 44 are good choices)

Soak gelatin in cold water until softened. Dissolve softened gelatin in boiling hot water. Add sugar and stir until gelatin and sugar are completely dissolved. Add juices and sherry, stir well. Pour into a serving bowl, mold, or individual dishes of choice. Refrigerate until set. Serve with whipped cream.

This makes a light elegant dessert, particularly after a heavy holiday meal.

Kate Failing
INDIANOLA, MS

Baked Apples and Cranberries

2 cups cranberries
3 cups apples - cut in bite-size pieces
1 1/4 cups sugar
1 stick butter - melted
1 1/2 cups oatmeal
1/2 cup brown sugar
1/2 cup pecans

Mix first three ingredients and spread in baking dish. Mix next four ingredients and spread over fruit. Bake at 350° for 40 minutes. Freezes well. Great with turkey for holidays.

Mimi Alexander
INDIANOLA, MS

Curried Fruit

1 can sliced pineapple
1 can peach halves
1 can pears
1 can apricot halves
Maraschino cherries
3/4 cup brown sugar
4 teaspoons curry

Drain fruit. Arrange in baking dish or in stacks in pan. Combine sugar and curry. Sprinkle over fruit. Bake 30 minutes at 350°. Serves 8 to 10. Delicious with ham or chicken.

Mrs. W. E. Failing
HOUSTON, TX

Rosie's Baked Pears

12 large cooking pears
2 cups sugar
1/2 teaspoon cinnamon
1/4 teaspoon vanilla
1 stick butter

Wash, peel, core and cut pears in halves lengthwise. Place in 4" deep baking dish. Sprinkle dry ingredients over top; slice butter and dot across the top. Cover; bake in 350° oven for one hour. We often bake these in aluminum freezing pan - store in freezer. Reheat 10 - 20 minutes.

Mrs. Robroy Fisher
GREENVILLE, MS

Homemade Ice Cream

1/2 gallon sweet milk
1 3/4 cup sugar
1 can condensed milk
6 eggs
1/2 teaspoon salt
2 teaspoons vanilla
1/2 pint whipping cream

Scald milk in large boiler. Slowly add beaten eggs, sugar, salt, and condensed milk. Mix well. Cook on very low heat until thick. Remove from heat and add 1/2 pint whipping cream and put in ice cream freezer.

Mrs. James Corder
INDIANOLA, MS

Old-Fashioned Ice Cream Custard

3 quarts milk
3 cups sugar
3 rounded tablespoons
    flour
Pinch of salt
9 eggs (medium to large)
1 pint cream or 1 large can
    evaporated milk
3 teaspoons vanilla

Put milk on to scald. Start beating eggs and when real fluffy add sugar, flour, and salt mixed together. When milk coats a spoon real heavy add egg mixture; cut heat off under the milk and fold custard constantly until well mixed. Cool.

When ready to freeze add cream, vanilla, and enough milk to fill can.

Mrs. Wallace Carter
ROLLING FORK, MS

Lemon-Pineapple Ice Cream

1 1/2 quarts milk
8 eggs
2 cups sugar
1 tablespoon vanilla
1 quart heavy cream
1 small can crushed
    pineapple
Juice of 5 lemons
1 cup sugar

Make custard of milk, eggs, sugar and vanilla. Add to this cooled custard 1 quart heavy cream, 1 small can crushed pineapple and juice of 5 lemons. (Add sugar to lemons). Freeze in ice cream freezer.

Katie B. Gooch
INDIANOLA, MS

Lotus Ice Cream

6 lemons
3 cups sugar
6 cups light cream
3 cups milk

Slice away and discard the ends of 2 lemons. Using a sharp knife cut into thin, almost transparent slices. Remove the seeds and cut in half to make crescent shape. Squeeze the remaining lemons and combine the juice with the sugar. Add the lemon slices, cover and refrigerate overnight. Stir, combine the cream and milk and pour into the churn of an ice cream freezer. Cover, and if possible, place the churn in an electric freezer for about 10 minutes. Do not freeze at this point.

Add the lemon mixture to the cream. Freeze according to the directions and keep frozen until ready to use. Yield: 9 servings. Delicious after a heavy meal.

Tom Barron
INDIANOLA, MS

Homemade Peach Ice Cream

1 pint whipping cream
1 pint half and half
3 cups of sugar
1 quart of soft peaches
Juice of two lemons
1/2 teaspoon almond
    extract

Peel and mash the peaches thoroughly. You can use a blender for this. Add one cup of sugar, 1/2 teaspoon of almond extract, and lemon juice to the peaches. The lemon juice will help prevent the peaches from turning black. Combine the half and half, whipping cream, and 2 cups of sugar and stir until all the sugar is dissolved. It is best to make up this mixture the day before you plan to freeze it as this will help make a smooth textured ice cream and will increase the yield. Handcranked ice cream is always the best. No electric churn can equal the texture of a hand cranked one.

Fill the churn only 3/4 full to allow for expansion. After packing the churn with alternate layers of ice and salt, crank the churn slowly at first until you feel a slight pull. Then triple the speed for about five or six minutes – 120 turns a minute. At this point, add the fruit mixture, repack the freezer with ice and salt and churn the ice cream a little while longer, again at a slow pace. It should normally take about 15-20 minutes to make a batch.

Be very careful while making the ice cream not to let any salt get into the ice cream container. The amount of sugar depends on how much acid the fruit has. If you find the recipe too rich, you can substitute milk for part of the cream.

Cay Brooks Ely
SHAW, MS

HOLT COLLIER

Born a slave in 1846, Collier served as a Confederate sharpshooter and cavalryman. Famed as a bear hunter, he guided Pres. Theodore Roosevelt on a hunt near Onward, MS, in 1902. When Roosevelt refused to shoot a bear Collier had roped, cartoonists coined the term "Teddy Bear." Collier was buried here in Live Oak Cemetery in 1936.

Ice Cream Pie with Almond Hershey Sauce

1 box vanilla wafers
1 1/2 sticks butter or
    margarine
12 almond Hershey bars
36 full size marshmallows
1 pint whipping cream
1/2 gallon vanilla-choco-
    late ice cream
Slivered almonds, toasted

Make a crust of the wafers and butter. Line bottom of 12" x 15" pan. Put almond Hershey bars and marshmallows in top of a double boiler. Stir frequently, mixture will be stiff. Whip cream to stiff peaks. When bars and marshmallows are well blended, turn off heat but leave over hot water while you fold in whipping cream until well blended. Pour over vanilla wafer crust.

Soften ice cream. Cut in slices and cover top of Hershey bar mixture. Smooth. Scatter slivered almonds over ice cream. Put in deep freeze. Serve with whipped cream and cherries.

Mrs. Frank Pigford, Jr.
CHAMPAIGN, IL

Peppermint Ice Cream Pie with Hot Fudge Sauce

20 Oreo cookies
1/4 stick butter (melted)
1 1/2 quarts peppermint
    ice cream

Sauce:
1 tablespoon butter
1 ounce semi-sweet
    chocolate
1/3 cup boiling water
1 cup sugar
2 tablespoons Karo
1/2 teaspoon vanilla
1/2 teaspoon salt

Crush Oreo cookies and moisten with melted butter. Press into 9 inch pie pan. This crust is delicious; for a thicker crust use more Oreos. Fill crust with peppermint ice cream.

Melt butter and chocolate and add boiling water, sugar and Karo. Boil 5 minutes. Add vanilla and salt. Spoon 2 teaspoons of hot fudge sauce over each piece of pie as it is served.

Sue Eastland McRoberts
JACKSON, MS

Pistachio Parfait

1 cup sugar
1/4 cup water
3 egg whites
1 tablespoon vanilla
1 teaspoon almond extract
1 pint heavy cream
Green coloring
1/2 cup finely chopped
   pistachio nuts
Whipped cream

Boil sugar and water until syrup will thread when dropped from tip of spoon. Pour slowly, while stirring constantly, on the beaten whites of eggs, and continue the beating until mixture is cold; then add flavoring. Color cream a delicate green and beat until stiff. Add to first mixture with nut meats. Freeze. Garnish top with whipped cream, sweetened and flavored with vanilla, and sprinkle with chopped nuts.

Mrs. John Neill
GREENWOOD, MS

Praline Parfait

2 cups dark corn syrup
1/3 cup sugar
1/3 cup boiling water
1 cup chopped toasted
   pecans

Combine all ingredients in a sauce pan and bring to boil over medium heat. As soon as mixture reaches a boiling stage, remove from heat immediately. Cool and store in a covered jar.

To make a Praline Parfait spoon alternate layers of vanilla ice cream and the sauce in a parfait glass, ending with a layer of sauce. Top with whipped cream and garnish with pecan halves.

This parfait is even better with coffee ice cream. If you can't find this, mix instant coffee with vanilla ice cream and freeze.

Wister Henry of Wister Henry Gardens
BELZONI, MS

Coffee Tortoni

1 egg white
1/8 teaspoon salt
1 cup heavy cream
1 teaspoon vanilla
1 tablespoon instant coffee
2 tablespoons sugar
1/4 cup sugar
1/8 teaspoon almond
   extract
1/4 cup toasted almonds

Combine egg whites, coffee and salt; beat until stiff. Gradually add 2 tablespoons sugar; beat until satiny. Whip cream; add 1/4 cup sugar, vanilla and almond extract. Beat until stiff. Fold with nuts into the egg mixture. Pour into eight (2 ounce) paper cups; freeze. I like to sprinkle some chopped nuts over the top, or serve with a cherry on top. Best to always double recipe. It keeps well in refrigerator.

Mrs. Raymond Craig
GREENWOOD, MS

Heavenly Dessert

6 egg yolks
1/2 cup sugar, heaping
1 teaspoon vanilla
1 teaspoon bourbon
1 pint whipping cream
Almond macaroons
Sherry

Beat yolk and 1/2 cup sugar until thick. Add vanilla and bourbon. Fold in 3 cups whipped cream. Crumble up macaroons and put in bottom of buttered removable tube pan. Dribble with sherry. Pour in 1/2 mixture and add more sherried macaroons. Freeze this before adding layer of last half of mixture. Finish with crumbs on top. Freeze over night. Serve with berries and whipped cream.

Lynn Eastland
INDIANOLA, MS

Lemon Frozen Dessert

3 egg yolks
1/2 cup sugar
1/4 cup lemon juice
1 lemon rind, grated
3 egg whites
1 cup whipping cream
Vanilla wafer crumbs

Cook egg yolks, sugar, lemon juice, and rind in top of double boiler until thick. When cool, add egg whites beaten stiff, then fold in whipping cream (whipped).

Line tray with wax paper and put layer of vanilla wafer crumbs; then pour lemon mixture in tray and put vanilla wafer crumbs on top and freeze. Serves 6 to 8.

Mrs. Guy Price
LYON, MS

Orange-Cranberry Freeze

1 can (1 pound) jellied
  cranberry sauce
1 6 ounce can frozen
  orange juice concentrate
  (undiluted)
1/2 cup sugar
1/8 teaspoon salt
1 cup heavy cream,
  whipped
1/8 teaspoon red food
  coloring (optional)

Combine sauce, juice concentrate, sugar, and salt. Beat with electric or rotary beater to blend. Fold food coloring in whipped cream. Put in 1 quart mold, loaf pan, or refrigerator trays. Freeze until firm.

Sue Eastland McRoberts
JACKSON, MS

Frozen Rainbow Dessert

1 pint whipping cream
1/2 cup sugar
1 cup nuts, chopped
24 almond macaroons
1 pint lime sherbet
1 pint raspberry sherbet
1 pint lemon sherbet

Crush macaroons in plastic sack with rolling pin and add to sweetened cream and nuts. Put 1/2 of this mixture into 9" x 14" pan. Spread lime sherbet, then raspberry sherbet, then lemon sherbets in layers. Cover with other half of cream mixture. Put in freezer. Allow sherbets to soften slightly before spreading. Serves 16.

Mrs. W. C. "Chuck" Trotter
INDIANOLA, MS

Pies and Puddings

―――――□―――――

Apple Pie-Delta Style

Serve with globs of whipped cream or French vanilla ice cream. Luscious and loaded with calories.

2 cups flour
1 teaspoon salt
1/2 cup shortening
1/2 cup cheddar cheese
6 tablespoons cold water
1/2 teaspoon cinnamon
1/4 teaspoon ginger
1/4 teaspoon cloves

Filling:
5 or 6 very tart apples
3/4 cup sugar
2 tablespoons flour
1/8 teaspoon salt
Lemon juice
1 teaspoon cinnamon
1 teaspoon nutmeg
1 teaspoon allspice
Plenty of butter

Mix shortening and cheese into flour and dry ingredients until the particles are about like rice. Use a fork to mix. Sprinkle water, 1 tablespoon at a time, over small portions of the mixture and only enough to hold the pastry together. Handle the dough as little as possible. Roll out into two oblongs 1/8 to 1/4 inch thick and place one in deep pie pan. Reserve other.

Peel and slice apples into the spiced cheese pastry-lined pan. Mix the dry ingredients together and sprinkle with lemon juice over each layer of apples. Dot each layer with butter dabs. Cut second pastry oblong into strips and lay in a basket weave patter atop the pie. Bake 400° 30 to 40 minutes.

Variation: Normandy Apple Pie. Follow Your Own Recipe for vanilla custard or creme patissie. Stir in 3 tablespoons ground blanched almonds and 1 teaspoon Kirsch. Peel, core, and slice 2 tart apples. Melt 4 tablespoons butter in frying pan and cook apples covered, until soft. Fill baked pie crust with the custard. Arrange the sliced cooked apples in a pattern on top. Sprinkle generously with confectioners' sugar. Heat 1 ounce of Calvados and pour over apples. Flambé.

Rear Admiral Clyde Van Arsdall
GULFPORT, MS

―――――

Boston Cream Pie

4 eggs, separated
1 cup sugar
1 cup flour
4 egg yolks beaten light
1 teaspoon vinegar, beat in
   yolks, add to whites

Beat egg whites until stiff. Add sugar and beat. Add flour, 1 tablespoon at a time. In separate bowl, beat yolks into vinegar and then add to main mixture. Put in ungreased pyrex pans, dusted with flour. Bake at 300° for 30 or 35 minutes or until pie springs back when touched.

Filling:
4 cups sweet milk
2 whole eggs
5 tablespoons flour, sifted
3/4 cup sugar
2 cups cream
Grapenuts cereal, crushed

Mix all ingredients in double boiler and cook until real thick. Let cool. Put in refrigerator until ready to split cakes and fill. Whip cream. Ice cakes and sprinkle rolled Grapenuts on top of cream. Keep in refrigerator. This makes two pies.

Mrs. S. M. Hunt
GREENWOOD, MS

Weidman's Bourbon Pie

1 box Nabisco chocolate
   snaps
1/2 cup melted butter of
   margarine
21 marshmallows
1 cup evaporated milk
1/2 pint whipping cream
3 tablespoons bourbon

Crush chocolate snaps; mix with melted margarine. Pat into 9-inch pie pan and bake in oven until set. Cool and fill with above mixture.

   Melt marshmallows in undiluted milk, do not boil. Chill. Whip cream and fold into marshmallow mixture. Add bourbon, pour into cooled chocolate crumb crust and refrigerate four hours or until set. If desired, top with whipped cream and chocolate crumbs.

Jane Diggs Rinehart
INDIANOLA, MS

Mama's Caramel Pie

1 cup milk
2 egg yolks
1 cup brown sugar
1 1/2 tablespoons butter
1 1/2 tablespoons flour
1/2 teaspoon vanilla

Cook in double boiler and pour into baked pie shell when slightly thickened. Beat egg whites with 2 tablespoons sugar and use for meringue. Lightly brown the meringue in a medium oven.

My grandmother, Mrs. James Howell (Helen McLean) Peebles' recipe.

Mrs. Brax Provine
GREENWOOD, MS

Chess Pie

4 egg yolks
1 whole egg
1 1/4 cups sugar
1/2 cup butter
2 tablespoons flour
2 tablespoons cream
1 teaspoon vanilla
Pinch salt

Beat all eggs until stiff, add other ingredients, and beat well. Pour in raw crust and cook in 375° oven until done.

This recipe is an Indianola favorite - an original of Mrs. Harvey Trice of Memphis.

Inamay Heathman
INDIANOLA, MS

Lemon Chess Pie

5 eggs
2 cups sugar
1/2 cup butter
1/4 cup lemon juice (3 lemons and some rind if desired)
2 tablespoons water
1 tablespoon flour
1 tablespoon corn meal
1/4 teaspoon salt
1 (9 inch) pie crust

Cream butter and sugar. Add flour, salt, corn meal, and water. Add eggs one at a time. Add lemon juice; pour into unbaked 9" pie crust. Bake 50 - 60 minutes at 350°.

Mrs. Eagle Boyd, Jr.
HAZEN, AR

Lemon Tarts

1 cup flour
1/2 cup butter
1/2 teaspoon salt
1/4 cup powdered sugar
2 eggs, well beaten
1 cup sugar
1 teaspoon baking powder
3 tablespoons lemon juice
3 tablespoons flour

Mix flour, butter, salt, and sugar together until mealy consistency. Press into 9" square pan and bake 20 minutes at 350°.

Mix remaining ingredients thoroughly and pour over hot crust. Bake for 25 minutes at 350°. Cut into small squares (dip knife into cold water intermittently). Sprinkle powdered sugar on top. Taste like bite size lemon chess pies.

Mrs. J. A. Ely, Jr.
SHAW, MS

Cheesecake De Luxe

2 1/2 pounds cream cheese,
    softened
1/4 teaspoon vanilla
    extract
1 tablespoon grated lemon
    rind
1 3/4 cups plus 1/3 cup
    sugar
3 tablespoons all-purpose
    flour
Pinch of salt
5 eggs
2 egg yolks
1/4 cup cream
Graham cracker crust
1 quart strawberries
1/4 cup water
1 tablespoon cornstarch
1 teaspoon butter

Soften cream cheese 30 seconds in microwave. Stir. Repeat. Preheat the oven to 475°. Beat cream cheese until fluffy. Add vanilla and lemon rind. Combine 1 3/4 cups of the sugar, the flour and salt. Gradually blend into cheese mixture. Beat in eggs and egg yolks, one at a time, and the cream. Beat well. Pour mixture into the prepared crust. Bake for 8 to 10 minutes. Reduce the heat to 200°. Bake for 1 hour 15 minutes, or until set. Turn off the heat. Allow the cake to remain in the oven with door ajar for 30 minutes. Cool on a rack. Chill.

To prepare the glaze, wash and hull the strawberries. Crush enough berries to make 1/2 cup. Boil the crushed berries, 1/3 cup of the sugar, the water and cornstarch 2 minutes, stirring. Add the butter. Strain and cool. Arrange the whole berries over the top of the cheesecake and pour the glaze over the berries. Chill. Use ready made graham-cracker crust.

Will Barnwell
INDIANOLA, MS

Chocolate Silk Pie

1 stick butter
3/4 cup sugar
2 eggs
1 1/2 teaspoons vanilla
1 1/2 ounces melted
  chocolate
9" pie shell
1/2 pint whipping cream

Cream butter and sugar well until fluffy. Add eggs separately and mix thoroughly. Add vanilla and chocolate and allow to set in cooked and cooled pie shell.

Top with whipped cream and grated chocolate. Serves 6.

Joyce Van Cleve
INDIANOLA, MS

Coconut Pie

1/2 cups sugar
1 tablespoon butter
  (rounded)
3 eggs
1 teaspoon vanilla
1/2 cup milk
1/8 teaspoon salt
1 cup coconut (fresh)
1 (9 inch) pie shell

Cream butter and sugar until fluffy. Add eggs and beat well. Add vanilla, milk, salt, and coconut. Cook in unbaked shell. Preheat oven to 425°. Cook at this temperature for first 10 minutes. Reduce heat to 325° for next 25 minutes. Serves 6.

Joyce Van Cleve
INDIANOLA, MS

Date Torte

14 dates, chopped
14 soda crackers, fine
1 cup pecans, chopped
3 egg whites
1 teaspoon vanilla
1 cup sugar

Beat egg whites until stiff; add sugar gradually. Fold in remaining ingredients. Grease 9 x 9 baking pan lightly with butter and bake at 350° about 25 minutes. Serve with whipped cream. Serves 9.

Mrs. Shelby Goza
ROSEDALE, MS

Speedy Fudge Pie

2 squares unsweetened
  chocolate
1 stick butter
1/4 cup flour
1 1/4 cups sugar
3 eggs
1 teaspoon vanilla

Melt chocolate and butter in top of double boiler. Add flour and sugar that have been mixed together, then 3 eggs beaten together. Add vanilla. Bake in buttered pie pan - 30 minutes in 350° oven. Serve with ice cream and chocolate sauce.

Helen Little
FT. SMITH, AR

Grasshopper Pie

16 Oreo cookies
1/3 cup melted butter
25 marshmallows
1/2 cup milk
2 ounces creme de menthe
1 ounce white creme de
  cocoa
1/2 pint cream, whipped
1 square chocolate

Make crust of cookies and butter. Press into 9" pie pan. Melt marshmallows in milk on low heat. Cool. Beat liqueurs into mixture. Fold in whipped cream. Pour into crust. Grate chocolate on top. Refrigerate 24 hours.

Mrs. Malloy French
INDIANOLA, MS

Jefferson Davis Pie

1 stick butter
2 cups brown sugar
4 egg yolks
2 tablespoons flour
1 teaspoon cinnamon
1 teaspoon nutmeg
1 cup cream
1/2 cup chopped dates
1/2 cup chopped pecans
1/2 cup raisins

Cream the butter and sugar well. Then beat in egg yolks one at a time. Sift flour and spices together (add a pinch of salt if desired). Blend into egg mixture until smooth. Gradually blend in cream. Stir in fruit and nuts. Bake in 9 inch pie crust at 300° for about 40 minutes. Remove from oven and top with meringue made with 4 egg whites beaten with 1/2 cup sugar. Brown about 5 minutes. Serves 6 or 8.

Mrs. James Corder
INDIANOLA, MS

Lemon Cream Pie Filling

"In the Scandinavian tradition of my grandmother, Mrs. J. D. Larsen."

2 cups sugar
3/4 cup flour
1/4 teaspoon salt
3 cups milk
6 eggs, separated
2 tablespoons butter
1/2 cup lemon juice
2 teaspoons grated lemon rind
3 egg whites, beaten softly

Meringue:
4 egg whites
1/4 teaspoon salt
3/4 cup sugar
1/2 teaspoon grated lemon rind

Mix sugar, flour, salt and milk in top of double boiler. Cook 15 minutes over hot water, stirring until thick. Add slightly beaten yolks and cook 3 minutes. Add and cool to lukewarm temperature.

Caution: Be certain cream mixture is lukewarm. Then add lemon juice, otherwise it will curdle. Fold in whites and pour into pre-cooked pastry.

Beat whites until soft peaks are formed. Add slowly 1 teaspoon sugar, and beat one minute. Then add remaining sugar and salt gradually. Spread atop lemon mixture. Top with lemon rind and bake at 425° until delicately brown (5 minutes). Cool.

Recipe makes 1 large pie or 10 tarts or may be frozen and served as an icebox dessert or pudding.

Mary Eda Allen
INDIANOLA, MS

Lemon Heaven Pie

1 (8 inch) pie shell
4 eggs
1/2 cup sugar
1/4 cup lemon juice
Grated rind of 1 lemon
1/4 teaspoon cream of
    tartar
1/4 cup sugar

Make 8 inch pie shell and cool. Beat together in top of double boiler 4 egg yolks, sugar, and lemon juice. Cook over boiling water until very thick, stirring constantly. Take from over hot water and let cool slightly. Blend in grated lemon rind.

Beat until foamy 4 egg whites. Add cream of tartar. Beat until egg whites are glossy. Fold half of egg whites and 1/4 cup sugar into cooled mixture. Pour into cooled crust. Beat gradually into other half of egg whites. Pour over mixture and bake 15 minutes at 300°.

Mrs. Elizabeth Kelly
INDIANOLA, MS

Lemon Meringue Pie

1 whole egg
3 egg yolks
1 1/2 cups boiling water
Pinch salt
1 tablespoon butter
1 1/2 cups sugar
3 tablespoons flour
1/3 cup lemon juice
Grated rind of 1 lemon

Meringue:
3 egg whites
6 tablespoons sugar

Beat eggs, add sugar to which the flour is mixed, and the boiling water. Cook over low heat, stirring constantly. When it is of thick custard consistency, remove from heat and add salt, lemon juice, rind, and butter. Pile into cooled pastry shell.

Make meringue by gradually adding sugar to egg whites. Top pie and bake in 350° oven until meringue is brown.

Mrs. Rogers K. Haydon
ITTA BENA, MS

Mother's Molasses Pie (Ada D. Neill)

1 cup sugar
1/2 cup molasses
1/2 stick butter
3 eggs, pinch salt, pinch soda
1 teaspoon vanilla flavoring

Melt butter; add sugar; add 3 eggs, and beat a little; put in molasses and stir in a little pinch of salt and soda. Add vanilla. Put in pie crust and bake in middle of oven. Bake at 400° for about 2 minutes. (If bottom of pie rises to top, bake a little longer on 400°). Turn back to 300° and bake about 55 minutes.

Mrs. Arthur Clark
INDIANOLA, MS

Mystery Pie

3 egg whites
1 cup sugar
1/4 teaspoon baking powder
1 teaspoon vanilla
20 round buttery crackers, rolled fine
1 cup chopped pecans
Whipped cream

Grease 9" glass pie pan. Beat egg whites until stiff, then fold in sugar, baking powder and vanilla. Beat until stiff. Fold in cracker crumbs and chopped pecans. Pour mixture into pie pan, bake at 350° for 20 minutes. To serve, top with whipped cream. 6 to 8 servings.

Mrs. Homer McKinney
MCKINNEY BAKERY, INDIANOLA, MS

Orange Pie

4 egg yolks
1 cup evaporated milk
1 grated orange, juice and all
1 cup sugar
1 tablespoon flour
1 tablespoon butter (room temperature)

Meringue:

4 egg whites
2 level tablespoons sugar to each egg white

Beat egg yolks, sugar, and butter together. Add flour, grated orange, and milk. Mix. Pour into unbaked pie crust. Cook in 350° oven until firm. Cover with meringue. Bake in slow oven of 300° for 15 minutes.

To make meringue, beat egg whites to a stiff dry froth. Add sugar, one tablespoon at a time, beating the egg whites constantly until the meringue is stiff, but glossy and creamy in consistency.

Minnie Tiler
TUNICA, MS

Peach Cobbler

3/4 cup water
1 cup sugar
1 cup self-rising flour
1 stick oleo
1 large can peaches
Cinnamon

Preheat oven to 400°. Mix water, sugar, and flour in a bowl. In a large iron skillet melt oleo. Pour flour mixture over butter. Do not mix. Then add peaches. (Do not mix) Sprinkle cinnamon on top. Bake until brown and bubbly, about 1 hour.

Karen K. Carpenter
INDIANOLA, MS

Karo Pecan Pie

1 cup sugar
1/2 cup dark Karo
4 tablespoons margarine
3 eggs
Dash of salt
1 cup pecans, broken
1 teaspoon vanilla

Mix sugar, karo and margarine in a small pan and bring to a boil. Remove, and immediately stir in 3 eggs which have been beaten quite well in a large bowl. Then add a couple of dashes of salt, 1 teaspoon vanilla and finally fold in 1 cup broken pecans, turning it over sufficiently to insure that all nuts are well coated. Pour into unbaked 9" pie crust and bake at 375° for 35 to 40 minutes.

This recipe doubles nicely, and in so doing, I usually use 5 extra large eggs instead of 6.

Mrs. W. C. Trotter, Jr.
GREENVILLE, MS

Pumpkin Pie

3 egg yolks
1/2 cup sugar
1/2 cup milk
1 envelope gelatin
3 egg whites (beaten until stiff with 1/2 cup sugar added to them)
1 1/4 cup canned pumpkin
1/2 teaspoon salt
1/2 teaspoon ginger
1/2 teaspoon nutmeg
1/2 teaspoon cinnamon

Mix yolks, sugar, pumpkin, spice, milk and cook until like custard. Have gelatin dissolved in cold water and add to hot pumpkin. When cool, fold in beaten egg whites and sugar. Pour into baked pie crust. Chill. Serve with generous amounts of whipped cream.

Mrs. Ned Green
HELENA, AR

Sour Cream Pies

1 cup sugar
2 heaping tablespoons
   flour
1/3 teaspoon cloves
1/2 teaspoon nutmeg
1/2 teaspoon cinnamon
2 cups sour cream or
   evaporated milk
4 egg yolks
1 tablespoon butter
1 teaspoon vanilla
1/2 cup chopped pecans
1/3 cup raisins
1 prepared pie shell or
   individual pie shells

Combine dry ingredients in double boiler. Add milk, eggs, butter and vanilla. Cook on low heat, stirring until thick. Add nuts and raisins. Cool. Add vanilla. Spoon into small pie shells; top with whipped cream. 6 to 8 small pies.

Miss Mattie Warren Oliver
INDIANOLA, MS

Strawberry Pie

1 quart strawberries
1 cup sugar
3 tablespoons cornstarch
Pinch of salt
1 baked pie shell - graham
   cracker or plain
Juice of 1 lemon

Mash 1 pint of berries - add 1 cup sugar, cornstarch, lemon juice and salt. Cook until thick and bubbling.

Remove from heat and cool slightly. Add remaining pint of whole berries. Pour into baked pie shell and set in refrigerator until cold. Top with whipped cream.

Mrs. Carroll Gartin
LAUREL, MS

French Strawberry Pie

1 package vanilla pudding
1 1/3 cup milk
1/2 teaspoon grated lemon
  peel
1/2 cup sour cream
1 (9 inch) baked pastry
  shell
2–3 cups whole strawber-
  ries
1/4 cup red currant jelly
1 tablespoon orange juice

Make up pudding according to package directions except that you use 1 1/3 cups milk and add the lemon peel. Then beat in 1/2 cup sour cream. Spread mixture in pie shell. Cover top with 2–3 cups whole strawberries, which have been washed, hulled and dried. Mix the jelly and orange juice together and then drizzle on top to glaze the berries. (I often double the portions for the glaze). Chill until set.

Jan Robertson
GREENVILLE, MS

Sweet Potato Pie

2 cups mashed cooked
  sweet potatoes
3 eggs beaten
1/2 cup white sugar
1/4 cup brown sugar
1/2 stick butter
1/2 teaspoon cinnamon
1/2 teaspoon nutmeg
1 small can evaporated
  milk

Mash butter with potatoes and add sugars, cinnamon, nutmeg, milk and eggs, well beaten. Fill pastry shell and cook in medium oven for approximately 35 minutes.

Mrs. Bob Barron
INDIANOLA, MS

Sweet Potato Meringue Pie

3 large sweet potatoes
2 tablespoons butter
1/2 cup sugar
1/2 teaspoon cinnamon
1/2 teaspoon nutmeg
1 egg
2 egg whites
4 teaspoons sugar

Peel and boil potatoes until soft. Drain. Mash well with the butter and pinch of salt. Add sugar, cinnamon, nutmeg and well beaten egg. Fill baked pie shell and cover with meringue made of beaten egg whites and the 4 teaspoons of sugar. Brown in 425° for 5 or 6 minutes.

Dot Myers
INDIANOLA, MS

Twinkie Pie

1 package semisweet
  chocolate drops
3 eggs, separated
1/2 cup sugar
1/2 teaspoon vanilla
3 to 4 packages Twinkies
1 cup chopped pecans
1/2 pint whipping cream

Grease Pyrex square or rectangular casserole with butter. Melt chocolate drops. Add egg yolks to chocolate slowly. Beat egg whites with sugar; add vanilla. Fold in chocolate. Layer in pan, Twinkies (cut in thirds lengthwise), chocolate, nuts. Repeat. Top with cream. Serves 8 to 10.

Eleanor N. Failing
INDIANOLA, MS

Banana Pudding

3/4 cup sugar
1/4 cup flour
Yolks of 2 eggs
Whites of 2 eggs
2 cups milk
1 teaspoon vanilla

Place in double boiler 1/4 cup milk blended with sugar, flour and egg yolks. Add the remaining milk and cook until the mixture thickens. Cool slightly and slowly add the whites of eggs which have been beaten until it stands in peaks. Add vanilla and sliced bananas to taste. Pour in footed dessert glasses and put refrigerator to cool. May also be served over lady fingers. Add a dollop of whipped cream when served.

Mrs. J. R. McPherson
PARAGOULD, AR

Bread Pudding

1 cup raisins
1/2 cup bourbon
6 cups coarsely cubed
  bread
2 cups half and half
1 1/2 cups milk
3 eggs
1 egg white
1 tablespoon vanilla
1 1/2 cups sugar
1/2 teaspoon cinnamon
1/4 cup butter, melted
3 eggs, plus 1 egg white

Soak raisins in bourbon overnight. Heat oven to 325°. Place bread in bowl and pour half and half and milk over them. Let stand 10 minutes; then crush with hands until blended. Add eggs (beaten), egg whites and vanilla. Combine sugar and cinnamon. Add to bread mixture and stir in raisin mixture. Pour melted butter into 13x9x2 baking pan. Spoon mixture into pan. Bake 30 minutes or until very firm. Cool. Cut into squares and pour Lemon Custard Sauce over and serve.

Mrs. Larry Hudson
MOORHEAD, MS

Lemon Custard Sauce

1/2 cup sugar
1/4 cup flour
1/8 teaspoon salt
1 1/2 cups milk
4 egg yolks, beaten
1/4 cup fresh lemon juice

Combine sugar, flour, and salt in small saucepan; mix well. Beat together milk and egg yolks; stir into sugar mixture. Cook over medium heat stirring constantly until thickened and mixture comes just to a boil. Remove from heat. Add lemon juice. Serve warm.

Mrs. Larry Hudson
MOORHEAD, MS

Bourbon Parfait

18 large marshmallows
1/2 cup milk
1/4 cup bourbon
1 pint whipping cream
1/2 cup chopped pecans

Melt marshmallows with milk. Cool in refrigerator. With mixer on low speed add bourbon (slow stream), fold in whipped cream and pecans. Serves 10 - 12.

Shirley Allen
INDIANOLA, MS

Caramel Pudding

3 egg yolks
3/4 cup sugar
2 tablespoons corn starch
1 1/2 cups milk
1/2 cup sugar
2 tablespoons butter
1 teaspoon vanilla
Whipped cream
Toasted salted pecans,
  chopped

Mix egg yolks, 3/4 cup sugar, corn starch, and milk and cook in boiler until thick, stirring constantly. Brown 1/2 cup sugar in iron skillet until melted. Add to above mixture. Add butter and vanilla. Cool. Serve in pastry tart. Top with whipped cream. Sprinkle with toasted salted pecans.

Mrs. Frank L. Tindall
INDIANOLA, MS

Supreme Au Chocolate (Chocolate Mousse)

4 ounces German sweet
  chocolate
4 eggs, separated
4 tablespoons sugar
3 1/2 ounces butter (no
  substitute)

Melt chocolate in bowl (over water in pan.) Add yolks and sugar a little at a time. Stir with fork. When all egg yolks and sugar are in, beat well with a wooden spoon. Beat in butter, bit by bit. Whip egg whites stiffly. Put into chocolate mixture - 1 tablespoon egg white, beat, then add remainder of whites slowly. Put into buttered bowl or buttered individual cups and chill at least 15 hours before serving. Serves 6.

Mrs. Adyn E. Schuyler
SUMNER, MS

Boiled Custard

4 large eggs
1/2 cup sugar
Dash of salt
2 cups whole milk
2 cups half and half
1 tablespoon pure vanilla
  flavoring

In mixing bowl whisk eggs, sugar, salt, milk and half and half. Strain into top of a 2 quart double boiler. Cook, stirring constantly, until mixture coats the spoon (about 45 minutes). Cool until warm before adding vanilla flavoring. I use this custard to make banana pudding. Serves six.

Shirley Allen
INDIANOLA, MS

Lorine's French Custard

1/2 cup sugar
1/2 cup boiling water
2 whole eggs & 3 additional egg yolks
Pinch of salt
4 tablespoons sugar
1/2 teaspoon vanilla
1 1/2 cups hot milk

Heat 1/2 cup sugar until it melts and browns over medium heat, stirring constantly with a wooden spoon. Slowly add 1/2 cup boiling water and let mixture simmer, continuing to stir. Pour into 1 quart casserole or divide evenly into six pyrex baking cups or fluted French custard cups. Do this about 10 minutes before you begin next step.

Beat eggs and egg yolks in a bowl with a heavy pinch of salt. Then add sugar, vanilla, and hot milk, but do not let mixture froth up (don't use electric mixer).

Slowly add this mixture into baking dishes. Do not let brown sugar mixture mix with egg mixture; and it should not if brown sugar mixture has begun to set. (Also a tilted spoon, held between baking dish and egg mixture helps prevent this.) Bake 1 hour at 250°.

Mrs. W. E. Howard
LAUREL, MS

Lemon Cups

1 cup sugar
1/4 cup flour
1/8 teaspoon salt
2 tablespoons melted butter
8-10 tablespoons lemon juice
3 egg yolks, beaten
1 1/2 cups scalded milk
3 egg whites, stiffly beaten

Combine sugar, flour, salt and butter. Add lemon juice and milk, then beaten egg yolks. Mix well, and fold in stiffly beaten egg whites. Pour into greased custard cups. Place in pan of hot water and bake 45 minutes at 325°. When ready to serve, invert cups on dessert plate. The effect will be cake with lemon custard over it.

Mrs. Joe Green
INDIANOLA, MS

Macaroon Pudding

1 pint milk
3 eggs
3/4 cup sugar
2 tablespoons gelatin
1 dozen almond maca-
  roons, broken
Almond flavoring
Whipped cream

Scald milk; beat eggs and add sugar. Dissolve gelatin and add to milk. Combine with almond macaroons and flavoring and chill. Serve with dollop of whipped cream.

Mrs. C. S. Whittington
GREENWOOD, MS

Mocha Sponge

6 squares unsweetened
  chocolate
6 eggs
2 envelopes gelatin
1/2 cup cold water
1 teaspoon vanilla
Pinch of salt
1 cup hot coffee, very
  strong
1 pint cream, whipped
Heavy rum to taste
1 1/2 cups granulated
  sugar

Melt chocolate in double boiler. Separate eggs. Beat yolks until lemon colored; add sugar gradually; beat some more; then add all chocolate slowly. Dissolve gelatin in cold water; then pour into hot coffee; stir and strain mixture. Mix well; add vanilla and salt. Fold in egg whites, beaten until stiff. Mix thoroughly and pour into an oiled ring mold. Chill. Serve with whipped cream flavored with heavy rum (or rum flavoring). Serves 6.

This recipe given me by Mrs. Francis B. Stewart, Charleston, SC.

Mrs. J. G. Prichard
INVERNESS, MS

Queen of Trifles

12 lady fingers, fill each
  with plum jelly
12 almond macaroons
1 dessert spoon sherry on
  each macaroon
1 cup slivered almonds
2 1/2 cups pineapple
1 recipe boiled custard

In a large bowl put a layer of jelly-filled lady fingers, then a layer of sherried macaroons, then slivered almonds and pineapple, then pour boiled custard over. Refrigerate. Serve with whipped cream. Serves 12.

Mrs. James Baird
INDIANOLA, MS

Index

———————□———————

Notes

Notes

To order additional copies of
Best of Bayou Cuisine
send $14.95 (plus $3.00 postage) to:

Best of Bayou Cuisine
P. O. Box 1005
Indianola, MS 38751

Or to order by credit card,
call toll-free
1-800-343-1583

All proceeds from the sale of this book go to further
the work of St. Stephen's Episcopal Church,
Indianola, Mississippi

**Quail Ridge Press is pleased to add *Best of Bayou Cuisine*
to its line of distinguished cookbooks.**

"Best of the Best" Cookbook Series:

Alabama	(28-3)	$14.95	*Missouri*	(44-5)	$14.95
Arkansas	(43-7)	$14.95	*New England*	(50-X)	$16.95
Florida	(16-X)	$14.95	*North Carolina*	(38-0)	$14.95
Georgia	(30-5)	$14.95	*Ohio*	(68-2)	$16.95
Illinois	(58-5)	$14.95	*Oklahoma*	(65-8)	$14.95
Indiana	(57-7)	$14.95	*Pennsylvania*	(47-X)	$14.95
Iowa	(82-8)	$14.95	*South Carolina*	(39-9)	$14.95
Kentucky	(27-5)	$14.95	*Tennessee*	(20-8)	$14.95
Louisiana	(13-5)	$14.95	*Texas I*	(14-3)	$14.95
Michigan	(69-0)	$14.95	*Texas II*	(62-3)	$16.95
Minnesota	(81-X)	$14.95	*Virginia*	(41-0)	$14.95
Mississippi	(19-4)	$14.95	*Wisconsin*	(80-1)	$14.95

Coming soon: **Colorado, Kansas, Louisiana II**

Individuals may purchase the full 24-volume set for a special "Best Club" price of $255.00 (a 30% discount off the regular price of $364.80) plus $5.00 shipping. Becoming a member of the "Best Club" will entitle you to a 25% discount on future volumes. Call for information on discounts for joining the "Best of the Month Club."

Other Quail Ridge Press Cookbooks

	ISBN SUFFIX
The Little New Orleans Cookbook (hardbound) $8.95	42-9
The Little New Orleans Cookbook, French Version (h/b) $10.95	60-7
The Little Gumbo Book (hardbound) $8.95	17-8
The Little Bean Book (hardbound) $9.95	32-1
Gourmet Camping $9.95	45-3
Lite Up Your Life $14.95	40-2
Hors D'Oeuvres Everybody Loves $5.95	11-9
The Seven Chocolate Sins $5.95	01-1
The Twelve Days of Christmas Cookbook $5.95	00-3
The Complete Venison Cookbook (paperbound) $19.95	70-4
Eat Your Way Thin $9.95	76-3
Kitchen Express (stand-up binding) $12.95	77-1
Best of Bayou Cuisine (paperbound) $14.95	78-X

ISBN Prefix: 0-937552-. All books are comb bound unless noted otherwise. Prices subject to change. To order, send check/money order to:

QUAIL RIDGE PRESS
P. O. Box 123 / Brandon, MS 39043

Or call toll-free to order by credit card:

1-800-343-1583

Please add $2.50 postage for any amount of books sent to one address. Gift wrap with enclosed card add $2.50. Mississippi residents add 7% sales tax. All orders ship within 24 hours. Write or call for free catalog of all QRP books and cookbooks.